Vandalized Lovemaps

ALSO BY JOHN MONEY

Hermaphroditism: An Inquiry into the Nature of a Human Paradox, 1952.

The Psychologic Study of Man, 1957.

A Standardized Road-Map Test of Direction Sense (with D. Alexander and H. T. Walker, Jr.), 1965.

Sex Errors of the Body: Dilemmas, Education and Counseling, 1968.

Man and Woman, Boy and Girl: The Differentiation and Dimorphism of Gender Identity from Conception to Maturity (with A. A. Ehrhardt), 1972.

Sexual Signatures (with Patricia Tucker), 1975.

Love and Love Sickness: The Science of Sex, Gender Difference, and Pairbonding, 1980.

The Destroying Angel: Sex, Fitness, and Food in the Legacy of Degeneracy Theory, Graham Crackers, Kellogg's Corn Flakes, and American Health History, 1985.

Venuses Penuses: Sexology, Sexosophy, and Exigency Theory, 1986.

Lovemaps: Sexual/Erotic Health and Pathology, Paraphilia, and Gender Transposition in Childhood, Adolescence, and Maturity, 1986; paperback 1988.

Gay, Straight, and In-Between: The Sexology of Erotic Orientation, 1988.

EDITED BY JOHN MONEY

Reading Disability: Progress and Research Needs in Dyslexia, 1962.

Sex Research: New Developments, 1965.

The Disabled Reader: Education of the Dyslexic Child, 1966.

Transsexualism and Sex Reassignment (with R. Green), 1969.

Contemporary Sexual Behavior: Critical Issues in the 1970's (with J. Zubin), 1973.

Developmental Human Behavior Genetics (with W. K. Schaie, E. Anderson, and G. McClearn), 1975.

Handbook of Sexology (with H. Musaph), 1977.

Traumatic Abuse and Neglect of Children at Home (with G. Williams), 1980.

Handbook of Human Sexuality (with B. B. Wolman), 1980.

The Pharmacology and Endocrinology of Sexual Function. Handbook of Sexology, Vol. 6 (with H. Musaph and J. M. A. Sitsen), 1988.

Sexology of Genes, Genitals, Hormones, & Gender: Selected Readings, 1989.

Dr. John Money
Dr. Margaret Lamacz

Vandalized
Lovemaps

Paraphilic Outcome of
Seven Cases in
Pediatric Sexology

PROMETHEUS BOOKS
Buffalo, New York

#19552949

Library of Congress Cataloging-in-Publication Data

Money, John, 1921-
    Vandalized lovemaps : paraphilic outcome of seven cases in
pediatric sexology / John Money and Margaret Lamacz.
        p.   cm.
    Bibliography: p.
    Includes index.
    ISBN 0-87975-513-X
    1. Psychosexual disorders—Etiology—Case studies.
2. Psychosexual disorders—Genetic aspects—Case studies.
3. Psychosexual disorders—Endocrine aspects—Case studies.
4. Generative organs—Abnormalities—Complications and sequelae—
Case studies. 5. Sex chromosome abnormalities—Complications and
sequelae—Case studies. I. Lamacz, Margaret, 1949-   II. Title.
    [CNLM: 1. Chromosome Abnormalities—case studies. 2. Endocrine
Diseases—case studies. 3. Genitalia—abnormalities—case studies.
4. Paraphilias—etiology—case studies. WM 610 M742v]
RC556.M67   1989
626.85′83071—dc20

                                                    DNLM/DLC
for Library of Congress   89-4037
                                                       CIP

For those whose lovemaps will be paraphilia-free in the 21st century if this book promotes the founding of pediatric sexology clinics and research centers, worldwide, as we hope.

Acknowledgments

The research and writing of this book was done with the support of USPHS Grant HD00325-31. Special thanks are extended to Mr. Ivy Garner, reference assistant in the Johns Hopkins Psychiatry/Neuroscience Library. Ms. Roberta Boyce did part of the word-processing, with extraordinary speed and skill. The dust jacket was professionally designed by the graphic artist, Ms. Sally Hopkins. Case material from the patients represented in Chapters 4 and 6 has appeared also in the *International Journal of Family Psychiatry* (Volume 5, 1984; Volume 7, 1986) and in *Lovemaps* (Money, 1986a).

CONTENTS

PREFACE

Hellfire-and-brimstone televangelism would have us believe that, as a religious nation, America fails. Wrong! We may not be particularly pious, but we are dedicated devil-hunters. The heritage of our Puritan forebears makes us ideological missionaries, charged with the moral responsibility of converting heretics, and criminalizing those who don't convert. We run our social and political history cyclically, justifying the privileges of redemption by mounting crusades against heresies and depravities, even those which are artifacts of our own devising.

Today, America is on another crusade, this time against the heresies of the sexual revolution. This so-called revolution of the 1960s and 1970s was no armed uprising, but rather a sexual reformation. We are now in the throes of the sexual counterreformation.

A reformation changes not only a people's doctrines, values, and beliefs, but also the pragmatics of their conduct and behavior toward one another. It is a general principle of any reformation that it is a response of people to technological innovation in society, either by borrowing or invention; or else to demographic change in society, namely, in the size of the population or its sex ratio or age ratio.

Technologically, the sexual reformation was a response, in part, to the discovery of antibiotics for the control of sexually transmitted diseases, especially, the twin scourges of syphilis and gonorrhea. In part it was a response also to the discovery of the oral contraceptive for women, the Pill. The uniqueness of the Pill was that it diverted the act of contraception from the genitalia to the mouth, and was the most effective method of giving women control over their own reproductive timetable. Also, it could be swallowed at any time of the day, not only in anticipation of the sexual act.

Demographically, the sexual reformation was a response in part to the onset of puberty at an earlier age; (an unexplained secular trend that had been going on for over a century); a great increase in life expectancy (from age 45 to 75-80, in less than a century); a dramatic lowering of the infant-mortality rate; and an explosion of population, worldwide, that justified or demanded smaller families and fewer offspring as the price of ecological survival.

Whereas the technology and demographics of the sexual reformation constituted scientific facts, the response to them constituted ideology—the ideology of sexual liberation. Liberation ideology repudiated the sex-negative ideology of Victorianism. It was explicitly permissive, without advocating untrammeled permissiveness and licentiousness. It did so by means of a semantic deceit: Whatever failed to qualify as sex-positive was disqualified from being sexual. It was classified instead as aggression—violence, assault, molestation, or abuse. Hence the false dogma that rape is not sex-negative, but a nonsexual and nonconsenting expression of male violence against women, although not of female violence against men.

The implicit logic of this semantic deceit has been much criticized, namely, that anything goes sexually provided it conforms to the criterion of consensuality. This criterion fails to come to grips with the issue of consensual sexological pathology, such as, for example, consensual sado-masochism, the outcome of which may be irreversible injury or death. Without a criterion to separate sex-positive from sex-negative, both categories may be defined either too overinclusively or too underinclusively. The sex-positive category is excessively constricted or underinclusive in the ideology of the counterreformation, and the sex-negative category is excessively enlarged or overinclusive.

Much of what the sexual reformation has categorized as sex-positive and permissible, the counterreformation has categorized as sex-negative and heretical. It has mounted its crusade against those whom it identified as the heretics of women's liberation, gay liberation, sex education, contraception, teenaged pregnancy, abortion, sexually transmitted disease, and pornography.

Three of the crusading strategies of the sexual counterreformation have been:

—the criminalization of sex, which affects particularly the pictorialization of nudity, the erotic entertainment industry, and the prosecution of those accused of sexual harassment, sexual coercion, and pedophilia.
—the professionalization of victimology, which has entailed the creation of a new arm of the law, the social science police, whose duty with respect to sexual victimology is to report suspected perpetrators, to

obtain, especially from children, a report of victimization, and to dislocate victims and "cure" them from the effects of abuse.

—the pathologizing of sex by inventing a hitherto unknown disease, sexual addiction, which is defined so as to include all that is sexual or erotic other than monogamous copulation.

The foregoing three strategies of the sexual counterreformation have had, all told, a destructive effect on the advancement of the science of sexology—its teaching, clinical application, and research. This destructiveness has been particularly acute with respect to the advancement of knowledge in pediatric sexology. Young academics shy away from pediatric sexological research, afraid of being stigmatized or even victimized by false accusations. Thus, investigation of the principles whereby children develop to be sexologically healthy or unhealthy in maturity remains mostly a void.

This book has staked a claim to a small portion of that void and has begun to explore it. It is the first of its kind, for it is a study of paraphilic development which is not retrospective, as is usually the case, but prospective. It is also the first of its kind in being a study of the origin of paraphilia before puberty, not later. In seven cases, it records from childhood onward factors in the evolution of a paraphilia. In all seven cases, there had been no diagnostic anticipation, in advance of puberty, of the development of the paraphilia. The patients had been diagnosed, most of them in infancy, with a hormonal and/or genital defect, for which they were being treated and observed in follow-up.

In five of the cases, the child grew up with visible evidence of a sex-organ anomaly. In another case, that of a girl, the child had atresia of the vagina which she first suspected in late childhood, if not earlier. In the first case, that of a boy, the early sex connection pertained not to an anomaly of the genitalia, but to their use in sexual rehearsal play followed by the automobile death of his playmate, which he experienced as God's punishment. Thus in all seven cases the precursor of the paraphilia was explicitly sexual. A paraphilia is itself a sexual phenomenon, albeit a sexuo-erotic one. Sex begets sex! Like begets like! The same principle applies to separation and loss.

According to the psychiatrist, John Bowlby (personal communication), actual or threatened abandonment, separation, or loss early in life begets later symptoms of abandonment, separations, or loss. Early in his psychoanalytic career, Freud held to the same principle, namely, that actual sexual molestation early in life led to sexual and sexually derived symptoms in adulthood. When he replaced the verity of actual molestation with the fantasy of Oedipal seduction (Masson, 1984), Freud misconstrued his data. The precursors of sexuoerotic syndromes of adolescence and maturity do not have their origins in fantasy, but in precursors that are themselves explicitly sexuoerotic and usually genitosexual as well. The data of this present volume confirm this principle.

Whereas a sexuoerotic outcome is contingent on a sexuoerotic antecedent, a pathological outcome is contingent also on antecedents that are sex-negative. The sex-negative antecedents may be traumatic, disciplinary, or stigmatizing. Traumatization may be accidentally, medically, or surgically induced, or illegally induced, as in abduction, molestation, or assault. Discipline may be abusive punishment, reprisal, humiliation, or penance. Discipline may be imposed in response to forbidden practices, including normal and healthy sexuoerotic play, either alone or with a playmate. Penance for secret infractions may be other-imposed or self-imposed. Stigmatization may be by ridicule, isolation, or selective treatment and may apply to anomalies of either the body or behavior.

Sex-negating antecedents in childhood produce sex pathologies in adulthood of which one of two main classes is sexuoerotic dysfunction or paraphilia, and the other genitoerotic dysfunction or hypophilia, the converse of hyperphilia. In each generation of population increase there are more children than parents who are exposed to sex negation. Consequently, with each succeeding generation, there is an exponential increase in the prevalence of dysfunctions contingent on ideological sex negation.

In public health, the short-term defense against an epidemic is containment, but the long-term defense is prevention. Short-term containment of paraphilias in the population may possibly be achieved, at least in part, by criminalizing them, and incarcerating and executing offenders in a Hitler-type of holocaust. By contrast, long-term prevention of paraphilias will be achieved only by biomedicalizing them. Epidemiological prevention requires intervention that, quite literally, prevents a syndrome from taking hold and developing. As applied to paraphilias, prevention is an epidemiological problem in public health. It entails cognizance of the principle that the paraphilias constitute a slow-spreading epidemic, and that the units of time by which to measure the exponential rate of its spread are not hours, days, weeks, or years, even, but generations. Although many details remain to be ascertained, a syndrome of paraphilia in maturity has precursors that trace back to childhood and even earlier into prenatal life. Prospective confirmation of this proposition is what makes this book important.

CHAPTER 1

Concepts Of Paraphilia

From Perversion to Paraphilia

To be without a name is to be without an existence, almost, or to be unrecognized, unidentified, and never spoken of. Historically, that had been the fate of *paraphilia* (from Greek, *para-,* beyond, amiss, or altered + *philia-,* love). "Paraphilia" is a biomedically impartial synonym for the morally judgmental term "perversion." It was formally introduced into the professional English-language literature in 1934 by the American psychoanalyst and sexologist, Benjamin Karpman (1886-1962), in a Special Article for the *Archives of Neurology and Psychiatry,* "The Obsessive Paraphilias (Perversions): A Critical Review of Stekel's Works on Sadism, Masochism, and Fetishism" (see Karpman, 1954, p. 629).

The term "paraphilia" had appeared earlier in translations of the writings of Karpman's own teacher and personal analyst in Vienna, Wilhelm Stekel (1868-1940) (see, for example, Volume 1 of his *Peculiarities of Behavior,* 1924, p. 83). Stekel wrote in his autobiography (1950, p. 233) that he had "changed perversion to paraphilia, following a suggestion by I. F. Krauss." Presumably, he had done so after his dispute in 1912 with orthodox Freudians. They did not take up the new term, but continued, as did Sigmund Freud (1856-1939), himself, to use only the old term, "perversion." Freud was not a sexologist with a theory of sex. His was a perversion theory of the neuroses, not a theory of perversion.

In 1980, "paraphilia" officially replaced "perversion" in the psychiatric nomenclature with the publication of DSM-III, the third edition of the

American Psychiatric Association's *Diagnostic and Statistical Manual of Mental Disorders.* "Perversion" is still used in the vocabulary of criminology and law. The corresponding vernacular term is "kinky sex" or "bizarre sex."

Historically, the perversions had been construed as signs of heresy and witchcraft, and perverts were burned alive or hanged. In colonial America of the 17th century, sodomy, adultery, bestiality, and rape were classified as crimes, punishable with the death penalty. The following quotation is from Bullough (1976, p. 520): "William Hackett, an indentured servant, engaged in the first act of bestiality to be recorded in the Massachusetts Colony. As a young man of eighteen, he was discovered one Sunday by a woman who, 'being detained from the public assembly by some infirmity that day, and by occasion looking out her window, espied him in the very act.' After several church members had spoken with him, Hackett confessed to the crime and admitted he had done such things before. The cow was burned before his eyes, after which he was hanged."

In penal codes of the 18th century, the sexual crimes subsumed under sodomy included oral and anal sex, homosexual contact, and bestiality. They were referred to as crimes against nature, so abominable and unspeakable that their names, quite literally, were not to be spoken. Thus, a suspect might even today be legally prosecuted and found guilty of an offense he or she has never heard specified by name.

In the secular law, the crimes against nature derived their name from the ancient ecclesiastical doctrine of the Natural Law, which had been incorporated into the canon law. In making the transition from secular law to forensic medicine, the name changed from "crimes against nature" to "perversions of the sexual instinct."

The perversions of the sexual instinct were the old wine of criminalized sex in a new bottle. What the church forbade and the court punished, the medical profession took in under a new name to investigate and maybe to treat. By not challenging the ancient privilege and power of religion and law to decree what is right and wrong in sex, doctors spared themselves the opprobrium of society and the accusation of being in favor of sinful and illegal sex.

Coincidentally, by putting their profession in the service of the law, forensic physicians became, de facto, medical police as well as doctors, jeopardized by a conflict of professional interest that still remains unresolved.

Perversions of the sexual instinct were defined according to the criterion, postulated in Natural Law, that the exclusive purpose of the sexual instinct is procreation. Thus, only penovaginal copulation in the male-superior position was defined as not a perversion. This extremely restricted definition excluded anything erotic or sexual, including masturbation, that would allow the nonprocreative wastage of semen.

The saving of semen for procreation alone has its origin in the philosophical remoteness of the past, namely, in the idea that wastage of the precious vital fluid would cause debility, disease, and death. The doctrine of semen conservation, widely disseminated in tribal medicine, has been on written record since around 600 B.C. in the Ayurvedic medical texts of India. It has an even earlier unrecorded history not only in India, but also in China.

Degeneracy Theory

Midway through the 18th century, semen-conservation theory underwent a revival that had an influence of enormous magnitude on the history of ideas in European and American medicine. The author of the revival was the Swiss physician, Simon André Tissot (1728-1797). The title of his book is *L'Onanisme, Dissertation sur les Maladies Produites par la Masturbation* (7th ed., 1781). It was first published in America as *Treatise on the Diseases Produced by Onanism* (1832).

According to the logic of Tissot's treatise, semen is the most valuable of all the vital fluids. One drop of it is equivalent to 50 of the most precious drops of blood. Lack of semen is what makes woman weak and mentally and physically inferior to man. Loss of semen drains away the vitality and degenerates both mind and body. A major source of degeneracy from semen wastage was, Tissot said, the social vice of whoring and promiscuity. He correctly associated the social vice with the social disease. Today known as syphilis and gonorrhea, the social disease was still then, more than a century before germ theory, considered one disease, not two. Making a logical blunder with devastating sexological consequences, Tissot paired the social vice with the secret vice—self-abuse or masturbation—as the second major source of degeneracy.

Tissot's second logical blunder, one that put the cart before the horse, was to attribute the practice of both the social and the secret vice to lust aroused by concupiscent thoughts and ideas—in today's terminology, erotic fantasies and dreams. Wet dreams while asleep were diagnosed as the disease, spermatorrhea, and said to be caused by concupiscence indulged in while awake.

Concupiscence was considered to be socially contagious, and to be caught by direct stimulation or by lewd talk or reading—photography had not yet been invented and pictures were not mass marketed. For those infected with concupiscence, the course was an ever worsening succession of sexual depravities and crimes, to quote the 18th century terms for perversions or paraphilias. The cures were quackery—a combination of diet, exercise, prayer, and will-power.

Tissot's degeneracy theory of disease caused by semen loss filled the medical void created when, as the fires of the Inquisition burned out in the 17th century, so also did its theory of disease caused by demon possession and witchcraft. Tissot medicalized degeneracy theory and made it compatible with the newest medical discoveries and ideas of his time. Even though it was so diffuse that it explained everything while explaining nothing, it had immense popularity and held the field without rival until modern bacteriology began with the discovery of the germ theory of disease in the 1870s (see, for a historical review, Money, 1985).

Degeneracy theory became applied to the explanation specifically of psychiatric and sexological disorders during the middle of the 19th century. A neglected fact of history is that in 1844 Heinrich Kaan (a comprehensive search failed to retrieve his dates), the personal physician to the Czar, published in Germany, in the German language, his book, *Psychopathia Sexualis* (Haeberle, 1978, p. 382; 1983).

In this book, Kaan mentioned in particular the love of boys, homosexual mutual masturbation, violation of corpses, coitus with animals, and contact with statues. There were two premises to his explanation of sexual psychopathology. One was circular, namely, the existence of a hereditary predisposition toward morbid fantasy (*phantasia morbosa*) which induces sensual excess, including self-abuse, which in turn increases the predisposition to morbid fantasy. The other proposition, borrowed directly from Tissot, was that morbid fantasy can be activated by eating rich and spicy food; sleeping in a sensual feather bed instead of on a hard mattress; wearing tightly corseted clothing; failing to get physical exercise and fresh air; and having too much idle leisure.

Richard von Krafft-Ebing (1840-1902) used not only the title of Kaan's book, but also its doctrine of degeneracy, when he published his own treatise forty-three years later, in 1886. Its complete title in the 1931 American edition is *Psychopathia Sexualis with Especial Reference to the Antipathic Sexual Instinct: A Medico-Forensic Study.* In this book, medicine staked out its claim against criminology for the scientific possession of the paraphilias. In the new age of bacteriology, there was new optimism that the paraphilias might yield the secrets of their etiology, prevention, and treatment to medical science.

Pioneer Survey

Krafft-Ebing's dual achievement as a pioneer was to record more extensive clinical data on the paraphilias than had ever before been recorded, and to formulate a theoretical explanation of them according to the principles of medicine then in vogue. His theory is built on an a priori assumption, namely, the existence of a sexual instinct, to which is added another a priori assumption, namely, the principle of degeneracy, to which is added, in turn, the principle of hereditary or constitutional taint.

Hereditary taint differed from what would today be called a hereditary trait. Hereditary degenerative tainting affected not only a single individual, but also an entire pedigree. Moreover, the magnitude of the taint could, like sin, be increased in the progenitors of each generation, so that parents accumulated more of it to pass on to their children until finally the pedigree became so hopelessly degenerated that it died out. The magnitude of one's degenerative taintedness could be increased within one's lifetime by agents such as alcohol, drugs, and mineral poisons, or by illnesses such as epilepsy, malaria, consumption, pellagra, venereal infection, and so on. For good measure, social and mental tainting were also possible. The prime suspect in the case of sexual tainting was masturbation. The principle of addictive and progressive tainting of an entire pedigree is the reverse of Darwinism— not evolution, but retrogression.

In Krafft-Ebing's schema, hereditary taint was responsible for degeneracy, and a degenerative brain and nervous system were responsible for, inter alia, paraphilic sexual pathology. The schema did not include a principle to explain how a diffusely degenerative brain produced a specific syndrome. However, the concept of general brain degeneration was compatible with specific, superimposed determinants.

Thus, Krafft-Ebing accepted from Alfred Binet (1857-1911) the explanation of fetishism as a product of associative learning, with the proviso that only in a degenerative brain would such an association take place (see also, Associative Determinism).

Similarly, he accepted the concepts of sadism and masochism as retrogressions of, respectively, the masculine and feminine sexual instinct to a more primitive evolutionary state, with the proviso that the retrogression would occur only in a degenerative brain.

Along the same lines, the surmise that "psychic hermaphroditism" or bisexuality was possibly a consequence of incomplete masculine and feminine brain differentiation was compatible with the principle of brain degeneracy. So also was the surmise of a female brain in a male body, and vice versa, in cases resembling those that today are called transexual.

By contrast, the principle of a brain tainted with hereditary degeneracy was superfluous to the explanation of sexual psychopathology secondary to brain lesions from accidental trauma, stroke, or epilepsy. Krafft-Ebing reported such cases as examples of nonhereditary degenerative change, and thus paved the way for completely dispensing with the principle of hereditary taint.

Krafft-Ebing's theoretical formulations and their shortcomings set the agenda that his successors are still working on, more than a century later, in attempting to explain the paraphilias biomedically instead of criminologically. The items on the agenda, taken up sequentially in what follows, are the principles of hereditary, phylogenetic, neuropathological, associative, intrapsychic, and biographical determinism.

Hereditary Determinism

In Krafft-Ebing's day, the ideas of the French naturalist, the Chevalier Jean-Baptiste de Lamarck (1744-1829), on the inheritance of acquired characteristics had not yet succumbed to the experimentally established Mendelian laws of inheritance. Thus, there was no impediment to Krafft-Ebing's explanation of perversions of the sexual instinct on the basis of the Lamarckian inheritance of degeneracy as an acquired characteristic. Not only might a hereditary taint be acquired and transmitted, but also, generation by generation, its magnitude might be progressively augmented until the pedigree became totally degenerate and extinct.

Krafft-Ebing's concept of hereditary taint in today's terminology would be a predisposition, and not necessarily hereditary. A hereditary taint is far removed from the concept of hereditary trait, which is not surprising in view of how little was known about heredity before the 20th century.

In 1886, the year when *Psychopathia Sexualis* first appeared, the principle of Mendelian inheritance was not yet publicly known. Gregor Mendel (1822-1884) had published his famous data on the hybridization of peas in 1866, but they went unnoticed until 1900. Thus, they were unknown also to Krafft-Ebing's Italian contemporary, the psychiatrist and criminologist, Cesare Lombroso (1836-1909), when in 1876 he published *L'uomo delinquente*, translated as *Criminal Man* (reprinted, 1972) [see also, his *Crime: Its Causes and Remedies* (1913)].

Lombroso did not explicitly repudiate the old principle of degeneracy, but he more or less replaced it with the principle, adopted from Valentin Magnan (1835-1916), of arrest at, or reversion to, a more primitive evolutionary stage or type—for which Lombroso used the term, "atavism." To the principle of atavism, Lombroso added the "signa degenerationis" of Benedict Morel (1809-1873), as the physical signs and symptoms of atavism (see also, Phylogenetic Determinism).

In Lombroso's theory of hereditary parallelism, atavism would show itself twice—once as a reversion to morphological deformity and asymmetry, and once as a reversion to uncouth and criminal behavior—and there would be a correlation between the two. Empirical observations and measurements would demonstrate the strength of the correlations. Lombroso was the founder of a new specialty which he named criminal anthropology.

Lombroso's search for anthropometric correlates of behavior became for William H. Sheldon (1899-1977), at Harvard, a search for a typology of behavior and its anthropometric correlates. His findings on *The Varieties of Temperament: A Psychology of Constitutional Differences* appeared in 1942, and on the *Varieties of Delinquent Youth* in 1949 (see Sheldon and Stevens, 1970; Sheldon, Hartl, and McDermott, 1970).

The search for anthropometric correlations did not lead to any new discoveries or predictions related to the paraphilias or other sexual psychopathologies. As a criminological theory, atavism was a tree that bore almost no fruit. The exception pertained to those morphological deformities and asymmetries that, as the science of genetics advanced, would prove to have a genetic determinant and, in many instances, to be signs of a particular syndrome. In some such syndromes, there might be psychological or personality correlates, related perhaps to criminality, but on an irregular rather than a systematic basis.

Some of the morphological stigmata catalogued by Lombroso would, after the technique of chromosome counting had been discovered by Tjio and Levan in 1956, be found to be associated with an anomaly in the number of chromosomes. The matching of either chromosomal or anatomical anomalies to anomalies and pathologies of sexual behavior has proved to be inconsistent and unpredictable, however. One exception applies to men with the supernumerary-Y syndrome (47,XYY). In them, the prevalence of paraphilia is higher than in ordinary 46,XY men, as is also the prevalence of bisexuality. By contrast, in men with the supernumerary-X chromosome (47,XXY, Klinefelter's syndrome) the prevalence of transexualism is higher than expected (see Money, 1988, Chapter 1; and Money unpublished data; Schiavi et al., 1988).

The idea that certain individuals or segments of society were predestined by hereditary inferiority to be degenerates of one sort or another had as its converse the idea of hereditary superiority and the maintenance of racial purity by the weeding out of inferior stock. This was the doctrine of the social eugenics movement that gained immense and widespread popularity in Europe and America from the latter part of the 19th century onward (see, for example, Ludmerer, 1972). The unfit were sterilized and castrated. Those classified as unfit were, inter alia, mentally defective, epileptic, insane, criminal, or sexually perverted.

Sexologists of the eugenics era, struggling to gain scientific acceptance and professional respect, rode the bandwagon of social eugenics. In much the same way, today, professional victimologists, specializing in sexual child abuse, ride another bandwagon—namely, that of equating suspicion with guilt until proved innocent, on the basis of the false doctrine that children never lie about sex.

The social eugenics movement became the volcanic explosion of racial purity in Hitler's Germany that unleashed a catastrophic social tsunami and destroyed millions. Among the victims, some were those who had self-righteously ridden the social eugenics bandwagon. Never for a moment had they even hallucinated that there might be a change in the rules of racial purity by which they, themselves, would be classified as racially unfit (Pfaefflin, 1986). Victimologists, beware!

Social eugenics destroyed itself in the German holocaust, and left a volcanic cloud of distrust hanging over the genetics of anything related to the theory of sex differences or sexual pathology. For example, the genetic explanation of homosexuality as a degenerate perversion fell by the wayside and gave way, in the political battle for gay rights, to the explanation of homosexuality as a sexual preference.

The phoenix of sexual genetics still waits to arise from its own ashes. Despite the explosion of research in molecular genetics and mapping of the human genome, research into the molecular genetics of sexual dimorphism has no priority, and research into the molecular genetics of paraphilia does not exist. Even in diseases that are both genetically transmitted and degeneratively destructive of brain tissue, for example, Huntington's and Alzheimer's diseases, paraphilic research is excluded.

Degeneracy as an explanation of paraphilia has been eclipsed, except in the vernacular. Thus, in media reporting, degeneracy theory survives in the term "sexual degenerate." So also, demon-possession theory survives in the term "sex fiend"; and atavism survives in the term "sex monster."

Phylogenetic Determinism

To be sick is to be unhealthy, and to be healthy is to be not sick. To be normal is to not be deviant, and to be deviant is to be abnormal. The norm is defined either statistically or ideologically. Prior to the two Kinsey surveys (1948; 1953), there was no statistical definition of sexual normality insofar as, under the terms of the sexual taboo, people kept quiet about their sex lives. Ostensibly, they had conformed to the orthodoxy of the ideological norm that had been enforced by peer pressure, the law, and the church.

When Krafft-Ebing wrote *Psychopathia Sexualis,* he was not troubled by the issue of mapping the boundary between the sexual instinct and its perversion. He simply accepted the conventional wisdom of the day, namely, that every manifestation of the sexual instinct, except the specific procreative act of genital copulation, was a perversion—masturbation, wet dreams, and oral sex included.

Historically, this procreative criterion had been incorporated into the canon law, from which it passed into secular law. It was accorded the prestige of being a law of nature. It was medically acceptable insofar as it was firmly anchored in phylogenesis and defined the sexual instinct on the criteria of species survival.

Species survival, however, does not, per se, restrict the sexual instinct to the criterion of procreation alone. That issue has been much argued in the century of sexology since Krafft-Ebing, especially with respect to the legitimacy of infertile and contracepted copulation, oral and anal copulation, homosexuality, and masturbation. The legitimacy of these and other nonprocreative sexual variations constituted a vexing problem of the relativity of standards for the two sexologists Paolo Mantegazza (1831-1910) and Iwan Bloch (1872-1922), who were also scholars of ethnography. Each of them avoided the chaos of relativity, and of having no standards at all, by endorsing the principle of procreation as the criterion for the normal, nonperverted functioning of the sexual instinct (see also Associative Determinism).

Procreation is the primordial principle of phylogenesis, and the first to have been called upon in the sexological explanation of the paraphilias. It overlaps with a second phylogenetic principle, also called upon for explanation of the paraphilias, namely, that of male/female complementarity which extends beyond the procreative juxtaposition of the male and female genitalia to include other aspects of masculine and feminine roles. Krafft-Ebing (1931, p. 85) adhered to the standard stereotypes of male and female when he wrote, "In the intercourse between the sexes, the active or aggressive role belongs to man; woman remains passive, defensive."

Aggressivity in the male and passivity in the female have become standard, stock-in-trade principles of all sexological theory. In pathology, they have become a basis on which to elaborate explanations of sadism and masochism. Their theoretical potential is multiplied, however, when they are used in transposition, so that masculinism is associated with female and femininism is associated with male. The occurrence and the degree of the transposition then provide ample opportunity to engage in the exercise of elaborating additional explanatory permutations and combinations.

Krafft-Ebing engaged in this exercise, drawing on his predecessor, Karl Ulrichs (1825-1895), to explain homosexuality and to differentiate it from transvestism, which might be combined with either heterosexual or homosexual copulation, and from the transposition which would eventually become known as transexualism. The term "homosexual" had been coined by K. M. Benkert in 1869 (Bullough, 1976, p. 637).

For the next century, homosexuality would itself be named as a perversion of the sexual instinct, which perhaps accounts for the fact that neither Krafft-Ebing nor his successors recognized explicitly that the various other perversions, the paraphilias, may appear in association with either a homosexual or heterosexual orientation or, in some cases, a bisexual one.

Many hundreds of thousands of words were written about homosexuality by Krafft-Ebing's contemporaries and successors in sexology as they attempted to find causal explanations for its variability as exclusive versus situational, monosexual versus bisexual, chronic versus transitory, active versus passive, cross-sex impersonating versus own-sex exaggerating, and overt versus latent. Their explanations of causality reflected the medical vogue of each era: constitutional, degenerative, socially contagious, hormonal, and intrapsychic, singly or severally.

The third phylogenetic principle that has been called upon in the sexological attempt to explain the pathologies of sex is that of evolutionary reversion, or atavism, the manifestation of a more primitive stage of development secondary to either an arrestment of development, or to a reversion or regression to a more primitive stage.

The idea of developmental arrest or regression presupposes a succession of stages of development as, for example, in embryological development, epitomized by Ernst Haeckel (1834-1919) in the aphorism, ontogeny recapitulates phylogeny. The successive stages of phylogenetic development are the stages of evolution from primitive to more complex, first propounded in 1859 by Charles Darwin (1809-1882) in *On the Origin of Species by Means of Natural Selection*.

The concept of evolutionary reversion found its way into sexological theory not directly from Darwin, but by way of grafting evolutionary theory onto the degeneracy theory of Tissot, newly revived by one of Darwin's contemporaries, already mentioned, the French psychiatrist, Benedict Morel. Morel's book, first published in 1857, two years ahead of Darwin's, had a lengthy title: *Traité de Dégénérescenses Physiques, Intellectuelles et Morales de l'Espèce Humaine et de ses Causes qui Produisent ces Variétés Maladies* (Treatise on Degeneracy as a Cause of Physical, Intellectual and Moral Defects in Mankind). (See Hoenig, 1977.) For Morel, Adam was the "type primitif" created perfect, in the image of God. After the Fall, degeneracy and deterioration took their toll in each generation. Morel's "signa degenerationis," the signs of degeneracy (see also Hereditary Determinism), were not only moral and intellectual, but also morphological. They could be seen, in serious cases, as asymmetries and malformations of the features and parts of the body.

Morel's resurrection of Tissot's doctrine of degeneracy had wide appeal in European psychiatry. Its influence on sexology was direct, through Krafft-Ebing. However, Morel's upside-down version of evolution had no chance of survival in competition with Darwin's version of evolution which replaced it. In the Darwinian revision, Morel's "signa degenerationis" were reconstrued as evidence of evolutionary arrest or reversion—a throwback to a primitive evolutionary stage of development, brought about by degeneracy. The British psychiatrist, Henry Maudsley (1835-1918), in his *Physiology and Pathology of the Mind* (1867) attributed some forms of psychopathology to evolutionary inferiority or deterioration, for which heredity might be held responsible, though not exclusively so. There was still a place for Tissot's degenerative bugaboo, masturbation, in Maudsley's doctrine of masturbatory insanity. There was also a place for neurological inferiority or deterioration, either of which might be secondary to heredity. Hughlings Jackson (1835-1911), Maudsley's contemporary in British neurology, linked the concept of evolutionary reversion with heredity in the explanation of neurological disease in an 1884 paper on "Evolution and Dissolution of the Nervous System" (see Sulloway, 1979).

As already mentioned, the principle of evolutionary reversion in combination with hereditary inferiority found its chief exponent in Cesare Lombroso, the Italian forensic psychiatrist and criminologist (see also Hereditary Determinism). He popularized the term "atavism," meaning reversion to a more primitive stage, and used it to explain not only criminal sexual psychopathology, but criminal pathology in general. His emphasis was on transmission of atavistic inferiority within a pedigree, and he did not exclude Lamarckian inheritance of acquired characteristics.

The principle of evolutionary reversion, relieved of dependence on hereditary inferiority and with closer affinity to Haeckel's principle of recapitulation than Darwin's evolution, was transmogrified by Sigmund Freud into the principle of intrapsychic fixation at a primitive or infantile stage of development, or else regression to that stage. Psychosexual fixation and regression were used as explanations of not only sexual psychopathologies—in psychoanalytic vocabulary "the perversions"—but also, in association with repression, of neurotic and psychotic pathologies in general (see also Intrapsychic Determinism).

In the aforesaid historical examples, the principle of evolutionary reversion was invoked to explain sexual phenomena that met with social disapproval as unhealthy or undesirable, or with social condemnation as pathological or criminal. In sociobiology, the new application of Darwinian evolution to social behavior (Wilson, 1975; Weinrich, 1987), the view of these same phenomena has been rotated 180 degrees. The evolutionary principle now invoked for their explanation is the principle of adaptive advantage, which subdivides into parental investment and kin selection. For example, the adaptive advantage of homosexuality is that it produces childless members of the kinship to assist in providing for the children of the kinship, so that they will survive and be able to transmit the genes of the kinship to the next generation.

Another example is the adaptive advantage of rape by a multiple rapist. Raping, it is claimed, selects for dominance. Provided it results in multiple pregnancies, it allows the dominant male to multiply his investment in parenthood and transmit his genes to a larger number of offspring.

Sociobiology does not address the issue of the limit of social tolerance, and the right of society to intervene, irrespective of the adaptive evolutionary advantage of sexual behavior classified as paraphilic.

In the foregoing historical review of phylogenetic determinism, three principles have been called upon to explain the psychopathologies of sex. They are the principles of procreation, male/female difference, and evolutionary reversion. The fourth principle was formulated so recently that its name, the principle of phylisms (Money, 1986a, Chapters 12 and 13; 1986b, Chapters 10 and 32) is not yet widely disseminated.

The principle of phylisms owes its existence to the science of ethology (see, for example, Lorenz, 1952; and Eibl-Eibesfeldt, 1971), and in particular to its redefinition of the concept of instinct. Traditionally, an instinct has been construed globally and amorphously as a biological force or drive that activates behavior consistent with itself. Ethologically, instinct is construed as having phylogenetically determined components all concordant with one another, namely, an innate recognition mechanism and a matching innate releasing mechanism, with a matching fixed action pattern, also innate, and an innately scheduled chronology within the limits of which the association of the recognition and releasing mechanism with the action pattern may become permanently imprinted. To illustrate: turkey hatchlings recognize the squat shape of the hen turkey, which triggers the release of the brood-following response, which, within the first few hours after hatching, sets in the brain of the hatchling an imprint of the mother bird as the moving shape always to follow. By contrast, if the hatchling is hand reared by a waddling human being whose shape triggers the release of the brood-following response, then the imprint is to the human being. Moreover, the imprint persists so that the bird will subsequently make courtship displays toward the human being, despite having lived, meanwhile, as a member of a flock of turkeys.

The behavior that is released by the concordant matching of recognition and releasing mechanisms, correctly timed, may be fixedly stereotyped, simple, and reiterated without change, so that it is accurately characterized as a fixed action pattern—for example, premature detumescence of the penis that happens invariably when it is in proximity to the partner's vagina, but never in solo masturbation. Alternately, it may be functionally stereotyped, complex, and adaptable, within limits, when repeated—for example, being pairbonded as a lover. In that case, it is more appropriately termed a fixed unit of functional adaptation. In human beings, a unit of functional adaptation exists mentally, in imagery and ideation, as well as motorically.

The fixed action pattern or unit of functional adaptation manifested predictably in response to concordance between the innate recognition and releasing mechanisms is what constitutes a phylism. A phylism is formally defined as: a unit of response or behavior of an organism that belongs to an individual through its phylogenetic heritage as a member of its species (Money, 1988).

Phylisms apply to the explanation of paraphilia insofar as a phylism may become enchained in the service of sexuoeroticism, even though, in its pristine manifestation, it is neither sexual nor erotic. Once enchained, it becomes fixed and functionally repetitious. To illustrate: in pedophilia, the phylism for parent-child pairbonding becomes enchained to the phylism for lover-lover pairbonding, and remains permanently so. The agents or factors responsible for this enchainment cannot be stated a priori, and they almost certainly are variable from case to case. Either the recognition mechanism or the releasing mechanism may be implicated, or the chronology of their activation may be off schedule.

Irrespective of which component mechanism of a phylism is implicated, what happened to implicate it is yet another issue. The possibilities include genetic defect, prenatal or postnatal pathology secondary to infection, pharmacologic toxicity, nutritional anomaly, metabolic defect, and postnatal errors or anomalies of sensory input and associative learning. The full catalogue of etiological factors for all forty-odd of the paraphilias remains to be ascertained.

The unsolved Rubik cube of Darwinian evolution is the riddle of why the male/female mating behavior of subprimate mammals is hormonally preprogramed in the brain, prenatally, so that at maturity they are virtually "hormonal robots," whereas primates have greater variability and human beings have the extraordinary range of variability manifested as the paraphilias. There is no explanation other than that of the science-fiction hypothesis that, when in evolution the human brain forfeited its franchise as a protohuman robot so as to become a thinking, speaking, syntactical, logical, and mathematical brain, it was obliged to pay the price of forfeiting also its robotic male/female procreative phylisms. In other words, in the human species, the evolutionary diversification of sexuoerotic and linguistic potentiality were correlated, and they remain so.

Neuropathological Determinism

There are in Krafft-Ebing's *Psychopathia Sexualis* sixteen pages in which he deals with idiocy (three cases), brain injury (two cases), late-stage syphilis (five cases), and epilepsy (twelve cases). Idiocy was categorized as an innate mental weakness, and the other disorders as acquired mental weakness. In reference to the acquired type, Krafft-Ebing wrote: "Perversions of the sexual instinct seem to be infrequent; and here the immoral sexual acts seem to depend on abnormally increased or uninhibited sexual feeling which, in itself, is not abnormal." Insofar as this statement is inconsistent with some of the case reports, it would appear that in Krafft-Ebing's etiological doctrine, perversion of the sexual instinct exists a priori, as an independent entity, and not as a symptom of manifest pathology of the brain. Nonetheless the very mention of brain pathology sufficed to identify it as needing future consideration.

In the century of sexology since Krafft-Ebing, new knowledge of the functional role of the brain in sexual psychopathology has accrued slowly. One source of evidence has been clinical epilepsy (reviewed in Money and Pruce, 1977). Interference with sexual function is specific to psychomotor or temporal-lobe epilepsy rather than other forms of epilepsy, and is manifested characteristically as a deficit or loss. Following brain surgery for the removal of a temporal-lobe epileptic focus, if the seizures go into remission, then the recovery of sexual function, although not guaranteed, is likely.

As in the case of hypofunction, the literature on sexual hyperfunction associated with epilepsy is sparse. There are occasional reports of episodic attacks of genitally intense arousal unrelieved by orgasm that are controllable only with antiepileptic medication. They constitute a rare form of epileptic seizure.

There are occasional reports, also, of temporal-lobe epileptic seizures with associated genital arousal and fetishistic attachment to an object. Neurosurgical intervention, if successful, controls the seizures, the genital arousal, and the fetishistic attachment.

Even though the occurrence of epileptic or epileptiform seizures in synchrony with genital and/or erotic arousal is a phenomenon rarely reported, the very fact of its existence is of significance for the neuropathological theory of paraphilia. It is consistent with the observation, not uncommon among paraphilic sex offenders who are in long-term clinical follow-up, that, when they embark on a performance of the paraphilic ritual, they are in an epileptiform, trance-like state, or paraphilic fugue. There are other clinical features of temporal-lobe epilepsy of which the counterparts may be found in paraphilia, for example, hypergraphia, obsessional hoarding of paraphernalia, preserving self-incriminating evidence, and circumstantiality of conversation—all pertaining to the paraphilia.

In the clinic, it is not uncommon for a patient to have a dual diagnosis of epilepsy and paraphilia, and to have a history of epileptic attacks separate from paraphilic fugue states. Likewise it is not uncommon for a paraphilic diagnosis to coexist with a history of traumatic head injury or with a history of manifest neurologic dysfunction. Nonetheless, the systematic neglect of function and dysfunction of the brain in paraphilic diagnosis and research has been extreme. One exception pertains to an investigation of hemispheric asymmetry and impaired lateralization of the dominant hemisphere of the brain in sex offenders versus controls (reviewed in Flor-Henry, 1987). The criteria were cognitive test performance and EEG coherence, and the findings were inconclusive.

Experimental brain studies in animals yield more data than do human clinical and brain-surgery data, but both are consistent in indicating that in addition to the temporal lobe, the amygdala and hippocampal region of the limbic cortex, as well as the hypothalamus, play a major part in the organization of sexual function and its pathology.

The majority of animal studies in brain/sex research have addressed the issue of pathology only from the viewpoint of male/female dimorphism, and the differentiation of dimorphism under the control of hormones in fetal and neonatal life (reviewed in Money, 1988).

This line of research had its beginnings under Eugen Steinach (1861-1944) and was first reported in 1912 and 1913. Steinach transplanted hetero-typic gonadal tissue into castrated neonatal guinea pigs, and produced "feminization of males and masculinization of females," in both the body and behavior (Steinach, 1940, pp. 239-40). In the 1920s, the sex hormones were first isolated and soon thereafter, synthesized. Magnus Hirschfeld (1868-1935) was the first sexologist to grasp the potential significance of Steinach's hormonal discoveries for sexology. He incorporated the concept of hormonal determinism into his explanation of homosexuality.

Research on hormones and the brain has yielded some data on hormonal induction of cross-sex dimorphism of the fetal brain, that is, the mascu-linization of the female brain and of subsequent mating behavior, and vice versa. Whether these data have explanatory relevance for the representation of human sexual orientation in the human brain, as Hirschfeld had hoped, will remain conjectural until ethically acceptable advances in the technology of brain research have been discovered. The same applies to male/female brain differences with respect to the prevalence and varieties of paraphilia.

The relationship between hormones and male/female dimorphism in the brain is diphasic. Phase one is prenatal. Phase two is in maturity. In phase one, steroidal sex hormones influence the templates which are pre-cursors of what will subsequently be filled-in and completed as male, female, or mixed. In phase two, steroidal sex hormones activate the filled-in template, but they do not determine the content of its read-out. Thus, the sex hormones do not determine what the content of a paraphilia will be. Nor does the level of sex hormones circulating in the blood stream correlate, point for point, with the intensity of a paraphilia or the frequency of its appearance either in imagery or practice. Rather, there is a minimum level of sex hormone that the brain needs, and any surplus is wasted. Even prepubertal children are able to be protosexual. The sex hormones added at puberty are absolutely essential for fertility. They activate sexuoeroticism beyond its prepubertal level, but, even without pubertal hormones, if they are suppressed, sexuoeroticism resumes functioning at the prepubertal level.

The rationale for using a sex-hormone suppressant or antagonist, which for men is an antiandrogen, is that it is able to lower the circulating androgen in the blood stream to the level of prepuberty. In the United States, Androcur, cyproterone acetate (CPA), the European antiandrogen, is not approved, and Depo-Provera, medroxyprogesterone (MPA), is approved for clinical use.

For the paraphile, treatment with Depo-Provera gives him the opportunity to gain more effective governance over the expression of his paraphilia. It does so not simply by lowering the secretion of the androgen, testosterone, from his own testicles, but by having also a direct calming effect on sex-regulating brain cells of the preoptic area of the hypothalamus. In a study done on adult male rhesus monkeys, Depo-Provera was absorbed into the cells of the preoptic area of the hypothalamus as rapidly as fifteen minutes following an intramuscular injection (Rees, Bonsal and Michael, 1986).

Depo-Provera has seldom been used for women paraphiles, mainly because it closely resembles their own female hormone, progesterone. Its effectiveness for female paraphiles needs further evaluation. Paraphilia in women, like many other aspects of female sexuoeroticism, suffers from research neglect.

The antiandrogens, MPA and CPA, both are synthetic sex steroidal hormones related to progesterone. Estrogen itself, in males, is an antiandrogenic sex steroid. It was formerly used for the treatment of sex-offending paraphilias in males. It invariably feminizes the male breasts and so is disfavored. Other sex steroids with antiandrogenic properties have not been given clinical trials for the treatment of paraphilia. Nor has there been a clinical trial with the nonsteroidal antiandrogen, flutamide, which has the special property, not of lowering circulating androgen, but of blocking the uptake of androgen by cells that have receptors for it.

The most recent nonsteroidal antiandrogenic discovery pertains to synthetic analogues of the molecule of the neuropeptide, LHRH (luteinizing hormone releasing hormone), secreted from brain cells of the hypothalamus to stimulate the nearby pituitary gland to secrete luteinizing hormone which, in turn, stimulates the gonads (ovaries or testicles) to secrete their hormones. Normally, the release of LHRH is not continuous, but pulsatile, at approximately half-hour intervals. If the fluctuating levels are kept constant, by means of treatment, then LHRH fails to stimulate the secretion of LH which, in turn, fails to stimulate the secretion of sex hormones from the gonads. Hence, in men, it has an antiandrogenic property. The LHRH analogues, leuprolide acetate and buserelin acetate (LHRH-ethylamide), are estimated to be 80 to 100 times more antiandrogenically potent than LHRH (see Soloway, 1986).

LHRH analogues have been used for the treatment of prostatic cancer, but not yet for paraphilias. Because they are brain hormones, they promise to open a new chapter of research on how the brain functions sexually, both in general and in relation to the paraphilias. So also does the use of lithium carbonate, of which there is preliminary evidence that it simulates antiandrogenic hormones in the successful treatment of paraphilias.

Associative Determinism

Krafft-Ebing met the first challenge to his use of the principle of degeneracy in the form of Alfred Binet's stimulus-response principle of associative learning (see Hoenig, 1977; Pinkava, 1987). He met the challenge by accepting the associative principle with the proviso that degeneracy provided the necessary predisposition for the associative learning of a sexual pathology (see also Pioneer Survey).

Alfred Binet, the French psychologist renowned for having invented the intelligence test, directed his sexological attention to fetishism, a paraphilic condition in which the sexuoerotic response is aroused by an unlikely stimulus. There are two classes of fetish, the smelly-tasty ones, for example, a smelly shoe or undergarment, and the touchy-feely ones, for example, a lock of hair, or a silky, furry, or rubber garment. Binet explained the coupling of fetishistic stimulus and response as the outcome of their having been associated in a fortuitous but indelible encounter in childhood.

Binet's interest in childhood was taken up by his contemporary, Albert Moll (1862-1939), who in 1909 consolidated his earlier work in the volume translated from German as *The Sexual Life of the Child* (1912), the first book on juvenile sexual behavior and development. Moll adopted Binet's associationism concept, though without giving up the concept of a congenitally weak or defective constitution, and applied it in the treatment of paraphilic and related disorders in adults with hypnosis. The function of treatment was to loosen the paraphilic stimulus-response association by inducting aversion, under hypnosis, to the paraphilic inclinations and behavior.

The concept of associative pairing, as used by Binet and Moll, came from the British empiricist school of associationist psychology which had been founded by John Locke (1632-1704). It was a concept made to order for transliteration into Pavlovian reflexological conditioning and, indeed, by 1923, Vladimir Bekhterev (1857-1927) (quoted in Pinkava, 1987) did precisely that. Bekhterev applied the concept of conditioning broadly to include not only perversion (paraphilia) but also inversion (homosexuality).

Today's heirs to the associationism of Binet, Moll, and Bekhterev have one line of descent by way of Hull's drive-reduction learning theory. Miller and Dollard (1950) used this theory to explain how a stimulus, assumed to be sexually neutral, could be paired with an orgasm-inducing stimulus, and so become the object of a derivative or conditioned sexual drive.

Drive theory, however, has been eclipsed by B. F. Skinner (b. 1904) and his school of operant conditioning, on which has been constructed the psychotherapeutic edifice of behavior modification. An early essay into the applicability of conditioning principles to the genesis and treatment of paraphilia is that of Marks (1972) on fetishism.

Behavior modificationism prides itself on having no theory other than the pragmatics of associative conditioning and deconditioning, unencumbered by teleological philosophy and metaphysics. Whereas there are hundreds of published reports on behavior modification applied to the treatment of paraphilia, there is no comprehensive theory of the paraphilias, only piecemeal hypothetical constructs (see, for example, Bandura and Walters, 1963). The issues of degeneracy, heredity, and predisposition are ignored as irrelevant. A simplified explanation of etiology in terms of associative learning and conditioning suffices—and likewise, with respect to treatment. Krafft-Ebing would be entitled to claim, as he did of Binet's associationism, that the stimulus-response explanation of etiology of paraphilia applies only in certain predisposed individuals. Scientifically, whereas it is no longer legitimate to equate predisposition with hereditary degeneracy, exactly what does constitute a predisposition remains, for the most part, unknown. Unknown does not, however, mean nonexistent—it means waiting to become known.

A second line of descent from Binet's associationism is social constructionism, the academic child of social psychology, sociology, and cultural anthropology. Social constructionism, like behavior modification, claims no theory other than stimulus-response associationism. The stimulus is the social construct or script (Gagnon and Simon, 1973), and the response is its cognitive incorporation within the individual self—rather like a regional diet. Insofar as the members of a society share the same menus or the same sexual mores, social scripting is adequate as a description of the script they share, whereas it fails to be an adequate explanation of the origin of the script, or of the origin of minority scripts.

A positive value of scripting theory is that it draws attention to the extensive range of sexual scripts in different societies, historically and ethnically. The cultural relativity of what each society defines as orthodox and unorthodox, legal and illegal, moral and immoral, had first been approached as a subject of sexological scholarship by the Italian physician, already mentioned, Paolo Mantegazza, author of *Trilogia dell 'Amore* (in English, *The Sexual Relations of Mankind,* 1937). Mantegazza explained the perversions as the outcome of restrictive sexual norms that excessively restrict and impede the coming together of the sexes, and thus facilitate perversion, including masturbation, as a substitute. For him, conjugation in penovaginal copulation was the only legitimate form of sexuality.

Another proponent of comparative sexology for whom copulation was the criterion standard was Iwan Bloch. He has become known as the sexologist who coined the term, "sexualwissenschaft," which is translated as "sexology." First published in German in 1907, his *Sexual Life of Our Times* appeared in an American translation in 1937. Bloch interpreted the ethnographic diversity of the perversions and their widespread occurrence as evidence that, in themselves, they had neither a moral nor a forensic significance, but must be regarded more or less as biological variations of the normal impulse. Nonetheless, that did not contravene society's right of intervention, with prophylactic measures to prevent perversion—such as keeping children away from harmful influences, no sex-segregated crowding together, no mutual onanism, no contact with perverts, no access to obscene books and pictures, no places of ill repute, and plenty of hard physical exercise at puberty. Bloch was equivocal in construing the evidence of comparative ethnic sexology with respect to the principle of social tolerance of diversity on the one hand, and the principle of social contagion on the other. He invoked will power to identify those who would resist contagion.

Will power has no pragmatic value in explaining individual resistance to social contagion. The inherent deficiency of associationist determinism, namely, that it fails to explain individual difference and uniqueness, is shared by the principles of social contagion, social scripting, and behavior modification. All three fail to give a sufficient explanation of why one person becomes a paraphile and another does not. If their associationism explanation were, per se, sufficient, then the paraphilic scripts that are prosecuted as pornography would turn the censors, judges, attorneys, and juries who see them into paraphiles. Such is manifestly not the case. Paraphilic pornography has sexuoerotic appeal only to those who already have the matching paraphilia in their own sexuoerotic imagery and ideation—like attracts like! There must be at least one other variable to account for why a person is capable of responding to one particular type of paraphilic pornography and not others. Associationism does not address itself to this issue. Hence the failure of associationism to explain why paraphiles fail to conform to the sexual orthodoxy scripted by society.

The newest contender with a claim to rectifying this failure goes by the in-vogue name of addictionology. Sexual addiction (Carnes, 1985; 1986) is a newly coined term for a disorder as fictitious as thirst addiction, hunger addiction, or reading addiction. Genuine addictions always have a predicate, and, as in grammar, it predicates an object, thus, for example: addiction is to alcohol or coffee, to chocolate candy or ice cream; and to murder mysteries or porno novels, respectively. Sexual addictionology does not address the specificity of addiction. Instead, it decrees that the only non-addictive form of sexual expression is lifelong heterosexual fidelity and commitment in monogamous marriage. Everything else is the gateway of sin through which exits the broad road that leads to sexual depravity, degeneracy, and addiction. Within addictionology, the wheel of degeneracy has made a full turn!

Intrapsychic Determinism

Krafft-Ebing died in 1902, old enough to have left the legacy of *Psychopathia Sexualis* to Freud, but too young to leave on record his reaction to Freud's 1905 publication of *Drei Abhandlungen zur Sexualtheorie* (Three Essays on the Theory of Sexuality). One may assume, however, that Krafft-Ebing would have recognized that his own explanation of sexual psychopathology could not absorb Freud's principle of intrapsychic determinism as it had done Binet's principle of associative determinism.

The psychopathologies of sex were, in the vocabulary of Freud, the "perversions," the name they still go by in most of contemporary psychoanalysis (see, for example, Stoller, 1975). Freud's explanation of the perversions is postulated upon the phylogenetic principles of recapitulation and evolutionary reversion (see also Phylogenetic Determinism).

Haeckel's principle that ontogeny recapitulates phylogeny was popularized by Wilhelm Boelsche (1861-1939), a novelist who was also a popular science writer. Haeckel had written on gastriculation, the process which he studied in marine sponges, whereby the cell mass invaginates to create a primitive stomach with a mouth and, later, an anal orifice—with, later still in higher organisms, genitalia. Boelsche popularized this gastrea theory as portraying the phylogenetic evolution of sexual sensitivity from the external skin to the gastreal mouth, and thence to the primitive cloaca, the anus, and finally the genitalia (Sulloway, 1979, p. 262). Boelsche's popularization went further, and portrayed the parallel between the morphology and method of reproduction in phylogenetic evolution, beginning with oral fusion and progressing through cloacal exchange to genital union. Recapitulated in individual development and reconstrued as instinctual, these evolutionary stages constitute, in Freudian theory, the developmental stages of infantile "polymorphous-perverse" sexuality—oral, anal, phallic, and genital.

In Freud's intrapsychic explanation of perversion, the principle of evolutionary reversion was dually represented as fixation, if development had been arrested, and regression, if development had progressed and then gone backward. Provided the outcome of either fixation or regression was the persistence of a prior stage of infantile polymorphous-perversity, then it would be named perversion (Freud did not differentiate all of the perversions, syndrome by syndrome). By contrast, if the perversion were modified and disguised by the superimposition of repression, then the outcome would be named neurosis.

To be complete, the intrapsychic explanation of perversion must include an explanation of the selectivity of fixation and regression in perverting only a minority of individuals, and not the majority. There are various options: degeneracy, hereditary taint, or neuropathology, for example. However, these options are not intrapsychic, but extrinsic.

Another option is traumatic interference with development which, in the case of the development of sexuality, might be brought about by premature or illicit sexual stimulation. Traumatic interference is not consistent with an exclusively intrapsychic explanation, insofar as traumatic interference originates extrinsically and is, therefore, a specific instance of associative determinism—as when genital arousal might become prematurely associated with being masturbated by a nursemaid, for example, or with being seduced, possibly incestuously, by an older person. In 1895, Freud gave credence to both of these possibilities. Whereas he did not formally relinquish the possibility of a harmful effect of masturbation, he completely abandoned the formulation of hysterical neurosis as the outcome of premature seduction. Freud's 1897 turning point toward a theory of intrapsychic determinism that was, in toto, consistently and exclusively intrapsychic is well known and, at the present time, acrimoniously controversial (Sulloway, 1979; Masson, 1984).

Within an exclusively intrapsychic system of explanation, there is a logically finite number of alternative intrapsychic principles with which to explain intrapsychic fixation and regression. One is the intrapsychic principle of idiopathic determinism, according to which it is preordained that fixation and regression will take place in the development of selected individuals only. A second is the intrapsychic principle of chronological sequence, according to which there is a phylogenetically ordained schedule for the various aspects of intrapsychic development, divergence from which induces fixation or regression. A third is the intrapsychic principle of periodicity, according to which intrapsychic development is phylogenetically preordained to take place in a fluctuating, cyclic, or pulsatile manner, without which fixation and regression will take place.

None of these three principles appears in Freud's system of intrapsychic explanation, although it is known from his letters to Wilhelm Fliess (1858-1928) that, after giving due consideration to the principle of periodicity as propounded by Fliess, he did not use it (Sulloway, 1979).

A fourth principle by which to explain fixation and regression intrapsychically is the principle of conflict or incompatibility between two or more components of the psyche, one being more powerful or dominant than the other. It is known, also from Freud's letters to Fliess, that the principle of conflict was prominent in two of Fliess's evolutionary formulations, the one of inherent intrapsychic bisexuality, and the other of sexual attraction by way of olfaction and the nose versus vision and the eyes. In Freud's formulations, the principle of conflict, transmuted into the principle of intrapsychic conflict, occupied a prominent position in his system of intrapsychic determinism. It applies to instinctual conflict and to hierarchical conflict between the instinctual id, and the ego and superego. Freud was equivocal about an exclusively intrapsychic origin of the superego. The major contests are in the arenas of bisexuality and the Oedipus complex.

In the arena of bisexuality, the intrapsychic contest is between heterosexuality and homosexuality. Either side may win. Homosexuality, by definition, is a perversion. Therefore, defeat of the perversion entails an alliance with repression. Repressed homosexuality does not disappear but becomes latent homosexuality, able to reappear only in the disguise of neurotic symptomatology, for example, paranoia. What is missing in this paradigm of intrapsychic determinism is that it lacks two principles, one to explain why and in whom heterosexuality will win the contest, and another to explain why and in whom homosexuality, a perversion in psychoanalytic terminology, will win without being transformed into a neurosis. The principle of intrapsychic conflict fails to fulfill its promise of providing an explanation of homosexuality as a perversion.

In the arena of the Oedipus complex, the intrapsychic contest is between infantile sexuality and infantile abstinence. The Oedipal triumph of being victorious over the rival, same-sexed parent would be the perversion of incest with the other-sexed parent. The tragedy of not being victorious is ensured by an Oedipal alliance with repression, and the penalty of defeat is castration anxiety. Under the threat of castration anxiety, sexuality can reappear only in the disguise of neurotic symptomatology. Here again, the principle of intrapsychic conflict fails to explain those who survive the Oedipal rivalry without neurosis, to be, instead, if not perverted, then healthy.

One way out of the dilemma of both latent homosexuality and castration anxiety is to make a doctrinal revision whereby latent homosexuality and/ or castration anxiety become the intrapsychic forces used to explain all of the perversions, except homosexuality and Oedipal incest, as if they were neuroses. The psychoanalyst with a lifetime of experience with paraphilic sex offenders who did precisely this, and used the term "paraphiliac neuroses," was Benjamin Karpman (1954, p. 579). He wrote: "Latent homosexuals may resort to paraphilia, or their sexual life may evidence pathology without recourse to paraphilia. Virtually all paraphilias spring from unconscious homosexuality; these perversions give rise to a number of sex crimes. Fellatio, cunnilingus, paederasty [anal coitus], when enacted in a heterosexual setting express unconscious homosexual trends" (p. 610).

Karpman wrote also that "unconscious incest pervades all neuroses, psychoses, and paraphilias" (p. 603). Karpman was not excessively dogmatic regarding the Oedipus complex and castration anxiety. By contrast, in a recent brief presentation on psychoanalytic theory and sexual deviation, Kline (1987) espoused Otto Fenichel (1897-1946), and his version of castration anxiety, in such statements as: "the fetish is an attempt to deny the lack of a penis; the male transvestite combines the homosexual's identification with his mother and the fetishist's denial that a woman has no penis; exhibitionism is an attempt at denial of castration; and voyeurs are fixated on experiences that aroused their castration anxiety."

The hazard of intrapsychic determinism is that, as in the foregoing examples, it is too readily converted into a dogma. A dogma is validated by the number of its converts and, conversely, of its victims, rather than by the pragmatics of its empirical productivity.

Biographical Determinism

The sexual life in the individual has "various phases, beginning with the stage of puberty to the extinction of sexual feeling," wrote Krafft-Ebing (1931, p. 7). "The advance of puberty develops the impulses of youth, hitherto vague and undefined, into conscious realization of the sexual power. The psychological reactions of animal passion manifest themselves in the irresistible desires of intimacy, and the longing to bestow the strange affections of nature upon others. . . . The sexual instinct manifested in childhood, independently of the physiological processes of puberty, may always be regarded as an accompanying symptom of a neuropsychopathic constitutional condition" (pp. 55-56). After quoting the case of a girl who "masturbated from her fourth year, consorted with boys of the age of ten or twelve, and had thought of killing her parents so that she might become her own mistress and give herself up to pleasure with men," Krafft-Ebing commented: "In these cases of premature manifestation of the libido, the children begin early to masturbate; and since they are greatly predisposed constitutionally, they often sink into dementia, or become subjects of severe degenerative neuroses or psychoses."

Krafft-Ebing was in conformity with orthodoxy of his era by equating the sexuality of childhood with pathology. To do so was to be heir to the degeneracy legacy of Tissot, to the morbid fascination of moralizing professionals with the evils of masturbation. In the second half of the last century, and well into the 20th century, hundreds of publications on sexual hygiene warned parents and youth of the terrible consequences of not being chaste and abstinent.

The early proponent of this tradition in America was the Reverend Sylvester Graham (1794-1851) in *A Lecture to Young Men* (1834). One of his disciples was John Harvey Kellogg, M.D. (1852-1943), an antisexual fanatic and vegetarian who invented corn flakes as a meat substitute and antimasturbation food. He wrote *Plain Facts for Old and Young, Embracing the Natural History and Hygiene of Organic Life* (1888) on his honeymoon.

As sexology expanded in the wake of *Psychopathia Sexualis,* Albert Moll was the first sexologist who had the temerity to question the orthodox doctrine of childhood sexuality as being itself always a manifestation of pathology as well as being premonitory of pathological adult sexuality. As early as 1897, in *Untersuchungen ueber die Libido Sexualis* [translated as *Libido Sexualis: Studies in the Psychosexual Laws of Love Verified by Clinical Case Histories* (1933)], he referred to the theory of childhood play put forward by Karl Groos (1861-1946). In *Die Spiele der Thiere* (1896) [translated as *The Play of Animals: A Study of Animal Life and Instinct* (1898)], Groos had developed the evolutionary concept of play as a necessary preactivity or practice of instinctive behavior in preparation for maturity. Moll and Groos both included sexuality among the preactive instincts of childhood (Sulloway, 1979, p. 250). Moll adduced substantiating evidence from other species.

Moll's full statement on childhood sexuality as a precursor of adult sexuality in both health and pathology appeared in 1909 under the title, *Das Sexualleben des Kindes* [translated as *The Sexual Life of the Child* (1912)]. There he wrote: "The experiences of childhood, which have not as yet any relationship with sexual life are, nevertheless of great significance in relation to the subsequent upbuilding of the sexual life, and above all in relation to the development of the psychosexual sentiments." Then he added in reference to a case example: "What applies, here, to a pathological instance may also be assumed to be true of the normal sexual life."

Moll refuted the traditional doctrine that childhood masturbation is a perversion of which the inevitable outcome is perversion of sexuality in adulthood. Similarly, he adduced evidence to refute the doctrine that same-sex contacts in childhood are inevitably the forerunner of the perversion (the term then currently used) of homosexuality in adulthood. Moll warned that a history of any one of the perversion-like sexual phenomena of childhood is compatible with sexual normalcy in adulthood. Moreover, the appearance of similarity between juvenile and postpubertal sexuality did not automatically make them identical.

Moll's concepts of developmental determinism and of the normalcy of libidinal development in childhood were assimilated by Freud who, according to Sulloway (1979), read and annotated *Libido Sexualis* in the summer of 1897. In September of that year, he relinquished his seduction theory of hysterical neurosis and replaced it with the beginnings of his own developmental libido theory of infantile sexuality and intrapsychic determinism (see also Intrapsychic Determinism).

In explaining cases of sexual pathology in adulthood, when the anamnesis showed antecedent evidence backdated to childhood, Moll resorted to traditional explanations of their pathogenetic significance. His explanation of the divergence between a healthy versus a pathological outcome of childhood sexuality in adulthood was, de facto, statistical. All biological processes manifest variations and anomalies Moll noted, and for him the sex instinct was no exception.

Havelock Ellis (1859-1939), Moll's British contemporary in sexology, shared with him the scientific spirit of documentary phenomenology and empiricism. He assembled and compared hypotheses, theories, and doctrines that documented the wide range of other people's attempts to explain the variations of human sexuality. He assembled also an archive of sexual biographies that documented the wide-ranging diversity of sexual variability in the population at large, and not only in the clinical and criminal population. When the first of the seven volumes of his magnum opus, *Studies in the Psychology of Sex*, appeared in 1897 (see Ellis, 1942), the entire edition was confiscated as obscene. Publication in English was then transferred from London to Philadelphia. When the final volume appeared in 1928, distribution was still restricted to the medical and legal professions. Purchase by the general public was not legally permitted until after 1930.

The scholarship of Moll and Ellis demolished the notion of an absolute line of demarcation separating the sexual biographies of those whom society accepted as normal from those whom it did not. The next logical step was the one taken by Alfred Kinsey (1894-1956), namely, to poll a very large sample of the general population in order to ascertain the statistical prevalence of orthodoxy and unorthodoxy in the sexual biographies of people at large (Kinsey, et al., 1948; 1953). Kinsey's successors at his Institute for Sex Research applied the same statistical survey technique to an investigation of the sexual biographies of 1,356 white male sex offenders, subdivided according to the nature of the offense (Gebhard, et al., 1965). The comparison groups were 888 male prisoners accused of nonsexual offenses, and 477 nonoffender males.

The statistical survey method lends itself to the ascertainment of statistical frequencies and correlations in a large sample of sexual biographies. It is designed so as to test a preexisting explanatory conjecture or hypothesis, and it may lead to additional conjectures or hypotheses for future statistical testing. However, frequencies and correlations, per se, do not constitute an explanation. They may, indeed, be fortuitous, or too fragmentized to be compatible with any conceptually consistent and coherent explanation or theory. The hazard of fragmentization is ubiquitous. It is present whenever a single-variable research design is superimposed on a phenomenon that is multivariately determined. In contemporary sexological research, univariate research design is in vogue. It is the bane of biographical determinism, for the sexual biography is determined not only multivariately, but also sequentially.

Biographical determinism that is multivariate and sequential is exemplified in *Lovemaps* (Money, 1986a) and in Chapter 2, "Lovemap Synthesis," that follows.

CHAPTER 2

Lovemap Synthesis

Lovemap Biography

Biographical determinism is chronological, broad-spectrum, and diversified. It is chronological insofar as it develops or unfolds sequentially. It is broad-spectrum insofar as it is multivariate—in other words, multiple constituent determinants are compatibly incorporated into a coherent whole. The constituent determinants may themselves be classified as genetic, phyletic, neurocortical, hormonal, immunologic, nutritional, toxic, stimulus-responsive, intrapsychic, and so forth. Biographical determinism is diversified insofar as it has diverse outcomes. In the case of the sexual biography, for example, the outcome may be as diverse as normophilic or paraphilic; and, if paraphilic, as thematically diversified and disparate in consequences as are the forty-odd named paraphilias.

A paraphilia is a manifestation of a lovemap that is, according to the ideological criterion of everyday orthodoxy, unorthodox. In street parlance it is "kinky." A lovemap is a postulated functional entity, synchronously in the brain and the mind, analogous to native language. It is formally defined as: a developmental representation or template, synchronously functional in the mind and the brain, depicting the idealized lover, the idealized love affair, and the idealized program of sexuoerotic activity with that lover, projected in imagery and ideation, or in actual performance (Money, 1986a; 1988).

Historically, geographically, and sociologically, the cultural response to the overt manifestations of paraphilic lovemaps has varied, and has been contingent on their thematic content, their strength and nonsuppressibility, and their manifestation in ideation and imagery alone, as compared with their being enacted in live performance, as well. Some have been categorized as whimsically playful and quaint. Others have fallen into the category of being intrusively annoying and inconvenient. Paraphilias in a third category have been characterized as maleficently offensive and injurious. Those legally decreed to be crimes have been distributed across all three categories, and criminal paraphilias with victims have not been distinguished from those that are victimless.

The right to live and let live applies two-sidedly, to those with a paraphilic lovemap, on one side, and to those eligible to be victims, as in paraphilic serial lust murder, to take an extreme case, on the other. The moral and legal right of society to intervene on behalf of the rights of potential victims, without depriving the bearers of a paraphilic lovemap of their rights, requires a principle that will allow the rational setting of a dividing line between social tolerance and social intervention. This is the principle of personal sexual inviolacy (Money, 1979; 1986a, pp. 4-6), namely, that no one has the right to impinge on someone else's personal sexual inviolacy by the imposition of the demands of his/her own paraphilic lovemap, without the other person's informed consent. A contract of informed consent entails that the terms of the contract be specified explicitly, so that the end is fully predicated by the beginning. In a sexual engagement, that means no surprise outcome unilaterally imposed on one partner by another.

Two paraphilic lovemaps that reciprocally match one another, as in sadomasochism, for example, may provide the basis for a consensual contract between two partners. Alternatively, one of the partners may accommodate to the paraphilic lovemap of the other partner, even to the point of collusion. The converse of accommodation is exclusion—the inchoate recognition of being left out of the imagery of the partner's paraphilic lovemap, and of being only an accessory, or a stage property, in a drama of love unrequited.

Paraphilic lovemaps are stable, usually over a lifetime. Their paraphilic content may be simple, unadorned, and homogeneous; or it may be compound, elaborate, and heterogeneous. The content may manifest itself promptly at puberty, or after a delay, with an interval of variable duration before imagery and ideation are transformed, if ever, into performance. The unfolding of the lovemap may be complete, on the first occasion, or in installments, like a drama with acts, scenes, and intermissions, each of variable duration. The series of installments may be misconstrued as separate paraphilias, instead of progressively enacted components of one multiplex paraphilia.

As in the case of native language, in the human species the lovemap is not innate, nor is it prenatally foreordained in all its details. It is not preprogramed, in toto, in the genome. The extent to which the genetic code may be responsible for programing prenatal components of the lovemap, however, remains to be ascertained. By analogy with native language, it would appear that the brain must be a human brain, and that it must be healthy and intact, if the lovemap is to be healthy and intact.

Among linguists, there is increasing consensus that there is a "deep structure" of a linguistic template that predisposes the infant brain to assimilate and speak a native language, and to do so sooner and more effectively than when acquiring a second language at a later age. Of course, no one will deny that the actual native language enters the brain through the ears, or alternatively through the eyes of the nonhearing, or the skin-sense of touch of those without either sight or hearing.

According to the experimental and clinical evidence reviewed in *Gay, Straight and In-Between* (Money, 1988), the deep structure of a lovemap template almost certainly predisposes its possessor to the subsequent assimilation and manifestation of stereotypes of being masculine or feminine. Even this basic dualism, however, is dependent on postnatal input through the senses before the masculine/feminine ratio in the lovemap becomes as native as the native language.

It is possible that other features of the deep structure of the lovemap template remain yet to be identified—such as, for example, different male/female predispositions toward mating dominance, or toward dependence on the eyes versus the skin senses for sexuoerotic arousal, or toward paraphilic versus hypophilic syndromes if lovemap differentiation goes awry. Whatever male/female differences might be identified, then it is far less likely that they will be attributable to genetics, directly, than to indirect genetic or other influences on the prenatal sex hormonalization (or dehormonalization) of male/female dimorphism of sexual pathways in the brain (see also Neuropathological Determinism).

Individual variance in the deep structure of the lovemap template, prenatally, may be exaggerated, diminished, or left unchanged in the course of the completion of the template, postnatally. Paraphilic intrusions on the course of its completion may be either intrinsic or extrinsic. Intrinsic intrusions that have already been recognized in some youthful paraphiles are pathological impulsiveness secondary to the 47,XYY syndrome; idiopathic quasi-autistic temperament type with failure to troopbond; traumatic head injury with residual temporal lobe damage; and spells or fugue states of an epileptiform nature (see also Neuropathological Determinism).

Extrinsic intrusions that may direct the postnatal completion of the lovemap template toward paraphilia are, according to present evidence, related to the phase of childhood sexual rehearsal play, with playmates, that covers especially the period between 4-5 to 8-9 years of age. In human juveniles, as in other primate species, sexual rehearsal play is a preparation for maturity. Rhesus monkeys deprived of juvenile sexual rehearsal play by being raised in isolation do not become competent in copulatory presenting and mounting as adults and do not reproduce their species. Juveniles that are released to play with age mates for as briefly as half an hour a day may become capable of copulation but only after a delay from the expected age of 6-9 months to 18-24 months and only in about one-third of cases. These latter juveniles, even though they do copulate when mature, have a low birth rate (see also Money, 1988).

As a species, human beings who are heirs to Western civilization have a long cultural heritage of negative strategies for dealing with juvenile sexual rehearsal play. These are strategies that thwart, warp, and distort the normophilic development of the lovemap so that the outcome is a vandalized lovemap. The strategies of vandalism include indifference and neglect instead of the active promotion of normophilic development; humiliation, prohibition, and abusive punishment of sexual rehearsal play; and coercive traumatization, wrong timing, and wrong matching of ages in sexual rehearsal play. The malignancy shared by all of these sources of lovemap pathology is the Catch-22 dilemma, or entrapment, inherent in any type of taboo activity, namely, that you're damned if you do reveal it, and damned if you don't. Therefore, no help is available.

Opponent-Process

Irrespective of whether the paraphilia-inducing intrusion on the completion of the lovemap is intrinsic, extrinsic, or both, the final common pathway is the one already expounded by which a phylism that is not sexuoerotic becomes enchained in the service of sexuoeroticism (see also Chapter 1, Phylogenetic Determinism). As in the manner of imprinting, once the enchainment occurs, it is persistently resistant to disenchainment.

The paradox of phylismic enchainment in the formation of a paraphilic lovemap is that it controverts the reward/punishment law of learning enshrined in both psychology and common sense. In other words, negative experiences that were traumatizing, harmful, humiliating, disgusting, or punishable become transmogrified from negative to positive. Instead of being avoided, they are sought after. Instead of being penalized, they are rewarded—with orgasm. Instead of being erotic turn-offs, they become erotically thrilling.

There was no solution to this paradox until the psychologist Richard Solomon (b. 1918) discovered a new law of learning, the law of opponent-process (Solomon, 1980). Aphoristically stated this law means that aversion turns into addiction. For example, a juvenile who upchucks and is deathly sick from smoking a first cigarette, rapidly becomes a nicotine addict. Or, the sky-diver's initial terror soon flip-flops into ecstasy, and he becomes addicted to the paraphernalia and the sport.

Psychopharmacologically, the likely explanation is that the flip-flop occurs when terror in the brain releases a counteractive flood of brain opiates which produce an ecstatic euphoria. That converts the parachutist into a junkie for sky-diving. Likewise, in the paraphile's history, there is a flip-flop from sexual terror to sexual ecstasy. The stimulus that had been aversive has become addictive. Its pursuit is reiterated, over and over. The addiction is to the stimulus, for example, the fetish of the fetishist, or the harness and whips of the masochist. The paraphilia is the pursuit of the stimulus, each repetition of the pursuit being ritualistically a replication of the others. This is the paraphilic ritual.

Reiteration of the paraphilic ritual occurs in dreams and fantasies, as well as in actual performance. It is insistent and demanding and, in the autonomous way of somnambulism, takes on a life of its own with its own schedule, in defiance of rationality, consequences, and voluntary control. It cannot be controlled by will power, and is unresponsive to punishment or even the threat of execution.

The addictive euphoria or ecstasy of the paraphilic ritual is erotic or orgasmic. Most, if not all, paraphiles, male and female, are hyperorgasmic—a daily quota of four or more orgasms, for example. The neuroendocrine dynamics of as many as ten ejaculations a day in male paraphiles still await explanation. The release of orgasm may be dependent on the performance of the paraphilic ritual, or on a replay of its imagery, as if on a mental videotape. Performance of the ritual may be preliminary to the culmination of orgasm, which may be delayed until the ritual is replayed in imagery.

Paleodigms

The popular belief that paraphilic rituals are caught by social contagion, either directly from the example of other people, or indirectly from written or pictorial instructions or representations, pornographic or otherwise, is incorrect. Also incorrect is the alternative proposition that a paraphilia is reinvented each time it recurs or, more precisely, each time that a nonsexual phylism is enchained in the service of sexuoeroticism.

Phylisms have not only a long evolutionary history, but also a long cultural history. They have been encoded into ethnic customs and conventions of social behavior. Their original significance may have been retained or altered by having been enchained in the service of some other function, as in paraphilias. The larger context into which they are encoded has a significance of its own which in some instances constitutes a *paleodigm* [a term newly coined from Greek, *paleo,* ancient + *deigma,* example (Money, 1989a)]. A paleodigm is an embodiment of prescientific folk wisdom in a saying or a story that encodes a cause-and-effect explanation which has a significance that penetrates the idiom of everyday language, and that influences behavior.

The paraphilias are, inter alia, paleodigmatic syndromes, insofar as their rituals may be deciphered as exemplifying seven grand paleodigmatic stratagems. These seven are as follows.

Sacrifice and Expiation. This grand stratagem encodes the paleodigm of sin and its expiation or atonement through sacrifice. In this case, the sin is the experience of lust in genitoerotic arousal and orgasm. The ultimate in paraphilic sacrifice is serial lust murder. Its converse or antipode is the self-arranged risk of one's own accidental autoerotic death, by self-asphyxiation, for example, or by accidental self-electrocution. Alternatively, the risk of one's own erotic death may be self-stage managed, with another actor or actors coopted to perform in what may conclude as an accidental erotic homicide. Another form of paraphilic sacrifice is the punishment inflicted or received in a sadomasochistic performance.

Marauding and Predation. This grand stratagem encodes the paleodigm of capturing and possessing another human being by force, entrapment, or abduction. In military history, when victorious armies raped the women of the enemy they had defeated, rape was defined not as the sexual coercion of the female, but as the misappropriation of another man's property, for she belonged to either her father or her husband. In contemporary usage, the heterosexual meaning of the term "rape" has been changed to signify vaginal penetration insisted upon after a female, who may be a wife, paramour, or date, says no to a male (rape of a male by a female is rarely considered). Rape defined in this way bears only peripheral relationship to the clinical syndrome named raptophilia (the Latin derivative) or biastophilia (the Greek derivative). In the syndrome of raptophilia, the raptophile's genitoerotic arousal and, eventually the orgasm, are contingent on having a partner who, as a captive, is forced to yield sexually under conditions of threat, assault, and injury.

Mercantilism and Venality. This grand stratagem encodes the paleodigm of obtaining goods or services by bartering and trade, of which a specific instance is the payment of the bride price or the provision of a dowry in an arranged marriage. A mercantile or venal paraphilia is one in which the paraphile's genitoerotic arousal and orgasm are contingent on negotiating some form of payment. In the orgasm trade, lust is a commodity, bought and sold, independently of love and affection.

Fetishism and Talismanism. This grand stratagem encodes the paleodigm of being in possession of an object or artifact that has extraordinary power of causality that enables its possessor to control events and to make the otherwise impossible come to pass. A paraphilic fetish or talisman is an object or artifact that, as a stimulus of genitoerotic arousal and orgasm, substitutes for the person who is its owner. There are two categories of paraphilic fetishes and talismans. One comprises the touchy-feely or hyphephilic artifacts that are derived from human-body contact, especially with skin and hair. The other comprises the tasty-smelly or olfactophilic artifacts that are derived from human-body tastes and smells, especially sweaty and crotch smells.

Stigmatism and Eligibility. This grand stratagem encodes the paleodigm of love at first sight—the irresistible attraction that draws an observer toward an erstwhile stranger, even at a distance, as if the meeting had been inevitably predestined by an inexplicable fate. Some people explain it as due to the chemistry of love. Since there are, as yet, no laboratory tests for the brain's chemistries of love, it is more down to earth to explain the attraction as the observer's sudden recognition that there is something about the stranger that exactly mirrors the imagery and ideation of his or her brain's own *lovemap* (Money, 1986a). An extreme example is the lovemap of acrotomophilia, which decrees that the partner must be an amputee. The acrotomophilic observer of the amputated stump becomes love stricken. If the stranger responds by being love stricken also, then the reciprocal match holds promise of becoming the proverbial marriage made in heaven. It is the romantic alternative to an arranged marriage in which the partners are matched by a broker, or by the elders of their family and kin. Though the qualities that trigger love at first sight are not necessarily discordant with family ideals, they may be so. Then they derive their power from what they signify as a repudiation and defiance of family ideals. Thus, the heir to a politically conservative fortune may be able to be smitten in love only if his/her lover meets the eligibility requirements of belonging not only to an ethnic stock that is socially anathema to the heir's family, but also to a radical political faction or religious cult that is equally anathema.

Solicitation and Allure. This grand stratagem encodes the paleodigm of what is known in the animal kingdom as assortative, conspecific mating while being in season or in heat. It may take the form of a mating dance or courtship display, the gestures of which are an overt presentation of the sex organs as an invitation to copulate. Except in live shows and movies for erotic entertainment, in the human species the mating dance is more likely to be a debutante ball or disco dance than a display of the naked genitalia. Solicitation and allurement become paraphilic when, instead of being invitational and preliminary to bilateral erotosexual involvement, they are engaged in unilaterally, and themselves constitute the trigger on which orgasm is dependent. Thus, the person being solicited or allured needs only to look, and is spared the defilement of genital contact, whereas people fear that the paraphilic exhibitionist, as well as the peeping Tom (voyeur), will be a rapist. Paraphilic rape (raptophilia) belongs in the category of marauding and predation, and rarely overlaps with paraphilic solicitation and allure.

Subrogation and Understudyship. This grand stratagem encodes the paleodigm of rescue and deliverance by one who nobly and altruistically takes the place of someone else who would otherwise suffer and be a victim. A paraphilic subrogate or understudy is one whose lust becomes released only if, by taking the place of someone else as sexual partner, he/she emancipates that someone else from the duty and obligation of being in the role of partner in lust. For example, there are some instances of paraphilic adultery in which the role of at least one of the adulterous pair is to rescue the other's spouse from having to perform sexually and to be thereby defiled by lust. There are also some instances of paraphilic incest in which the same stratagem applies. It may apply also in association with commercial prostitution, in which case prostitution as a career is paraphilic as well as monetary. Subrogation or understudy paraphilias may be either heterosexual, homosexual, or bisexual.

Paleodigms illustrate the principle that information coded in the mind and the cerebral cortex may influence behavior, even though the connection between the paleodigm and the behavior is not explicitly formulated. A paleodigm is not, per se, causative. However, in syndromes characterized by selectively ritualized behavior, the performance of which has an effect on someone else, paleodigmatics may be of significance for diagnosis, prognosis, and treatment.

Five Universal Exigencies

In terms of the philosophy of causality, the exclusive extremes of teleological determinism and reductionistic determinism are both eschewed in the lovemap synthesis. Synthesism is not eclecticism, for eclecticism collates differences, whereas synthesism unifies them. The unifying principle of lovemap synthesism is biographical determinism, which is a network of multivariate and sequential contingencies. Biographical determinism is dynamic, not static, insofar as it conceptualizes relationships between developmental sequences and contiguities. It is empirical and operational. It is temporal before it is causal. That is to say, it construes a connection between two variables, first as a temporal event, and as a causal event only after causality has been empirically justified—which is very rare. Even the conjunction "because" in a sentence is a booby trap!

Biographical determinism is saved from being a museum of collectors' items, with no system or organization, by its affiliation with exigency theory (Money, 1957; 1986b, Chapters 8 and 9). Exigency theory is not a theory of causality, but a theory of existential inevitabilities within which the nexuses of causality are predicated. The manifold inevitabilities of existence are constituents of five universal exigencies of being human. Our very survival is premised upon them, and so also are the stipulations and strategies of our survival.

Pairbondage. Being bonded together in pairs, as in parent-child or lover-lover bonding, is what the term "pairbondage" means. In everyday usage, bondage implies servitude or enforced submission. Although pairbondage is defined so as not to exclude this restrictive connotation, it has a larger meaning that encompasses also mutual dependency and cooperation, and affectional attachment. Pairbondage has a twofold phyletic origin in mammals. One is mutual attachment between a nursing mother and her feeding baby, without which the young fail to survive. The other is mutual attraction between males and females, and their accommodation to one another in mating, without which a diecious species fails to reproduce itself.

Male-female pairbonding is species specific and individually variable with respect to its duration and the proximity of the pair. In human beings, the two extremes are represented by anonymous donor fertilization, at the extreme of anonymity, and lifelong allegiance and copulatory fidelity, at the extreme of personal proximity.

Troopbondage. Troopbondage means bondedness among individuals so that together they become members of a family or troop that continues its long-term existence despite the loss or departure of any one member. Human troopbondage has its primate phyletic origin in the fact that members of the troop breed not in unison but asynchronously, with transgenerational overlap and with age-related interdependency. In newborn mammals, the troopbonding of a baby begins with its pairbonding with its mother as the phyletically ordained minimum unit for its survival and health. After weaning, in herding and troopbonding species it is also phyletically ordained that isolation and deprivation of the company of other members of the species, or their surrogate replacements, is incompatible with health and survival. Nonhuman primate species are, in the majority of instances, troopbonders like ourselves.

Abidance. Abidance means continuing to remain, be sustained, or survive in the same condition or circumstances of living or dwelling. It is a noun formed from the verb "to abide" (from the Anglo-Saxon root, *bidan,* to bide). There are three forms of the past participle, "abode," "abided," and "abidden."

In its present usage, abidance means sustentation, or to be sustained in one's ecological niche or dwelling place in inanimate nature in cooperation or competition with others of one's own species, amongst other species of fauna and flora. Abidance has its phyletic origin in the fact that human primates are mammalian omnivores ecologically dependent on air, water, earth, and fire, and on the products of these four, particularly in the form of nourishment, shelter, and clothing, for survival. Human troops or individuals with an impoverished ecological niche that fails to provide sufficient food, water, shelter, and clothing do not survive.

Ycleptance. "Yclept" is an Elizabethan word, one form of the past participle of to clepe, meaning to name, to call, or to style. "Ycleped" and "cleped" are two alternative past participles. "Ycleptance" means the condition or experience of being classified, branded, labeled, or typecast. It has its phyletic basis in likeness and unlikeness between individual and group attributes. Human beings have named and typecast one another since before recorded time. The terms range from the haphazard informality of nicknames that recognize personal idiosyncrasies, to the highly organized formality of scientific classifications or medical diagnoses that prognosticate our futures. The categories of ycleptance are many and diverse: sex, age, family, clan, language, race, religion, politics, wealth, occupation, health, physique, looks, temperament, and so on. We all live typecast under the imprimatur of our fellow human beings. We are either stigmatized or idolized by the brand names or labels under which we are yclept. They shape our destinies.

Foredoomance. "Doom," in Anglo-Saxon and Middle English usage, meant what is laid down, a judgment or decree. In today's usage it also means destiny or fate, especially if the predicted outcome is adverse, as in being doomed to suffer harm, sickness, or death. A foredoom is a doom ordained beforehand. "Foredoomance" is the collective noun that, as here defined, denotes the condition of being preordained to die, and to be vulnerable to injury, defect, and disease. Foredoomance has its phyletic origins in the principle of infirmity and the mortality of all life forms. Some individuals are at greater risk than others because of imperfections or errors in their genetic code. Some are at greater risk by reason of exposure to more dangerous places or things. All, however, are exposed to the risk, phyletically ordained, that all life forms, from viruses and bacteria to insects and vertebrates, are subject to being displaced and preyed upon by other life forms. Foredoomance applies to each one of us at first hand, in a primary way, and also in a derivative way insofar as it applies to those we know. Their suffering grieves us; their dying is our bereavement.

The five universal exigencies, when applied to the study of individual cases, as in the seven chapters that follow, systematically guard against the inadvertent neglect of data and their determinants, without which the biographical outcome would be insufficiently accounted for.

Biographical Outcome: Methodology

The seven biographies that follow constitute an opportunity sample that consists of the seven cases from among several hundred on file in the Johns Hopkins Psychohormonal Research Unit (PRU) that met three criteria for inclusion. These three criteria were: a history of endocrine and/or genital defect diagnosed in childhood; a history of treatment and long-term pediatric and psychohormonal follow-up; and a developmental history of paraphilic imagery and/or practice first recognized at or after adolescence and continuing into maturity.

PRU referrals have been from the Johns Hopkins Pediatric Endocrine Clinic (PEC). There has been no known referral bias that might have favored cases prone to the development of a paraphilia. Patients who reach the PEC from the surrounding catchment area may or may not constitute a random, nonbiased sample of cases with pediatric endocrine and/or genital defects.

By ordinary statistical standards, the size of the sample is small. However, in view of the infrequency of longitudinal outcome studies, it can be considered large. To the best of the authors' knowledge, there has been no other prospective developmental study of paraphilia.

Ideally, a sample would be large enough to warrant statistical comparison with a contrast group. In the world of health-care, however, some syndromes are so rare that it is not possible to assemble a large, clinically homogenous series of cases in one medical center, even in the course of an entire professional life.

Currently, all long-term outcome studies in sexology have the value of scarcity. That justifies restoration of the tradition, widely accepted a century ago, of publishing long and thorough case studies. There is a special place in sexology at this present phase of its history for the detailed single case report, particularly the report of a unique case that has the paramount virtue of showing that accepted theory or dogma needs to be changed in order to accommodate a new hypothesis. That new hypothesis then leads to the devising of a research design whereby it may be tested.

The single matched-pair research design is one in which two unique or rare cases are compared. They are matched on the criterion of being concordant in some respects, and discordant in others—for example, in intersex cases, concordant for etiology and diagnosis, and discordant for assigned sex and rearing. Eventually, more matched pairs of the same type may be found, thus allowing two matched groups to be compared statistically.

The seven biographies in this book are biographies of cases that are unique in the study of paraphilia, insofar as they were obtained prospectively, not retrospectively. Each is presented singly, as there has been no available companion case suitable for comparison and contrast regarding paraphilia. Thus, the seven biographies do not offer proof of causality, but rather hypotheses of where to search for causality.

The consolidated, psychohormonal files, not the actual patients, constituted the data base for the present study. Each PRU file has been built-up over the years by a succession of professional staff members.

The consolidated psychohormonal file contains not only the longitudinal psychoendocrine history, but also the pediatric, medical, and surgical history, and other pertinent laboratory, clinical, social, and academic reports. The contents of each file are arranged in chronological sequence, and subdivided according to the classification of a standard Table of Contents, namely, Endocrine and General Medical History, Surgical History, School History, Social Agency History, Psychological Testing, and Psychohormonal Unit Interviews and related data.

Each of the following seven biographical accounts began with checking and updating the consolidated psychohormonal file for completeness. If any records from other clinics, laboratories, or agencies were missing, they were retrieved. The most recent update interviews were recorded in person or, by appointment, via long-distance telephone. The interviews were conducted with the assistance of a written schedule of topics set forth in a systematic Schedule of Inquiry (for details see Money, 1986b, Chapter 8, and Money, 1989b).

After the records had been reviewed and completed, the pages of each file were numbered. In preparation for indexing and abstracting, four conceptual categories were defined, criticized, revised, and decided upon. The four categories are those under which the findings are presented in each biography. They are: Diagnostic and Clinical Biography; Family Pathology; Biography of Social Development; and Lovemap Biography. Within each category, a set of subcategories was defined so as to prevent oversights and omissions on the working sheets used for data indexing and abstracting. These subcategories were as follows:

Diagnostic and Clinical Biography: History of initial diagnosis; history of outpatient and inpatient pediatric medical and surgical treatment; history of parents' knowledge of the child's condition.

Family Pathology: Indubitable and explicit evidence of major feuding between the parents, between patient and parents, and between siblings and the patient; evidence of major psychiatric illness in immediate family members; evidence of major alcohol and/or drug abuse.

Biography of Social Development: History of peer group relationships and activities; academic history (including IQ and other achievement test data); vocational history.

Lovemap Biography: History of childhood sexual learning and sex rehearsal play; history of romantic dating in adolescence; history of sexuo-erotic imagery; history of sexuoerotic partnerships and pairbonding; primary sensory channels of sexuoerotic arousal.

The synopsis of each individual biography presents the developmental antecedents deemed to be of etiological significance in the genesis of the paraphilia. Then, in Chapters 10 and 11, the various antecedent variables that were shared and not shared are tabulated and compared, in preparation for the final conceptual analysis of Chapter 12.

CHAPTER 3

Biography 1: Pedophilia in a Male with a History of Hypothyroidism

Diagnostic and Clinical Biography

Biography 1 is that of a man of forty, with a history of treated congenital hypothyroidism of insidious onset in infancy. His lovemap differentiated as bisexual. The heterosexual component not only predominated, but also incorporated a paraphilic age discrepancy, first recorded in adulthood, such that the idealized lover was depicted as a peripubertal or early adolescent girl.

He was two years old when first seen in the Johns Hopkins Pediatric Endocrine Clinic (PEC). He was referred by his local physician for confirmation of a suspected diagnosis of hypothyroidism.

According to the referring physician's report, the child had been delivered by an uncomplicated cesarean section. There was no birth injury or infection. An umbilical hernia diagnosed at one month of age was treated successfully with the application of adhesive straps. At six months of age, an indirect right inguinal hernia was noticed but the surgery was deferred until age twelve months.

By the time the boy had reached the age of nearly two, there was inescapable evidence that his mental and physical development were retarded. The mother had had difficulty with feeding the baby, who "sucked poorly and took the bottle poorly." He had no teeth until he was seventeen months old, and did not stand until twenty months of age. His size at twenty months was that of a one year old. He did not speak even single words.

Following the suspected diagnosis of hypothyroidism at age twenty-one months, treatment was begun with one 0.25-grain tablet of USP dessicated thyroid, daily. Two months later the thyroid dosage was increased to 0.5 grain, daily.

When he was first seen in the PEC, the boy had been treated with thyroid for three months. At this time, his miniature size was the one visibly striking anomaly. Otherwise the body proportions were close to those expected in a two-year old. The behavioral characteristics typically expected in congenital hypothyroidism (Wilson and Foster, 1985), other than retarded development, were not conspicuous. The boy was alert, spoke a few words, and "resisted attempts to examine him vigorously and effectively." Only the history of retarded development and the small size gave credence to the hypothyroid diagnosis. Confirmation of the diagnosis required a radio-active iodine uptake test, after withholding thyroid treatment for three months. Thereupon, at age 2 yrs 3 mos, thyroid treatment was resumed, beginning with 0.5 grain daily. This dosage was progressively increased until, five months later, it was 1.5 grains daily, and by age 3 yrs 2 mos, 2 grains daily, at which level it was maintained throughout childhood.

Within the first four months after resumption of treatment, the boy grew 2 inches (5 cm), with a corresponding advance in all of his development. He became more physically active. He had a good appetite. By age three he could feed himself and he was toilet trained. His vocabulary had increased, and he could put three or four words together. In the examining room he appeared interested in his environment, was cooperative, and was not nervous or jittery. Whereas the height age had increased, the bone age had not advanced as rapidly as expected in response to thyroid therapy, and remained in arrears until puberty.

After an initial statural growth spurt, there was steady, gradual progress, physically. Prepubertally, the stature was rather short, with marked shortness of the extremities, but not the torso.

The onset of puberty was at the age of 12½. There was a rapid increase in height so that, at thirteen, the height age was a year in advance of the chronological age. The ultimate height was 5 ft 6 in (167.1 cm) which, according to the growth chart of the National Center for Health Statistics, places a male at the 5th percentile (Hamill et al., 1979).

The patient remained euthyroid throughout the subsequent years of follow-up until he was last seen at age forty. He had been followed into adulthood in the PEC until, at the age of twenty-seven, his complete endocrine care was transferred to an endocrinologist in his home town. Since there was no psychohormonal transfer available, he continued to maintain contact, sporadically, on a self-demand basis, with the PRU.

Family Pathology

When this boy was first seen in the PRU at the age of 5 yrs 2 mos, it was for the purpose of administering the first in a developmental series of intelligence tests as a part of a research study on the long-term outcome of IQ in treated hypothyroidism. It was against this background that information about psychopathology in his parents' marital relationship came out in a piecemeal fashion over an extended period of time. The full extent of the problem was eventually revealed by the boy's father, but not until eleven years after the initial psychohormonal visit.

During the intervening years the parents' reports were focused exclusively on the business at hand, namely, their son's intellectual and academic functioning. In this context, it gradually became apparent that the mother was an anxious and perfectionist worrier, obsessively self-monitoring her performance as mother of her only child. Her husband, who regularly accompanied his wife and son to the PRU, was aware of this trait in his wife. However, he did not show any hint of overt dissatisfaction or resentment. He appeared to be a docile man, adjusted to the role of undemanding and understanding husband and provider. He mentioned, but without additional comment, that his wife had had two nervous breakdowns and had recently avoided a third one by going to a psychiatrist in their home town.

Three years later it was his wife who stated that she had again become so anxious and worried about things in general, and about her son in particular, that she had resumed psychotherapy on a weekly basis. The interviewer's written comment recorded after that interview reads: "It was the perfectionism of having no stone unturned that brought the woman here today to get my opinion. Perfectionism and her ambition for her son have set her obsessionally wondering whether she is expecting too much of him, or too little."

The important piece of information not disclosed at this time was that, during the year, the boy's father had left home for two months after having discovered that his wife and another man, one of his friends, were having an affair. Neither of them mentioned this marital crisis. Instead, there was only the usual concern about the son and his mother's anxieties about him. It subsequently became clear that her relentlessly obsessive focus on her son deflected attention away from the adversarial status of the marriage which became known only six years later, when the boy was sixteen.

The appointment when the boy was sixteen had been requested by the father because of his son's school difficulties, and his own long-standing and "very serious marital problems that were now out in the open." Ordinarily both parents accompanied their son to the hospital, but this time the father came without his wife.

Both the father and the son appeared deeply disturbed by the latest developments in their family life. The son said that he saw his mother as subject to schizophrenia because she had a split personality, being some days loving and reasonable, and other days hateful and irrational toward him and his father. Under the circumstances, he had considered the possibility of removing himself from his position between fighting parents by going to a boarding school, if the family finances would allow it. Otherwise, he would move to live with his paternal uncle. He eventually implemented the latter plan.

The father's report began in these words: "No, we hadn't been on the marital rocks—normal problems I guess." As the interview progressed, he contradicted that initial statement by giving a story of long-standing marital discord, the onset of which predated their son's birth by several years.

As the story unfolded, the classic marital pattern emerged of a power struggle devoid of affection and respect. In the husband's eyes, the image of his wife was that of a managerial and assertive woman, wielding power by being sexually seductive, and then exploding in spells of hysterically dissociated anger, yelling, and hatred. By inference, his own image was that of being the injured party who withdrew from dispute and was sexually uncoercive. Though he retreated into nonviolent resistance and silent sabotage when under pressure, he did not recognize himself as being passively aggressive, par excellence.

According to his interpretation, the primary conflict with his wife that laid the foundation for their estrangement was rooted in sexuality. His wife, he said, had started her sex life at a very young age with her brother and then "would have sex with any fellow she went steady with." She would taunt him by saying that she had gotten sexual satisfaction from every one of her partners except him. This was her retaliation against him, for not having sought treatment for a long-standing problem of premature ejaculation. His own premarital sexual experience had been almost nonexistent, he said. He had "had sex relations with only one person, that was in the seventh grade, other than my wife." He continued with increasing embarrassment: "I guess I have puritanical morals. I don't know. I have the urge. I was in Paris for one year after the war, and I met this girl whose husband was overseas, a diplomat. In the first week, we could have had relations. Then I talked so that she knew my standards. After that, only necking above the waist, as they say, and petting below. So, my adequacy with other women, I can't answer that."

They had been married for six years when his wife asked him for a divorce because of another man with whom she had had an affair while her husband was a soldier in Europe during World War II. After he agreed, she changed her mind and he came back "like a fool." Three years later their son was born. When the boy was four, the father was called back into the army and spent several months in Korea. His wife accused him of leaving her—a deliberate abandonment of her and their small child. Five years later there was another temporary separation. This time it was, indeed, an abandonment, insofar as it was his unilateral decision to leave. This was the occasion when he had found out that she was having an affair with his friend. After only two months he was back home, guilt ridden because of their son. "I'd leave today, too," he added, "except for my son. I can't leave him with her. She's a heller with him too. Except if she's getting her own way."

He thought that the psychotherapy which his wife had been pursuing for several years might prove beneficial to the marriage. It turned out, by contrast, to be a sophisticated source of further harassment: "I've been psychoanalyzed by my wife," he said with sarcasm. "What my wife's psychiatrist told her was that I hate women. Some sort of father complex. Selfish. Inadequate. The time I left home was just after my father died. That means I lost his support and didn't do so good."

The extent to which he was detached and locked into a preoccupation with martyrdom was evidenced by what he omitted even to mention, namely, that just two years earlier his wife had had to cope with uterine and ovarian cancer. She underwent surgery and cobalt treatment, the success of which became indisputable only after many years of full remission, following the final marriage break-up.

At the conclusion of this account of his marital drama, the man did not see any alternative but to separate. "I have no love for her whatsoever," he said. "I used to have, I think. I don't want to be near her anymore. I didn't use to be like that." His decision materialized a year and a half later, when the marriage ended in divorce.

For some time preceding his parents' divorce, at which time the son was 17½ years old, he was plagued with symptoms, namely, hair pulling, thumb sucking, sweating, throat-tightening, and transient hypertension, which could not be attributed to his endocrine condition. According to his own observation, they were associated with a high degree of severe tension that he experienced whenever he was around his parents. After his parents separated and he moved in with his uncle for four months, all of these symptoms disappeared. Then his uncle moved into a smaller house without accommodation for him. Consequently, he had to stay with his mother. Once again, "the tensions were impossible," and the same symptoms reappeared. He described his mother as having pendulum shifts from excessive affection to temper tantrums. He hated her affection as much as her temper tantrums. What scared him the most was his suspicion that his mother would be capable of seducing him (see Lovemap Biography).

His mother remarried a few months after the divorce. He moved back to his father's house at that time and has been living there ever since. His contacts with his mother became sporadic even though she was eager to see him more often. She was unhappy in her second marriage, and tried to make him her confidant, despite his overt reluctance. It was only shortly before her death from atherosclerosis, at the age of sixty-six, that he became more responsive to her initiative to improve their relationship. Their reconciliation took place just three months before she died. It was a theatrically dramatic scene, in which the mother confessed her errors and the son offered his forgiveness. He was thirty-three years old.

The son's relationship with his father remained devoid of affection, intimacy, or camaraderie, but was also free of major conflicts and tensions. The father supported his son financially throughout his undergraduate years, and subsidized his housing subsequently until, at the time of the last follow-up, the son was forty years old.

Biography of Social Development

The information pertaining to the boy's early social development derives from the records of the PEC at Johns Hopkins where he was followed for three years prior to the psychohormonal referral at the age 5 yrs 2 mos. Behaviorally, his development followed the course that is common to patients with early treated congenital hypothyroidism (Money and Lewis, 1964; Money et al., 1978), including a transitional period of hyperkinesis that paralleled the transition from hypothyroid to euthyroid.

Beginning at age 5 yrs 2 mos, his intellectual development was monitored during subsequent long-term psychohormonal follow-up. Table 3.1 shows the IQs in serial order.

It is evident in Table 3.1 that there was a gradual IQ improvement until age 12 yrs 7 mos, a feature sometimes encountered in treated congenital hypothyroidism. Then followed a highly atypical leap of IQ.

In early childhood, the school performance was more or less concordant with IQ. A few months after he entered a private kindergarten at the age of 5 yrs 6 mos, the teacher's report said that the boy was gradually developing the ability to concentrate on assignments, even though there was still noticeable hyperactivity. He repeated the first grade, because of difficulties in mathematics. The mother thought it was because he was "extremely nervous, excitable and unstable emotionally." The endocrinologist's observation was partly in agreement: "The boy (aged 6 yrs 8 mos) is constantly in motion, fidgeting and jumping from one thing to another. The movements are not erratic or choreiform in character. He seems intelligent and interested in everything."

TABLE 3.1

IQ Changes Classified by Age at Testing

Test	WISC	WISC	WISC	WISC	WISC	WAIS	WAIS
Age (yrs:mos)	5:2	8:6	12:7	14:6	15:11	27:8	29:11
Verbal IQ	79	91	105	128	124	128	122
Performance IQ	92	100	90	120	128	122	125
Full Scale IQ	84	95	98	126	128	127	125

Legend

WISC: Wechsler Intelligence Scale for Children
WAIS: Wechsler Adult Intelligence Scale

In fourth grade, he was transferred to the slow learner's class. According to his new teacher, he "displayed normal intelligence, learned at an average rate, and seemed to be well adjusted and happy." So as to be better able to supervise his learning, his mother took a volunteer job in a school for retarded children.

In retrospect, at the age of twenty-eight, the patient interpreted his childhood social difficulties as resulting from delayed intellectual maturation. He said that he did have friends of his own age, but played with children three to four years younger. "I tended to be excluded from my own age group," he recalled, "because I was a little slow catching onto the games and things like that. So, I tended to stay to myself." He resented his mother's protectionism and possessiveness. "She made me her comforter, but at the same time, she dragged me to psychologists and psychiatrists."

Between the ages twelve and fourteen, the sudden leap of 28 IQ points, from 98 to 126, occurred within the first two years of puberty. Thus, he had two major changes to deal with at once: puberty and an elevation of intellectual capability.

In later years, he recalled how, in his mid-teens, perhaps in tenth grade, he suddenly felt that new horizons had opened to him and he could see connections that weren't previously obvious to him. "I felt like a member of the nouveau riche, except that, in this case, I was going from the intellectually poor up to the wealthy, and learning how to adjust my behavior to the new, inherited knowledge or IQ. It took a while to adjust, to catch up to learning how to act at the country club level of behavior."

In spite of the sudden catch-up growth of intelligence, he failed the 12th grade. Looking back, again at age twenty-eight, he ascribed this failure to what he decribed as an increasingly intense "performance anxiety" and a fear of not being able to fulfill the revised, higher expectations of his parents and others. "When I was a slow learner," he said, "I was a slow learner. I acted like one and I was expected to live out my profession that way, or my career goals. Then when I came up for the IQ test here, I was told I was bright, and then I flunked high school. Then I went back for retesting, and the local psychologist said I was average. So then I was caught in a conflict. Am I smart or am I dumb? What am I? And ever since then they have been playing it back and forth. So that's a good reason to be a little schizophrenic, a little borderline personality, because you don't know where the hell you are, where the border is."

From the perspective of his psychohormonal counselor it was apparent that there were, in fact, some schizoid features that appeared in the boy's thought processes in early adolescence. During the period after the IQ elevated from 98 to 126, his conversation became garrulous. Thoughts took off at tangents and became overinclusive and grandiose. It was reminiscent of logorrhea, though not to a pathological degree. His writings, samples of which he proudly presented to his interviewer, tended to be florid and a bit pompously preoccupied with what amounted to his own quasi-theosophy.

Religiosity reached its peak when he was nineteen and disillusioned with his recent failure to graduate. As it became known much later, he was also, at around the same age, bitterly disappointed with the new discovery of a sexual inadequacy (see Lovemap Biography). It was, perhaps, sexual defeat which pushed him toward the religiose.

With the financial help of his father, with whom he was living, he eventually graduated from high school at age twenty. He made his first attempt to achieve financial independence by taking a warehouse job and renting his own apartment. He quit the job after nearly two years, with no new job in sight. Failure to find employment forced him to move back in with his father.

At twenty-two, he entered his local university undergraduate program in special education, and five years later graduated with a bachelor's degree. He planned to enroll in a master's degree program in a theological seminary and become a lay minister. The plan did not materialize until five years later. At age thirty-two, he wrote that he was in a program for a Master of Arts in Religion. "My goal is counseling in sexuality and further development of my spiritual nature," he wrote. "I have always had a religious aspect that needed a healthy expression." Just two months later, another letter contained the following reflection: "I realized that my seminary studies were only a way of putting off that which I have needed to do for years now, finding a job."

In fact, his major problem, which he recognized in his adulthood, was that he was unable to establish an independent life. Although he desperately needed a job to free himself from total financial dependency on his father, he found himself unable to pursue the necessary precedures involved in a job search. He reported that just the thought of having to fill out a job application form was enough to trigger an anxiety attack. Therefore, at thirty-five, he reverted to his old strategy of evading independent adulthood by enrolling in a post-bachelor college program to get a certificate for a legal research job.

He was forty years old when he resumed contact with the PRU after a five-year interval. He was still living with his father, and he had no income other than from a small inheritance. He worked as a volunteer advocate in rehabilitation. He talked, with his usual disarming boyish enthusiasm, about his achievements and persistence in his work, which had made him a local media celebrity. He was hoping to transform his volunteer position into a paid one. He did not consider the lack of steady income a major problem. He said he lived "fairly comfortably." His father did not charge him rent. Occasionally, he earned some money by doing small projects for a state agency.

His social life was limited to contacts with people with whom he worked and his former and present girlfriends. Throughout his adulthood he developed close friendships with women rather than men. He remained single. At forty his attitude toward marriage and family was ambivalent. He realized that a potential wife of his would have to be informed about this "inclination" toward young girls. "I think the person I'd marry would obviously have to be the person who wouldn't overreact and go berserk by even hearing the information." With regard to family, he knew that he could be a great father for a boy. He recognized the possibility of raising a daughter as too threatening, considering his paraphilia (see Lovemap Biography).

Lovemap Biography

When their son was 12 yrs 7 mos old and just entering puberty, his parents decided to have him participate in a sex-educational session with them and the staff of the PRU. He saw diagrams illustrating an elementary explanation of reproduction. The parents thought they would be able to give additional sex education at home, as needed, but that proved too difficult for them to do.

After the session, there was a two-year interval before the boy returned to the clinic, at age 14 yrs 6 mos, for a check-up of his thyroid status. On this occasion there was sufficient time for an individual session in the PRU dealing with his sexual history. He had had no source of sexual information, he said, other than what he had found out for himself in books. Though he spoke uninhibitedly about masturbation, he did not disclose, as he would do much later in life, that at around the time of puberty, "there were girls; and the boys were doing the circle jerk type of thing; lying on top of each other, shining a flash light on each other, pulling the pants down, and just looking—the doctor-nurse game."

From around this same age, he recalled, "there are two strong memories that I have." One was of a girl who "asked me to help her clear the ants out of her pants." He estimated that he and the girl were then ten or eleven years old. He did "a very thorough search" after she took off her pants. The girl got upset when he was "pulling the lips apart, playing doctor again, to see whether there were ants in there." She ran home, leaving him terrified of inevitable punishment, which did not, however, materialize.

The second strong memory was one of an experience in which he and three other boys had been rubbing their penises against the thighs of a girl from the neighborhood with whom they were playing. A week later, the girl was struck by an automobile and killed. "We were all feeling somewhat guilty about it," he recalled years later, as an adult. "I think the way I was generally raised, as you're punished for doing bad things, that certainly loomed over me, wondering whether there was a connection. I was always told, God will get you. It was just the trauma of those things so close together. The thing I can remember is that I was fooling around with her, and the next thing I knew she was dead."

He clearly recalled how flattered he was when, at around age thirteen, a fourteen-year-old girl invited him to play in the woods. "We were lying on each other, clothed, and I was moving back and forth, imitating intercourse," he said, "and I had an ejaculation probably within a minute or two."

During the course of his interview at age 14 yrs 6 mos, the query about sexual experience and imagery was prompted by the boy's report on his new hobby, weight lifting. The interviewer noted that "there was a great deal of weight-lifting narcissism," which is often associated with insecurity about gender identity and role. The boy's response to a query about his sexual interests did not, however, indicate overt ambiguity about his gender identity and role. By contrast with talk about actual experience, which was guarded, his talk about masturbation imagery was atypically explicit for a boy his age: "About a girl who might be naked," he said, "or about having intercourse with a girl. . . . A man has to lie down and a woman is lying on her back."

He masturbated regularly, he said, "at least once a day, but often more than once a day." Later in his teenage he invented a method of masturbation which he found very satisfactory. He put lubricant inside of a condom, put it on his penis, and then wrapped a cloth around it to simulate a vagina. He had a bed at just the right height so that he could kneel beside it with his simulated vagina resting on the bedding, as he thrust his penis back and forth. He had no apparent qualms about his masturbation activity and/or its frequency. There was only a short period in his life, around age eighteen, when he tried to restrict the frequency of masturbation, without success.

At sixteen, he said that he had started dating girls, but did not go beyond petting. He considered his erotic interest, imagery, and behavior to be exclusively heterosexual. His interviewer made a notation that "the boy's openness and frankness in discussing sexual experiences bordered on disinhibition similar to that seen in some patients with social pathology." Only later did it become evident that he had been editing his self-reports so as to persuade himself, perhaps even more than his listener, that he was unambiguously heterosexual. Information about homosexual experiences was disclosed only after he had had, at age eighteen, his first heterosexual intercourse. The partner was a girlfriend, aged fifteen.

This heterosexual initiation apparently eased his insecurity about sexual orientation, for he was later able to say: "I have been through the homosexual stage of development. At around age eight, it was a matter of group masturbation. Now I know I'm out of the homosexual phase, because girls are very attractive to me."

Four years later, in his early twenties, he was again not so sure about his sexual orientation. He said, in a telephone call to his much-trusted counselor, that he had resorted to a homosexual partner when no female partner was available, and felt guilty about that. At twenty-six, he was less reluctant to accept that he was, in fact, bisexual. He was now ready to give a full account of both heterosexual and homosexual experiences: "When I was younger I started off with heterosexual exploration," he said, referring to doctor-and-nurse and hiding-in-closet games. "And then a number of these guys in the neighborhood would be together for what we called circle jerks and exploration, things like that. And as time went on, I did start dating girls when I was around maybe fourteen or fifteen. At the same time I had one or two experiences in homosexual encounters. It was not an emotional gesture but simply a sexual encounter. Later I had an encounter with a man I worked with, but that was once or twice, and I didn't want to carry that to any further relationship on a continued basis. I'd been more or less the passive person and kind of shocked that somebody had made advances toward me; but at the same time, I felt a certain degree of pleasure involved in it."

In a follow-up interview, he expanded the foregoing report with more details of what had actually taken place, homosexually. According to his own wording, in one instance he had been "passive," meaning that his partner had masturbated him, and in another "passive-aggressive," meaning the two had engaged in "mutual masturbation without mutual attachment— it was a way to express sexuality." There had been no oral sex, and no anal intercourse. In actuality and in fantasy, the male partner was always an adult, never younger.

Throughout his twenties, the homosexual fantasies and occasional encounters were paralleled by heterosexual ones. Retrospectively, he considered himself to have been predominantly heterosexual, but extremely insecure. At thirty, he recalled his insecure attempts to establish a romantic relationship with women: "I had a heterosexual experience when I was eighteen years old," he recalled, referring to his first intercourse, "and I was scared to death of what to do. I had no idea. Part of the anxiety made me have a premature ejaculation. She told me at the end that she could get a better screw from her dog. I was devastated. I continued to have premature ejaculation after that—after the sensitizing to that, and I'd often be impotent."

He was aged twenty-three when he had had his first sexually satisfying relationship with a woman of his age. He had known her for a number of months prior to their first sexual encounter. From then on, over a period of months, their sex life "improved to a very satisfactory level." However, his newly attained self-confidence as a lover was not associated with falling in love with a partner of his own age. At twenty-seven, while reflecting upon this issue, he said: "I guess the last few years I've been at the university, I've had sporadic relationships with different levels of sexual involvement, but still it gets me into a kind of feeling of guilt, not really feeling free."

He was not yet ready, at age twenty-three, to acknowledge explicity to himself or to anyone else that his lovemap was, in fact, subject to the proviso which disallowed falling in love with anyone except a peripubertal or early adolescent girl. Although the first pedophilic episode in his sexual and erotic biography had occurred at age twenty-one, he did not formulate it as pedophilia, nor report it until five years later. In his retrospective report at age twenty-six, he said: "I was twenty-one, I guess, and I had just been recently rejected on an engagement, and felt quite depressed. I was visiting a family that had been known to be of questionable sexual activities. I had known the one young girl, nine or maybe ten years old. She came over and sat on me and kind of jumped up and down. She snuggled up to me, and all of a sudden, the next thing I knew was I was fondling her and massaging her, and then, in turn, I took her hand and brought it over to reach mine—my genitals. She was somewhat reluctant but then she continued, and at that moment I started ejaculating. I left shortly thereafter, and then suffered. It tormented me."

A year later, at twenty-seven, it was in the same off-handed way that he talked about incest. It happened in response to a query about his recent dream life. This was his response: "I had a dream a number of months ago of having relations with my mother. It shook the hell out of me, so I went to the university psychiatrist. This was something that I think had occured once before in my life, and I was trying to find an explanation of why a wet dream, and why a dream of the sexual relationship with my mother. I wasn't going in with a lot of panic, but with more interest— how that particular thing could occur. And I think I came out with it reasonably resolved. I don't know if this was symbolic or not, but I had been slowly accepting my mother on different levels. I had avoided her before and now I became more compassionate with her. It may have just been a sign of getting back that basic mother love that I had always felt I didn't receive."

Eight years later, at age thirty-five, two years after his mother's death, he took college courses in human sexuality and formulated his own explanation of his earlier relationship with his mother: "My mother always wanted me to stay with her and take care of her. Kissing. She always wanted to kiss when I came in. I couldn't stand it. I hated it because it was overpowering. It wasn't just the normal kissing. I could tell, she was just waiting for me to show up in that door so she could grab me. . . . Maybe I sensed that she was an overpowering mother-figure trying to seduce me."

On this same occasion, at age thirty-five, he formulated also his own explanation of his attraction to young girls. "The first time I was interested in young girls either erotically or friendshipwise was when I had gone from my low IQ to my high IQ, and flunking high school, feeling very inadequate about my personality. With that kind of inadequacy I felt safer with younger girls because their expectations, socially and sexually, were not the same. I was a premature ejaculator, impotent for a few years, until I met Cindy, the girl who was my age, and that was the first time I was really successful. But still after that I'd revert back again to younger girls because as soon as I didn't have my job—young girls look up to you. So I felt safer with that."

Between the ages of twenty-seven and thirty he had been noticing increased preoccupation with what he used to call "girl fantasies." He was no longer casual when, at age thirty, he requested an appointment to talk about his gradually weakening resistance against pedophilic temptations. "At points it becomes difficult," he said. "Just recently, I was in a room by myself and the girl was just laying there. I found it very difficult not to just turn her over. As I'm sitting here now, I'm getting an erection thinking about it."

Within the preceding few years, he had noticed that the intensity and frequency of fantasies of pubertal girls had increased to the point that he was afraid that he may start acting them out. He had not yet attempted to do so, except for the aforesaid episode at age twenty-one. "It's a combination of fantasizing, as I'm seeing girls in shopping centers, and just watching them. Then it sets off an erection response, and it's just kind of—I carry through a number of fantasies maybe, uh, everything from petting to possible intercourse depending on the age, I think. As they get older I think about having intercourse."

He now recognized that his maximum erotosexual response was contingent upon juvenile age and characteristics of female partners, namely, "girls between about ten and fourteen years old, not taller than 5 ft 4 in, reasonably good built, but with small breasts and long brown hair. The presence of pubic hair goes along with the turn-on. Yet I'm turned on by looking at those without pubic hair and with the small breast development, at least at the bud-size level."

Prepubertal girls were not sexually attractive to him, unless "they come off in maybe a seductive manner. The ten-year olds I can fall in love with, but it's not sexual as much as it is affectional. Although there are sexual elements in it, it's not as genital. It's more gentle. I can't picture intercourse with a ten-year-old girl. It's interesting. It's always either oral sex or petting or something like this. It's not until I'm clear that it's a twelve or thirteen-year-old girl, and that's when my fantasies with intercourse develop."

He could not keep himself from wandering around shopping malls in search of an opportunity to watch young girls. At home, he would use magazines or books specializing in pubertal girls' images. Occasionally, he would go to peep shows, where the so-called "Lolita films" were available.

He had only one long-continuing, bonded relationship. It was with Nita, a girl he had known since she was eleven, and he was thirty. She was an adopted child of the minister of the church to which he belonged, and where he did some volunteer work. The relationship started as "a big brother type of thing," he recalled. "When she was fourteen, we were holding hands, and then went to kissing. And then at 15½, we just sat down and discussed whether or not we should get further involved, and mutually we agreed. So from then on we were having a kind of on and off sexual relationship. I guess we went from standard intercourse, moved into oral sex, individually, and sixty-nine. Changing positions, top, bottom, sideways, twisting, rolling, and then we went into a lot of massaging with creams and lotions and vibrators. But it wasn't forced. It wasn't unnatural. It just developed in very small stages, always very comfortable for both of us."

Their affair continued until she was twenty-one and he was forty years old. It had broken up only a few months before the interview in which he recounted its history. It was in this context that he reviewed the different channels of erotic arousal. With Nita, he said: "I loved the smell when I moved down in her genital area, and the taste of licking . . . and also her hair, underarms, pubic area, and just the general sweat that builds up."

Stimulation of the skin senses was also very erotic for him. "If I had to weigh massaging against intercourse, then massaging comes first, because you can linger much longer. . . . We could go to the beach and she would pull my penis out. Then she would spend an hour rubbing it. She would go so gentle, and bring me to the point of getting to a peak, and then back off. . . . She would work her way down my back. It used to drive me wild."

Auditory stimuli were of background significance: "We almost always had music in the background," he said. Similarly: "Lowered light or candlelight puts us in the mood." Visually, "the lips, eyes, nose, are the big turn-on, and seeing her hair, swept over her face."

Without a partner present, visual imagery was the primary sexual stimulus: "In masturbation, I just get down, get the picture out, like the little girl here [he had brought some fashion magazine pictures with him], develop some fantasies, and then bring the masturbation to orgasm over a ten-minute period."

The pictures held the clue to the break-up with Nita, namely, that she had become an adult. His rationale, however, was that he "was tired of being yanked around by her and her mother." He mentioned vaguely that the "situation changed when the girl moved out on her own." He did not mention a possible connection between the timing of the break-up, and the fact that the girl had grown beyond the age and physique of being eligible for a pedophile or ephebophile. As a young woman moving toward adult independency, she could no longer meet the criteria imposed by his lovemap.

He was again hopeful about the possibility of establishing an erotic relationship with an adult woman. Within the last few months, he said, "I was finding myself very attracted to this female trooper [traffic police officer] and another woman who is a lab technician, who are both in their thirties. I felt with my feeling I could meet someone else, which I hadn't felt previously. I thought now was the time to make the break."

He sounded very convincing while making the foregoing statement about shaping his erotic attraction to adult women. However, barely an hour later, when on his way out of the PRU, he noticed a portrait in oils of an adolescent girl in a 1970s hippie outfit. He did not control his reaction: "Oh, God!" he exclaimed, "That's it! Where did you get it?" He was standing with his eyes glued to the painting. He said that he would pay any price to have it. In every detail, the painting depicted the characteristics of the ideal girl from his paraphilic fantasy. His reaction replicated what he had earlier said about seeing a young girl in the street: "As soon as I see her, all of a sudden, as soon as my eyes hit her, I just automatically, like a robot, just start following her. I am just fixated. And then after maybe five minutes of following her around, all of a sudden, I have an erection. Usually she walks off, or it's just I've realized that if I go too much longer, then I'll get noticed. It's not wise. I'm not going to do anything. I wouldn't touch her or anything, anyway. So if I can do without—and usually I don't need to be so obvious, although friends of mine have mentioned that I am."

Significance of the Case

Prenatal Precursors of Paraphilia. With regard to the future development of paraphilia, in this case the significance of the chromosomal sex is that it was 46, XY, as for a male, and concordant with the gonadal sex (testes), prenatal hormonal sex (masculinizing), and the genital sex (normal male morphology). Thus, these aspects of masculine differentiation were not affected by the prenatal determinants of congenital thyroid deficiency. There is no body of knowledge that would indicate a relationship between prenatal thyroid deficiency and the prenatal, gender-related differentiation of the sexual pathways of the brain.

Postnatal Precursors of Paraphilia: Prepuberty. From birth onwards this child had no specific diagnostic status, until at the age of 1 yr 9 mos he was diagnosed as hypothyroid. From then on, his mother's already exaggerated perfectionism on behalf of the child increased in magnitude. Her marital sex life was already in a deteriorated state, so that the rehabilitation of her only child became for the mother a consuming preoccupation. The effect on the child was to juvenilize his social development and retard the acquisition of normal boyhood autonomy and independence. He developed the self-concept of a cognitively handicapped thyroid invalid. His social maturation lagged, and became a source of stigmatizing isolation from his peer group. He bonded socially with chronologically younger children whose social age matched his own. His prepubertal sexual rehearsal play was limited to sporadic, show-and-tell, doctor-nurse play with boys and girls. One neighborhood girl with whom he and three other boys had been playing a penis-rubbing, frotteur type of game was killed, soon thereafter, by an automobile. He construed her death as a punishment for his own sin.

Postnatal Precursors of Paraphilia: Postpuberty. Puberty was spontaneous and masculinizing. Within the first two pubertal years there was a sudden leap in catch-up intellectual growth, reflected in an elevation of IQ from 98 to 126. In later years, he epitomized this change by equating himself with a nouveau riche, unprepared in the ways of spending his new intellectual capital. The catch-up in intellectual growth was accompanied by much slower catch-up growth in social maturation. Even at the age of forty, he lived like a college student planning for an adult career that never quite materialized.

As an adult he recalled that his one and only adolescent attempt at having sexual intercourse had resulted in rejection and ridicule. He subsequently tested his sexuoerotic capability in homosexual and heterosexual contacts with age mates. These contacts were transitory and had none of the intensity which he experienced in his first love affair.

Adulthood Paraphilic Outcome. The first love affair was with a girl of fifteen. It had begun incipiently when he was thirty and the girl was then eleven years old. It ended when the girl was twenty-one. There had been one premonition of age discrepancy when he was twenty-one and had ejaculated in his pants in response to fondling a girl of ten or eleven. Afterwards, he felt "tormented," and for the next nine years tried to confirm that he was sexually normal.

Paraphilic Stratagem. In this case the paraphilia is properly classified as ephebophilia rather than pedophilia, insofar as the partner eligible for a love affair is developmentally in the transition from puberty to advanced puberty and adolescence.

In ephebophilia, as well as pedophilia, the paraphilic stratagem is, in accordance with the principle of opponent process, the erotization of once-forbidden or aversive experiences. In this case, there is a history of forbidden childhood sexual rehearsal play, its significance blown out of proportion by self-blame for the ensuing accidental automobile death of the girl playmate.

There is also a history of maternal parenting in which, as experienced by the boy, parent-child bonding veered too aversively close to the forbidden erotization of lover-lover bonding. The fusion of parental pairbonding with lover pairbonding is a defining characteristic of both pedophilia and ephebophilia. Originally forbidden, the fusion becomes paraphilically reversed, and continues to maintain itself until the child grows up to the age of parenthood. Then the age roles reverse, but the fusion of lover-lover and parent-child bonding continues.

Its continuance is ensured in part by the pedophile's or ephebophile's own retarded sexuoerotic age, which is concordant not with his or her own chronological age, but with the age of the younger lover. In the present case, it is possible that the hypothyroid-derived retardation of mental age, in this instance until puberty, and of social age until long after, fed into the retardation of sexuoerotic age that has remained adolescent until the chronological age of forty. Whether or not there will be any catch-up growth in sexuoerotic age remains for the future to disclose. The patient has not given up hoping.

CHAPTER 4

Biography 2: Masochistic Disposition and Rejected Sex Reassignment in a Homosexual Male with Congenital Micropenis

Diagnostic and Clinical Biography

Biography 2 is that of a male, now in his thirties, who was born with a micropenis. In middle childhood, the masculine differentiation of his lovemap veered in the direction of male-to-female sex reassignment. The male/female bipotentiality of the lovemap created a suicidal upheaval of uncertainty in teenage. A trial period of heterosexuality failed and yielded to exclusive homosexuality, over which was superimposed a thin veneer of masochism combined with suboptimal assertiveness and career achievement.

There is no record in the clinical history of how the parents were told of their firstborn baby's genital defect. Although from the beginning the baby was referred to as a boy, a urological consultation was obtained because of the extremely small size of the penis with minor, first degree hypospadias of its meatus, at the corona of the glans, together with bilateral cryptorchidism. The urologist assured the parents that one testicle could be palpated high in the inguinal canal, and that the baby was indeed a male. It was too soon for the Barr body, discovered in 1948, to be used clinically as a test of genetic sex; and too soon for sex-chromosome karyotyping, as it was not until 1959 that human chromosomes were routinely visualized and counted in hospital genetics laboratories.

When the baby was six months old, the urologist reported that both testes could be palpated, and he euphemistically declared that the child would develop "normally." The pediatrician was not convinced, however, and referred the baby to Lawson Wilkins, the renowned Johns Hopkins pediatric specialist in intersexuality. It was decided, on the basis of the physical examination, that exploratory surgery should be performed in order to rule out the possibility of covert internal intersexuality. The external genitals comprised a normally formed, empty scrotum; undescended testes, the right unpalpable and the left questionably high in the inguinal canal; and a penis that appeared to be "a small fold of preputial tissue about 1 cm in length." Urination was from the tip of this micropenis, through a glans that was not quite perfectly fused.

Surgically it was established that the internal reproductive structures were masculine, with no evidence of intersexuality. The testes were bilaterally palpated with difficulty near the internal inguinal rings, where they were left in the expectation that they would descend spontaneously.

Postsurgically, the following statement was entered in the baby's medical record: "These findings clearly indicate that the patient is a male with an exceedingly small penis; with the absence of all female genital organs it would have been impossible to have converted him into a female even if this had been desired." Today, this criterion against feminization no longer holds. Even at that earlier time, in related cases of gonadally male inter-sexuality or hermaphroditism, the appearance and surgical correctibility of external genitals constituted in rare cases the criterion whereby female-assigned sex was decided upon. The possibility of feminization in the present case was mooted specifically by the psychologist and psychiatrist, by reason of the fact that the penis was too small ever to be made adequately functional for coitus in adulthood. There was no precedent of sex reannouncement in a case of microphallus, however. Moreover, the parents were strongly committed to getting help for a son.

The parents were first referred in person to the Johns Hopkins Psycho-hormonal Research Unit (PRU) on the occasion of the first follow-up visit when the baby was aged two. The referral was made in response to their quest for information regarding the psychologic as well as the somatic prognosis in their son's case.

Two years later there was another follow-up visit. At that time, a buccal smear was taken and it was found to be chromatin negative, as expected in a gonadal male. The chromosomal karyotype, 46,XY, was not actually verified until the patient was twenty-five years old.

At age four, the boy was subject to attacks of dermatitis, a symptom he and his father shared. Attacks had been more prolonged earlier in infancy. With advancing age they became shorter and less severe, though persistent sporadically through adolescence and into adulthood. The same applied to asthma attacks. Cortisone controlled the skin outbreaks, and antihistamine the asthma.

During the years of childhood, follow-up visits were scheduled one or more years apart. Some were at the boy's own request, for he took up the self-demand option of appointments with his "talking doctor." When he was ten years old, he disclosed the existence of a private dilemma regarding the idea of being a girl (see Lovemap Biography). He opted in favor of retaining male status, with the help of testosterone cream (0.2% testosterone propionate in stearin-lanolin cream) appied locally to the penis in an attempt to increase its size immediately, without waiting for the normal age of puberty. The cream did, as desired, bring about a premature induction of genitally localized pubertal development. In nineteen months the penis grew from 1 cm to 4 cm stretched length. There was a concomitant increase in morale. In adolescence, a final increment of growth increased the stretched length of the penis to its adult dimension, 6 cm long and 2 cm in diameter.

The onset of adolescent development was at age 13 yrs 7 mos, when it was decided to induce puberty with exogenous androgen, testosterone enanthate, 200 mg every three to four weeks, on which dosage masculinization was subsequently maintained. This decision was made on the basis of the lack of signs, upon physical examination, of the onset of puberty, together with the laboratory finding of elevated gonadotropins. The exact fate of the patient's own undescended testes will be definitely ascertained when he is psychologically ready for further gonadotropin testing and possible surgical exploration. For cosmetic appearance, the scrotum now contains silicone prosthetic testes, surgically implanted at age fourteen. At age eighteen, as a convenience while away at college, he substituted the oral form of testosterone (methyltestosterone 20 or 30 mg daily) for the injectable form (testosterone propionate). Compliancy was self-regulated, so as to strike a balance between being tired too often or "horny" too often.

The masculinizing effect of testosterone therapy was completely effective with respect to physique and appearance in adulthood. One encountered a muscular, hirsute adult male, six feet (183 cm) tall, with no balding, whom both men and women found handsome and attractive, according to the criteria used in everyday life. Nonetheless, the adversity of genital inadequacy took its toll.

Even though he learned, early in his life, to keep his secret to himself, he could not avoid exposure in the hospital examining room. The unavoidable childhood genital examinations became a source of nosocomially induced stigmatization. In an autobiographical sketch written in adulthood, he referred to his childhood hospital visits in these words: "Each year when I went to the hospital for my annual medical check-up, the student doctors and new fellows seemed to ask questions and make statements which were designed to annoy and make uneasy patients like myself. One particular question I distinctly remember being asked many years in succession: 'Was I satisfied with the size of my penis?' I vaguely remember others of similar ilk." He wrote these words hoping that the message would reach those in the medical profession who come into contact with intersexual individuals.

Family Pathology

This child was the oldest sibling and only son. There were two younger sisters. The father worked in a medically related profession. The mother, also a professional, had her office at home. Both parents accompanied their son on visits to Johns Hopkins until he was eight years old. Subsequently, he was accompanied only by his father.

Their son was still an infant when the parents made it clear that they did not seek comfort in false hopes. They were looking the hard facts straight in the face. Both parents were committed to following the guidelines for the management of their son's upbringing as delineated in the course of psychohormonal counseling.

On one occasion, when the psychohormonal counseling focused most explicitly on the problems that the boy, then still very young, might face in the future, the mother looked as though she could have burst into tears, but made an effort not to make it obvious. She admitted that she was pessimistic about being able to answer the boy's future queries about the prospect of growing a bigger penis, whereas the father was more optimistic.

In the early years of follow-up, the father, even though he did not openly express or show any anxiety, worry, or distress, was deeply concerned. He allowed that he was, in general, a man who swings with the punches and takes things as they come. It was easier for him to become self-effacing rather than to resist or retaliate. For about six months after his son's birth, he frequently had difficulty maintaining an erection while having intercourse. It was not until two years later, however, that he disclosed having had this problem. He said that whenever his thoughts would go to the baby lying in the next room, his erection would fail. The wife commented that he had been apparently pretty good at disguising his problem, as this had been the first time she had heard this piece of information.

The family dynamics gradually changed as two more children, both daughters, were born. In the father's description, his family had become "a typical American family, insofar as women take over, and sometimes they are very shrill about it." His own attitude was to take the line of least resistance. He and his only son teamed up in a father-son comradeship as if to counterbalance the mother-daughter alliances.

In adulthood, the son's retrospective recall of childhood was colored by resentment toward the mother: "My mother would inflict strange punishments on me for things which she considered wrong-doings. For example, I used to have a penchant for saying 'no' to my mother, if she asked me to do something which seemed especially disagreeable. If I said 'no,' my mother, more often than not, would make me write 'I won't say no' 100-200 times, or risk the loss of dinner or allowance. My father was never the disciplinarian, always my mother."

The teaming-up of the father and son became more apparent when the mother-son relationship deteriorated rapidly after the boy entered high school. The boy and his father agreed that the source of the trouble was that the mother became obsessively perfectionistic in her demands on the boy, while being more laissez-faire in her demands on his sisters.

Ostensibly, it was the boy's neglect of homework assignments that became the bone of contention between him and his mother. Ambitious for her family in the culturally Jewish tradition, the mother spurred her son on to academic excellence. One might have inferred a subliminal hope that a big intellect could offset a small penis. As time went on, mother and son became locked in an intensifying adversarial relationship in which continued academic underachievement became the son's chief weapon. The struggle escalated until the boy moved away from home to complete his education in a private boarding school.

Biography of Social Development

The boy's social development did not conform to the idealized stereotype of American boyhood in assertiveness, dominance, rivalry, fighting, and competitiveness in sports. As a boy, the father had not been too different.

When the son entered first grade, the father wrote a progress report. There were complaints from school that the boy was a poor listener and did not follow instructions well. He said he didn't like his teacher. She was a strict disciplinarian. Once after a distressing day at school, he was threatened with detention, whereupon he cried and vomited. That night he awoke from a nightmare and talked about difficulties at school, some with other children, which he was unable to resolve. None of the difficulties could be directly traced to the genital condition. Offered a change of teacher, he elected against it.

"In ordinary, outside-the-class behavior," the father wrote, "he has been quiet, completely nonaggressive (except occasionally toward his sister), and perhaps oversensitive and insecure. He will not join a group of children who are not well known to him. Under friendly circumstances, he gets along well with children of either sex. He avoids the rough and tumble play of boys, but enjoys other types of play. The teacher reported that at school he does not get along well with boys, but frequently plays alone, or with girls." There was no evidence of teasing or tormenting by peers. The boy, aware of adverse consequences in case of public exposure of his birth defect, successfully avoided any inquisitiveness on the part of his peers.

At the age of eight, for the first time he initiated a request for another appointment. Information about social development obtained during the visit confirmed prior evidence of extroverted sociability in general, despite limited participation in boys' sports: "I don't like to get beat up," he said. "My friend Sydney knows a lot about wrestling, and I do too—I can get him in some holds. Sometimes, it hurts. And I don't like to fight."

The father, whose own boyhood social development resembled the son's, made a point of spending time with his son, teaching wrestling, for example, which the boy enjoyed.

Of most of the boys in his class, he said: "Well, they're kind of rough, you know. And sometimes they don't want me to play kickball with them, and baseball. . . . They say I don't play good, and they want the best man on their side. So I just swing on the swings. Some other kids do, too."

After school, he was always responsive when his friends wanted him to join their play, but he was reliant on their initiative and leadership rather than his own. His recreational interests included swimming, gymnastics, bicycle-riding, and stamp collecting. His collection expanded into a very successful small dealership in adulthood. As a boarding student in high school, he took up tennis and soccer which, he said, helped him to make friends and not to feel an outsider. He also took up writing and produced both light verse and short stories (see Lovemap Biography). In college, he became an active organizer and leader in minority rights.

The IQ, taken at age ten on the Wechsler Intelligence Scale for Children, was Verbal IQ, 128; Performance IQ, 108; Full Scale IQ, 120. Two and a half years later, upon repeat testing, the corresponding IQs were 119, 107, and 115.

Up through his eleventh year, the boy's school grades were A and B. Then the first sign of academic underachievement began to appear. There was much contention between mother and son regarding neglect of home-work assignments. The struggle escalated in junior high school. Academic performance, formerly average or better, dropped to below average.

The boy suffered recurring attacks of intense depression with suicidal and self-mutilatory fantasies, and crying spells. At one time in adolescence there was a recurrent eidetic hypnogogic image of a gun: "This vision in my head, you know, of an unhandled gun, rising up and firing in the air, and boom, blowing my head to bits."

This imagistic experience was so traumatizing that the only defense against it was a compelling fascination with gun shops, and with thoughts of purchasing a gun and using it to complete the nightmare once for all. The purchase was never made.

Discovered in childhood, the calming effect of rocking, hair pulling, and head banging persisted throughout adolescence and early adulthood. As he described it, the motion of rocking induced a trance-like state, which provided temporary relief from depressive attacks. He resorted to rocking as a relaxation whenever time was available. It became more insistent in his adolescent years, when schooling problems and conflicts with his mother, because of his academic underachieving, became a source of chronic distress.

Disputes with the mother increased, until father, son, and mother eventually reached a consensus whereby the son completed the last two years of high school away from home at a private boarding school. There his grades improved.

From high school, he went to college and then graduated with a master's degree. He was accepted into a Ph.D. program in another institution, but did not complete the first year. Discontinuance of the doctoral training and transfer to a different institution and training can be construed, hypothetically, as a manifestation of achievement panic, insofar as academic success would lead ultimately to the rites and responsibilities of adulthood. Confronted with that hypothesis, he shared his reflection in a letter to his counselor: "You are right to a certain point about the self-sabotage. I never told you this, but the exam I had way back in November, I sort of fucked that one up on purpose. . . . I don't think my penis thing will ever end, because I will always have a constant reminder, as I have in the past. But you are right about the never wanting to be a mature man being synonymous with not making the grade degree-wise, because of my small prick. I always wondered what it was that was making me rather powerless to do anything about my schoolwork. My parents and former teachers always said I was lazy and sloughed things off."

To help finance his education, during the summers of his student years he worked as a counselor in diverse institutions serving the handicapped or emotionally disturbed.

He has always been masculine in appearance. When he came to the hospital, it was obvious to all those with whom he had contact that his clothing, hairstyle, moustache, and jewelry fitted the style of the times as appropriately masculine. So too did his body language.

Lovemap Biography

In rearing this child, the parents had drawn on recommendations given them by the psychohormonal counselor. Their son was only two years old when they received their first guidelines, such as the policy of straight-forward talk with the child without trying to spare him with evasions, euphemisms, and false hopes. They were encouraged to start preparing the way at school so that the boy, advised in advance to guard against exposing himself to teasing, could avoid being seen by other children.

At nursery school, the boy did not appear to be embarrassed by having always to sit to urinate. He mentioned to his mother something about sitting to urinate, to which she replied that she had known other little boys who also sit.

In kindergarten the next year, he still was obliged to sit, but without being self-conscious, as some other boys copied him. At four, he knew the reason for his hospital visits: "Because I have a little penis, you know. . . .That's just how I got borned." He had seen his playmate's penis, but did not reveal his own. His father said, jokingly, that he had become quite a connoisseur of penises and their size, even to the point of asking a visiting mother when she would change her baby's diaper so he could see the penis. There was no evidence from him at this time of an awareness of cryp-torchidism. He had seen the genitalia of his baby sister as well as the penis of his male playmate, and considered that he looked like the latter. Sometimes, he conceded, unconvincingly, he liked to play with his penis "just for fun," and the feeling was, "Oh, very good."

Inquiry into genital self-stimulation at age five produced replies that did not clearly differentiate adjustment of clothing from erotic good feeling, but it was clear that "my mother doesn't like me to play with my penis." Without evasiveness, the same lack of specificity persisted when the topic came up again at age ten, following treatment with testosterone ointment. The father had reported that his son habitually masturbated a fair bit, but in an absent-minded way, as when watching television without much concentration. The family policy was that masturbation should be private, not prevented.

The treatment with testosterone ointment at age ten did not produce any changes in localized genital sensations according to what could be ascertained from the boy. Digital manipulation of the genitals continued, but it seemed to be less an erotic act of masturbation than a pacifier, like rocking or thumb-sucking.

During childhood there were no reports of sexual rehearsal play, nor of romantic rehearsals and juvenile love affairs. Many years later, however, at the age of twenty, there was a retrospective recall: "When I was nine,

I had this crush on a guy in my third grade . . . just like the one I had at camp, this summer. It just struck me; I remember back to the third grade. I said to myself: 'It's just like the time I had this crush on this one guy in the third grade.' It was more than hero worship, or anything like that. It was that, well, he just struck me as being really, like handsome. And it wasn't like having the next door neighbor as a friend. I mean, I had to have this guy as a friend. . . . So I just assumed it was a crush, something like that."

The only evidence of potential duality of gender identity/role prior to age ten was the prevalence of pacific play over agonistic play. Then, at age ten, a highly differentiated duality was disclosed on the occasion of a follow-up visit scheduled at the boy's own written request. At the outset of the interview, the history records, he said that he had asked for the appointment because he wanted to talk to his long-term counselor, but that he had nothing special to report or ask. Pursuing a cue previously given by the boy's father, the counselor explored the "safe" area of academic and social achievements. In his usual candid way, the boy said that he doesn't go off with the other boys to play, but usually joins in the girls' group. He wasn't the only boy in their group. He mentioned specifically his friend, a diabetic, whom the other boys don't want to bother with, because he can't run fast enough. He himself could run fast enough, but for him the other boys were too rough, always fighting, and he didn't like to fight. He gave no evidence of attraction toward girls' toys, clothes, or domestic activities.

The counselor decided to further explore the significance of the boy's alignment with girls, by using the parable technique, namely, a narration of a relevant situation used as a personalized projective test. The narrative was about another boy with a small penis who wondered if God really had intended for him to be a girl—in fact, he once had a dream in which he actually turned into a girl. The boy's response to the story was that he himself had thought of changing to a girl: "Well, I would like to be born a girl." Asked why, he answered without delay: "Oh, because you can have a baby. . . . And that would be fun when it was a little child, you know. Yes, I know that [fathers can play with a baby]. I would rather be doing what a mother does. I've seen my mother do the things like ironing clothes and washing—and it's fun. I've ironed clothes a lot for my mother. And it would just be fun for me to be a little girl."

As the interview progressed, it was established that the boy had sufficient knowledge of the basics of human reproduction. He knew that the father's sperm was necessary to make a baby but "I probably wouldn't have a sperm. So why be a boy if you can't have a sperm and your penis is small?"

There then ensued an explanation of donor insemination and the sperm bank, and a lengthy conversation on how sperms get out of the penis. He was uncertain as to whether his own penis had ever become erect, and whether he had good feelings in it. Then the talk turned to pregnancy, and the way that the baby comes through the vagina, the same place where the penis goes. He maintained that he would rather be a girl, but if he could have a normal penis, he "wouldn't want to be a girl anymore."

The counselor then outlined two hypothetical treatment options, masculine and feminine, neither totally satisfactory and both without fertility, and asked if the decision between them would be difficult. His response was: "No, I want to be a boy. I would like to be a man. If you have to pay all that money just for an operation so you can have a vagina, and I would think to look like a girl, and can't get a baby out of you, what's the use of wasting all that money—if you have to go and get another baby?"

Supplied with information about the use of testosterone ointment to give an immediate boost in penis size, he had no hesitation in opting to try it, while leaving open the other option of reconsidering being a girl. In further conversation about the origin of his idea of changing sex, he said that he had read some media references to Christine Jorgensen, the transexual whose case had first astonished the world several years earlier (Jorgensen, 1967).

The return appointment was in three months, by which time the application of testosterone had begun to take effect. Eventually the boy did concede that the growth of his penis had definitely confirmed his decision to keep on being a boy. Before that, he had circumvented making reference to the last talk about being a girl. Then, directly questioned, he said he'd changed his mind because: "I thought it would be more interesting to be a boy, because there's a lot of things you can do, and girls can't be that many things. There's not that many girls can be airplane fliers, or train runners and engineers, or taxi cab drivers. . . . I just don't like the things girls do. They are nurses or stewardesses, or just plain American housewives. . . . If I'm a boy now and would change, maybe I wouldn't find the girls' things interesting, and I might just want to change right back to a boy. I might want to be an engineer and, if I was a girl, I'd have to change right back to a boy, because there aren't many girl engineers."

Six months later, once again, he fielded the question of feeling like wanting to be a girl: "Sometimes my penis, sometimes it feels like, you know, it has to be rubbed or something like that." Upon further questioning he explained the connection between the feeling in his penis and wanting to be a girl: "Well, I sometimes pretend I'm a girl and sometimes before going to bed, if I get out of the bath, I feel like I want to be a girl. So I put on a towel, pretend it's a skirt, and I'm a girl. But before I go to sleep, it goes away. Most of the time I don't have that feeling."

At this time he was aged eleven and still using testosterone cream. Further conversation established that his feeling of being a girl would more accurately be termed a masturbation fantasy. At this time masturbation produced good feeling, an uncertain degree of tumescence, and no ejaculation. The use of testosterone cream was discontinued before he turned twelve.

In follow-up interviews, inquiry on psychosexual imagery was open-ended and not addressed specifically to being female. In three follow-ups, over the next 2½ years, the topic was submerged by talk of heterosexual imagery and prospects. Developmentally the boy had remained prepubertal until, at age 13 yrs 7 mos, the first injection of testosterone enanthate to induce puberty had been given.

Eight months after the first testosterone injection, prosthetic testes were surgically implanted. Thereafter, follow-up visits were on an annual basis. The masculinizing effect of testosterone was as expected. It included an increased prevalence of erotic imagery, and of masturbation and masturbation fantasies which were talked about on the occasion of each visit. Erotic feeling in masturbation was localized in the usual place, the glans penis and the area of the frenulum (there had been no circumcision).

The theme of being female remained submerged for four more years. The boy referred to heterosexual erotic imagery only. He took the initiative in dating, but the relationships were companionable rather than romantic or erotic. He knew that he was holding back lest he be embarrassed by the size of his penis. He was not prudish about nudity, as in the communal shower at school, but he was threatened by the potential failure of a penis that he estimated to be less than three inches long in erection. He considered the possibility of professional surrogate sex therapy, but was too young to be accepted into a program. He was phobic to the idea and prospect of using a prosthetic penis or vibrator as auxiliary sex toys.

The sex-change theme had resurfaced as a studious interest when the boy, at age fifteen, purchased a copy of Harry Benjamin's *The Transsexual Phenomenon* (1966), newly published. Three years later, as a high school senior, aged eighteen, he wrote a knowledgeable term paper on the subject. In this context, he answered a question about the possible self-application his term paper might have: "Well, I don't know. Sometimes when I masturbate, I make believe that I switch, like I'm a woman and someone else is the man, or something like that. I can't seem to masturbate, and you know, to get the tension off any other way, so I just make believe that I'm a woman, or something like that, and somebody else is a man. And the boy, the man, in the fantasy doesn't have a face or anything. It's just somebody. And he's fucking me." In the fantasy, his own body was transformed into a female's, with breasts and a vagina.

The transexual fantasies were more likely to occur in stressful periods, especially when he was in "a real bad mood and had a lot of work or a lot of problems at school." There were also fantasies in which he was an uninvolved observer of other people's intercourse. If, in the fantasy, he allowed himself to be an active participant, he would picture himself as a man with a bigger penis having intercourse with "some girl."

Recalling when he first started to think about being female and having a vagina, he pointed to the age of about ten. "It was really funny," he said. "I used to masturbate when I was about ten years old, and I used to like—I'd take two pairs of socks and put them in a shirt and make believe that I was a woman, you know, and then stuff some shirt down my pants and pretend that I was pregnant, you know, and then I'd masturbate like that. . . . I remember one time wanting to change sexes when I was a little kid, real little, I don't know, seven, eight, or nine."

He wondered about his sexual future as a man: "I don't know. It might be tough, because my penis is very small, to have sexual intercourse. And it might be tough, if I marry, on my wife. . . . Well, it might not, because if I find out that, you know, my wife enjoys sex with a small penis, or something like that, then I just might believe that I was a guy with a large penis, and leave it at that. I might find out that my penis is big enough to fit, you know, her vagina. Then I might not have transexual fantasies."

No one had been told about the masturbation fantasies and their content prior to this present disclosure, but he had wanted someone to tell them to "because sometimes they are pretty weird."

The imagery of being a female did not include imagery of cross-dressing. He had never been in transvestite costume, nor had he impersonated a woman's mannerisms in private or public. To the contrary, he tried to exaggerate a man's aspects, he said, "just to see what the women will do. Sometimes I get nice stares."

The imagery of being female with a male partner did not extend to encompass imagery of being male with a male partner, as is evident in the following: "I can't really stand, you know, homosexuality that much because, you know, I don't mind homosexuals, but I'd hate to do it myself because it would strike me as perverted, you know. . . . I shy away from stuff like that, man to man. You know, it doesn't appeal to me, doing something like that, as a man, you know."

He was eighteen when he had his first romantic friendship. The partner was a mannish girl, a fellow high-school senior, psychologically troubled and, because of it, an outcast among most of the students. "She had never been kissed," he said, "when I kissed her in October. She told me, she groaned, she had to go to the psychologist because I kissed her. She wouldn't talk to me because, you know, it must have been a real traumatic experience to be kissed by a boy."

In summing up the interview in which the foregoing information had been revealed, the counselor gave his opinion that: "The man's side of things is too strong to let the other side ever come out much further than in fantasy." Wisely, in view of what lay ahead, the gateway to further discussion was left unconditionally open.

In the follow-up at age nineteen, a year later, although the psychosexual biography overtly remained essentially unchanged, there was an explosion of self-revelation, for the first time, of virulent attacks of suicidal depression. The attacks fluctuated in frequency over the ensuing years, loosely in parallel with fluctuations in the polarity of female versus male. Sleep dreams during this period of development combined explicit imagery on the themes of being in a tunnel or on a bridge while in an automobile; vehicular accidents and death; homosexuality and homosexual paternal incest in which he was the receptor; and being a female with a vagina.

Six months later penovaginal intercourse was first attempted. He wrote: "I could not get my penis in at first, but I found that if I put a pillow under her buttocks, I could get in about two to three inches. I'm glad that she didn't comment about how small my penis is because, if she had, I might have almost cried. The only trouble I had was that, if I came out too far, I wouldn't be able to get it back in, and as you know, there isn't too much leeway with the size of my penis. She liked it though, which I was glad about, and kept begging for more. In fact, now she's even boasting to a couple of her friends how many times we fucked that one night. And, sort of unfortunately, she's so gone on me that she's even talking about marriage."

After this first experience, he mostly evaded invitations, some of them unequivocal and explicit, to coital encounters. Nonetheless, he did attempt penovaginal intercourse again with a couple of partners. The sum total of his experiences led him to write that he had no heterosexual confidence in his sex life.

A month before his twentieth birthday, and now a sophomore in college, he was the young adult who volunteered to be interviewed in the psychoendocrine case presentation for Johns Hopkins senior medical students. Afterwards, he taped a summary interview in private, in which appeared a change toward acceptance of homosexuality. The change was manifest in masturbation imagery: "I have four kinds [of fantasies]. I can have myself in there, or I can have two different people in there with me looking at it—it's usually about a movie or something I've seen. I can have me as a lady. And me homosexual, that's the new one. And, let's see, homosexual, I'm the receptor, of course. And heterosexual with me in it, I have a large penis. And the one with me as a lady, I don't know what my—like I can see part of my body—I don't know what my face looks like."

Prevalence of the different types of imagery he estimated as: "Maybe 20% homosexual, and around 20% me as the lady, and around 20% me doing the fucking, and around 40% I'm watching the thing." The different types of imagery had different degrees of vividness. Watching others was clearest. The self with an enlarged penis came next. The self as a lady was: "Like I'm seeing through the fog." The self as a male homosexual received no mention regarding vividness.

He had come to the conclusion that at some time in the future he would probably try a homosexual experience, and gave the following explanation: "Well, when I couldn't fuck that second girl, I really felt bad about it. I felt like I'd failed, you know, and I decided—I was reading a book on homosexuality, Martin Hoffman [1968], and it gave some vivid homosexual interludes, and I thought it really sounded good. I thought it might be a nice idea to try that."

He tested relaxation of the anal sphincter digitally. He could not estimate when he might embark on an actual experience because: "I'd ruin my whole reputation at college. At the moment, I'm making jokes about homosexualism. All the kids in my dorm take it as a joke, and they'd never believe that I'd do it."

Reading the future with respect to sex change, he stated: "I think it would work if I was about, if I was still ten years old; but I don't think it would work right now, because I'd still see myself with a moustache and I wouldn't really like—I couldn't picture myself right now walking in the street with high heels or anything. Maybe ten years from now, if I decided then, it might work. But right now, if I changed into a woman, it would be like I was living in a dream state, because I might not believe that I was actually a woman."

There is in the psychoendocrine record a note, written by his counselor, as follows: "It was on this occasion that I first presented the hypothesis that gender polarity of female and male had fused with a linguistic polarity of French and English, respectively. [The patient] had begun studying French in high school and, with remarkable rapidity, began writing French verse. In English he wrote verse and short stories. The French verse was lyrical and refined in imagery. The English writings were forceful and more vernacular in imagery. Insofar as one can classify the content and style of writing by the sex of the author, the French verse was feminine, and the English verse and prose masculine." To this formulation, the patient's reaction was: "That's interesting, because . . . when I started doing French, I thought well, if I didn't really make it as a guy, you know, like I figured if you're going to change sex, you may as well leave the state or country, or something like that, because by the time you're seventeen or eighteen you know a hell of a lot of people in the United States, but you don't know anybody in Europe. I don't know; I guess I probably thought that maybe by learning French I could go to France or something like that, and nobody would recognize me."

At this time he had already finalized arrangements for his forthcoming year as a junior in college, namely, as an exchange student abroad, at a French-speaking university. When suicidal ruminations intruded on his plan, a rider became added: "For a while I was planning to kill myself when I came back," he said. The unplanned, but logical, alternative was to not return, but to remain overseas living as a female. Another logical alternative was to return home and become rehabilitated as a homosexual or bisexual man.

Obviously, the psychosexual agenda for the year abroad far outweighed the academic agenda. So it is not surprising that course grades were poor, except in conversational French. Psychosexually, there was much agonizing on whether or not to try a homosexual relationship. This issue remained, for the time being, unresolved. The sex-change issue was resolved insofar as the fictive French-language female did not materialize. Her place was usurped by an English-speaking male, severely depressed, grossly mal-nourished, physically debilitated, and dangerously ill when he returned to the United States to recover.

Even though the French-speaking female would not materialize, the past validity of being female was maintained. On the Sacks Sentence Completion Test, for example, on the item that began: "If I were young again," the completion was, "I would request a sex change." Eighteen months after living abroad he wrote in a letter: "I'm scared that my boyfriends or girlfriends are going to start judging their attraction to me by my small prick, rather than me. If you ever let parents who have a baby with a microphallus raise their kid as a male, you're a damn fool." In another letter, a couple of months later, vehemently rejecting the idea of a prosthetic, strap-on penis, he wrote: "I'd rather be gay the rest of my life than have to function heterosexually with the use of a dildo. If I had known all I know now when I was ten, I would have told you to cut my penis off at that time. I'm having fantasies about mutilating myself. That's why I need the Elavil back. Luckily for me, it's just fantasies."

His sex life during his senior year, back in the United States, continued to be heterosexual in expression, but bisexual in fantasy. "My friend and I have been having some excellent talks about sexuality and homosexuality," he wrote. "In talking with him I discovered that I really don't consider myself gay, or bisexual, or anything. I sort of feel neuter, stuck in the middle."

Though his friend himself was a member of the gay movement, for months the two maintained only a comradeship without sex: "I was afraid that I would discover that, if I went to bed with a guy, I wouldn't like it, and would have been bluffing myself the whole time in my fantasies. I decided that I had to conclude whether I liked it or not, and not pussyfoot around anymore." This was the matter-of-fact way in which he reported the first overtly genital homosexual interaction in his life, shortly before his twenty-second birthday. He enjoyed the experience, despite being beset by misgivings about the size of his penis and of being rejected because of it.

A year later, a letter contained a succinct statement of his ambivalence about being bisexual: "I've been having head problems every now and then, again. Fortunately, it's not as troublesome as two and three years ago. Maybe it's because I've noticed an interest in myself in chicks (romantic), but no real urge to get them into bed. I'm afraid of a possibility that could happen in a few years: that I would marry a girl because of a romantic fantasy and because I don't feel abnormal in the eyes of my family; and then I would have homosexual relations on the side. Here's something you'll probably find interesting. When I get a trick in bed, I feel satisfied if he fucks me in the ass. I get pleasure out of being touched and felt. I tried letting guys give me blowjobs, and I haven't been able to come. I sometimes can come being jerked-off by my partner, at times with great effort."

The positional problems of anal intercourse, with himself as the insertor, made him feel intolerably inadequate, and realistically so when the partner's primary turn-on was from deep anal penetration.

Whereas the problem of being able to establish a lasting erotic pairbond as a heterosexual lover had been primarily a deficit in his input into the relationship, in homosexual relationships it was the other way round. Partners toward whom he felt a strong and lasting attraction, and who at first reciprocated, did not continue the relationship erotically for as long as he was prepared to do. It was not possible for him to ascertain whether they were intrinsically fly-by-night lovers, or whether they rejected him because of the inadequacy of his penis size.

In his middle twenties, he identified himself personally and politically as gay. He was active in the gay liberation movement, and found morale-building support from working with like-minded colleagues.

His experience of masturbation imagery no longer included imagery of the self as a woman with a man. It was bisexual, though predominantly homosexual between two males. Explicitly erotic movies and graphics of male-male homosexual content were a better erotic turn-on for him than were heterosexual ones, though the latter were effective too. He was able to use explicit pictures as cues for masturbation imagery, should spontaneous imagery not present itself. Touch, however, according to his own evaluation, prevailed over vision as the major channel of sexual turn-on: "All this guy had to do was touch me on the knee, right here, and I just, sort of, you know"—he finished the sentence with his hands. Smell, taste and sound were rated as erotically noncontributory. Narratives, however, could be arousing.

"I don't know," he said, trying to foresee his sexual future. "I guess I'll try to stay with male friends, like if I can latch on to an affair with a guy. But, if I'm still floating around for a few more years like I have been in the gay thing, I'll try to find a woman, then, who maybe doesn't care if I sort of trip outside."

This prospective bisexual lifestyle did not materialize, but he did, in fact "float around," getting involved in casual short-lived relationships with other men. He would break a budding relationship in anticipation of rejection, as soon as it reached the stage when the potential sexual partner might find out about his small penis.

He was nearly thirty when he became involved in his first lasting homosexual relationship with a man ten years his senior. It was then that the masochistic traits, of which he was previously unaware, emerged to match his partner's mildly sadistic traits: "Well, my lover slaps me every now and then. You know, he'll hit me, you know. Hit on the back side, slap me in the face or punch me, you know, that type of thing. He is [sadistic] a little, yeah, a little. Sometimes I'll say, I'll call him daddy or papa, or just crazy stuff like that. So we'll play like that, and I'll say like, 'Papa don't hurt me,' and he'll call me a baby. Like little baby." He later supplemented the above report in these words: "We don't have sex. We haven't had sex in a year. But he'll slap my face and it gives me a sexual pleasure. Yeah, I get a charge. I don't usually get erections from it. It's just, I get a, a warm feeling, similar to that when I lie on his stomach, you know, I put my head on his stomach."

Masochistic ideation, first reported in teenage, remained in the contents of his adult dreams and daydreams: "Yeah, like falling off a cliff, being hit by a car, or something like that. Sometimes, before I go to bed, I'll have these thoughts where I'll be like watching a moving picture where my arms are getting cut up by a razor blade and the blood would run like paint, dripping down. The same thing with poking with the—like sewing needle, and the blood will come and just spurt like a little bubble."

It was in the context of the above disclosure that he recalled his fascination, during his college years, with sadomasochistic practices of two of his college mates, a masochistic girl and her sadistic boyfriend. He had identified with the girl rather than the boy. Another girl in his circle of friends had been a self-mutilator who burned and cut herself. One of his homosexual male friends was a urophile.

Significance of the Case

Prenatal Precursors of Paraphilia. With regard to the development of paraphilia, in this case the significance of the chromosomal sex is that it was 46,XY, as for a male, and concordant with the gonadal sex (testes) and the prenatal hormonal sex (nonfeminizing). These three variables were discordant with the external genital morphology insofar as the penis was extremely small. On the basis of the evidence of the sexual morphology, one may conjecture that the sexual morphology of the brain was more masculinized than feminized. However, there is no proof that this conjecture is correct.

Postnatal Precursors of Paraphilia: Prepuberty. On the basis of palpated testes, it was decided that, despite the minute size of the penis, the child would be assigned to live as a boy. The parents were mortified by having a first child, and only son, who was genitally defective. During the child's earliest infancy they were able to evade the problem by seldom mentioning it. As the child grew older, the mother's strategy was a neurotic one of attacking the child and not his syndrome. The father's strategy was one of more passive avoidance of the problem, but not of his son. The boy was unable to satisfy the demands his mother put on him. His juvenile response was to entertain the covert but explicit proposition of sex reassignment as a girl. In childhood he abstained from self-exposure in sexual rehearsal play, though he did have a crush on another boy at age 8.

Postnatal Precursors of Paraphilia: Postpuberty. The onset of masculinizing puberty was clinically induced at age 13 yrs 7 mos, at which age there were no signs of spontaneous hormonal puberty. The road to masculine achievement was slow. At times the boy came close to suicide as he was unable to solve the problem, present since childhood, of whether or not to undergo sex reassignment.

Each adolescent attempt at establishing a sex life for himself ended in a fiasco. In college, he and other students with severe psychosexual problems, for example, paraphilic masochism, established themselves as a friendship group. He became fascinated with sadomasochism, but only in a peripheral way.

Adulthood Paraphilic Outcome. He gave up on the possibility of establishing a heterosexual life after he discovered that his capacity for a love affair was with a male lover. In a relationship he readily fell into the subordinate role and into being a martyr, short of being a complete masochist. He found himself sexually aroused by being slapped around. The other aspect of his martyrdom was to have to forfeit sex in the relationship. He did not engage in bondage and discipline, in part because his lover required complete, obedient abstinence from sex in their relationship.

Paraphilic Stratagem. In this case, victimization by a birth defect and pathologically exaggerated maternal demands led to two strategies of coping. One was the strategy of gender transposition. The dilemma of gender transposition was solved according to the opponent-process principle, by a reversal of negative and positive. The negation of homosexuality changed to the positive of "coming out," which displaced the erstwhile possibility of sex reassignment to live as a girl and mature as a woman. The other strategy involved also the opponent-process principle, according to which the paraphilic erotization of suffering changed submissiveness, martyrdom, and masochism from negative to positive.

CHAPTER 5

Biography 3: Sadomasochism in a Male with Congenital Micropenis

Diagnostic and Clinical Biography

Biography 3 is that of a man, now in his early thirties, who in boyhood had a retracted and virtually invisible micropenis. His parents disavowed the existence of his congenital defect, so that his mortification was intensified. His lovemap differentiated, after a short interlude of ambiguity, as heterosexually sadomasochistic. He, himself, was represented in both the sadistic and the masochistic roles, but in fantasy only, not in performance.

The patient's birth defect of the sex organs did not come to medical attention until his mother took him at age 8 yrs 4 mos to a neurosurgeon for a neurological evaluation. She had suspected that the boy's slowness, clumsiness, and poor school performance might suggest brain damage resulting from accidental head injuries in early childhood. The neurosurgeon did not find any evidence of brain damage. Instead, he found that the boy's genitals were too small for his age, and advised a referral for endocrine evaluation in the Johns Hopkins Pediatric Endocrine Clinic (PEC).

Upon initial physical examination at age 8 yrs 9 mos, the length of the uncircumcised penis was 1 cm. The foreskin was abnormally redundant, and the scrotum was empty. The body was obese, with the weight 114.4 pounds (51.9 kg) and the height 58.5 inches (148 cm). A large amount of suprapubic fat completely covered the penis, so that it could be seen only after the folds of fat had been pushed away. The left testicle could be easily brought down, and was found to be small but of normal consistency. The right gonad and the prostate were not palpable. Subsequently, the right gonad was mobilized and considered to be a normal testicle. The buccal smear showed a male chromatin pattern. The karyotype, done ten years later, was 46,XY.

By convention, a penis of below average dimensions is defined as a micropenis when, on the criterion of stretched length, its measurement falls at least 2.5 standard deviations below the mean for age (Money et al., 1984). When a micropenis is an isolated birth defect, its etiology is usually unascertainable. In some cases a micropenis may be associated with either a deficiency of androgen secretion or an intracellular anomaly in androgen uptake during fetal development (Danish et al., 1980).

The most extreme degree of micropenis, as in the present case, is rare, and there is no uniform etiology. Even in those syndromes, for example, hypogonadotropic hypogonadism (Kallmann's syndrome), in which a variable degree of hypogenitalism is a diagnostic feature, its etiological origin cannot be satisfactorily explained. In the present instance, the child's micropenis might be attributed etiologically to toxic teratology: during the second month of the pregnancy, the mother had been hospitalized following what she defined as an accidental overdose of an unspecified barbiturate. It is known that barbiturates used during pregnancy may have a teratogenic effect on a fetus, including malformations of the genitalia (Nelson and Forfar, 1971; Reinisch and Sanders, 1982).

At birth, the baby's sex assignment as a male was not questioned. According to the mother, nobody noticed the genital abnormality. "None of the doctors said anything about the organs themselves being abnormal," she recalled during her first psychohormonal interview. "He wasn't any different. Didn't seem to me to be, and no one else brought my attention to it. I had no idea because the foreskin laps over, and a baby is small anyway." She was inconsistent when later she said that "the obstetrician couldn't do a circumcision because the organs hadn't developed right." There was additional evidence of the strategy of denial at work in her dealing with her son's birth defect (see Family Pathology).

The boy was admitted for further endocrine, psychohormonal, and surgical evaluation at Johns Hopkins, three weeks after the first outpatient visit. The surgeon's impression was that the peculiar appearance of the boy's penis was due largely to an adherent phimosis. A circumcision revealed a normally formed glans and urethral opening at its tip. Two months later another operation was performed, as the boy complained of difficulty in urinating from his penis, now retracted completely into the suprapubic fat pad. A Z-plasty above the penis was performed to release the penis from its surrounding tissue. In addition, some suprapubic fat tissue was removed.

The surgery resulted in a closer to normal appearance of the penis, which was now more exposed.

The boy became talkative more than formerly. He said he was now concerned only with obesity, and enthusiastically accepted the recommendation to start a low calorie diet. He was discharged with the recommendation to use testosterone propionate (0.2%) ointment, which promotes penile growth if applied locally. This treatment is designed to bring about pubertal enlargement of the penis prematurely. It has a good cosmetic effect until the age when the rest of the body undergoes puberty. The penis does not then undergo the further enlargement of a second puberty (Money et al., 1985).

In the present case, the topical application of testosterone ointment at age nine resulted in some increase in penis size. It also induced a scanty growth of pubic hair. After six months of treatment, the boy's mother, concerned with his "excessive development" decided not to renew the prescription, and application of the ointment was discontinued. The boy was then 9 yrs 3 mos old. The stretched length of his penis was 4 cm.

When he was 10 yrs 7 mos old, his mother took him to a local pediatrician who, on his own initiative, prescribed two hormones to advance pubertal enlargement of the penis, namely, chorionic gonadotropin (4000 units) and testosterone (10 mg), both daily. The duration of this treatment was not recorded. On the patient's return to the PEC seven months later, there was no significant change in his sexual development, except for full descent of his right testicle. The urinary level of the gonadotropins LH (luteinizing hormone) and FSH (follicle stimulating hormone) was prepubertal.

A year later, at the age of 12 yrs 5 mos, the patient had clear signs of the spontaneous onset of puberty. The stretched length of the penis was 6 cm, and the dimensions of both testes were 3 x 2 cm. Pubertal scrotal thinning and vascularization were present. No further endocrine treatment was needed.

At age eighteen, the patient was 6 ft 3 in (191 cm) tall, and his weight was 274.5 pounds (124.5 kg). His penis, though still small, was larger than predicted. It measured 7 cm x 2.3 cm unstretched length, and 13.3 cm, stretched length. The testes were 4.5 x 3 cm bilaterally. The LH and FSH levels were within normal limits (71 ng/ml and 224 ng/ml, respectively).

These findings remained unchanged at the last endocrine follow-up at age twenty-two. The patient was then followed in the Psychohormonal Research Unit (PRU) for another four years. By the time he reached the age of twenty-six, his height had increased to 6 ft 7 in (200.6 cm). He had managed to reduce his weight to 195 pounds (88.4 kg), but still considered himself too heavy.

Family Pathology

Early in the course of her first psychohormonal interview, the patient's mother unwittingly demonstrated her use of the strategy of making a statement and then undercutting it with another statement that partially rescinded or nullified it. Asked about how she and her husband got along, she replied: "Well, about like most people, I suppose." Laughing, she added: "We have little disagreements. Nothing unusual, but . . ." The interviewer finished her sentence with: "But you would marry him again?" Laughing still louder, she concurred: "Oh, yes. I waited twenty-four years for him," meaning that she married at age twenty-four. This way of joking was compatible with a response that had been made a few minutes earlier, also with laughter, when she characterized her relationship with her husband as: "We're business partners. But, uh, I enjoy it and he does too. Most of the time. Until I feel that I should spend more time at home." The family business was an instrument repair shop.

The other feature observed in the woman's behavior since the early stage of follow-up was her puzzling indifference with regard to her son's diagnosis. Her story was that she had been unaware of her son's birth defect until it was revealed during his neurological evaluation at the age of eight. She recalled, however, that prior to that the boy did complain about being "different from other boys," but she thought he referred to his penis being uncircumcised. She did not take any action, because "when you dread something," she said, "you have a tendency to put it off."

She continued to disregard the boy's condition even after the Johns Hopkins evaluation resulted in the diagnosis of micropenis: "I didn't think too much about it," she said, "because even then I thought maybe it was just a matter of hormone treatment and a matter of circumcision of some sort." She went to a local pediatrician to get a second opinion. "That's when I got the shock," she said. "He told me that it might be a situation of two sexes, it might be a reversed sexual situation. And I got, I guess, I sort of got panicky." She had calmed down as soon as she had been assured that sex reassignment was not considered in her son's treatment plan.

From then on, the issue of the micropenis became nonexistent again in her communication with the boy, family members, and even psychohormonal staff. It was evident, for example, in her telephone conversation with one of the psychohormonal staff, when her son was twenty-six years old. With no mention of penis size, her concern was that he might need another visit, because "his breasts are quite developed, and he doesn't seem to be slimming down like normal."

Throughout seventeen years of follow-up it was apparent that denial and substitution of secondary problems for the primary, but unspeakable one constituted her strategy of coping with the trauma of having a defective child. Under the circumstances, she could never become her son's ally in struggling with the adversities of the unspeakable condition.

The two older sons (there were no sisters) were apparently never informed about the reasons for their youngest brother's visits to a distant hospital. The middle brother, who once accompanied the patient, then eighteen years old, to the hospital, guessed that it was "a thyroid problem." This was concordant with the patient's previous statements that nobody at home ever mentioned his birth defect. The patient himself adopted that policy, so that he did not spontaneously talk about his defect even in the psycho-hormonal office. Instead, he often referred to his obesity as if it was the major problem and consistently avoided or denied the existence of any worries concerning his genital status. It was not until he was eighteen years old that he started talking about his genital inadequacy and its impact on his erotosexual functioning (see Lovemap Biography).

Judging on the basis of the family's image as presented by his mother, nothing indicated the existence of severe intrafamilial and/or intramarital tensions. Their existence became apparent only in the light of the patient's and his middle brother's reports. The father was unavailable for interview, as he did not accompany his wife and son to the hospital.

When the patient was nearly eleven, he likened his mother's behavior to that of his girl schoolmates: "My mother is a grown-up lady, but she's still mean like the girls at school. Instead of using her claws and feet she uses a belt. She doesn't have anything to press against me." Seven years later his perception of his mother had not changed. "She yells a lot, we don't get along very well," he said with resignation. One of his Sacks Sentence Completion Test responses was that mothers "don't listen." He then elaborated on that issue: "I get to hear her complaints about my father, complaints about me and about everybody else. She's very unpredictable as to the mood. One minute she can be yelling about everything in the world and the next minute she'll be laughing about something."

The patient's relationship with his father was not any better: "My father and I are not close at all," he complained. "He's hard to get along with. He's very conservative in a lot of ways. He's just not easy to talk to, never has been. He never helps me, looks down on me, never listens." Nonetheless, they worked together in the family shop.

His relations with his two older brothers were also disturbed owing to the fact that both of them victimized him by ridiculing or, at best, ignoring him. His mother, who was aware of his recurring conflicts with his brothers, attributed them to his oversensitivity: "If the brothers just look at him, he screams," she once said. "If someone is home, he stays in his room most of the time, listening to the radio. If no one is home, he will go into the family room and watch television."

The brother said of his parents that "there had been a lot of fighting in the marriage. Things are better now than a few years ago." What he had to say about his brother was disparaging, as in the comment: "He doesn't know his limitations. He thinks he can fix anything in the shop, but he can't."

By the time the patient was in his early twenties, and still living with his parents, his position in the family had not changed. His strategy was to "spend as little time at home as absolutely necessary. My family," he said, "never lets me do anything myself, treats me like I'm not there. They ignore me—like I'm trying to say something and they'll just not take me seriously."

During the last follow-up interview at the age of twenty-six, he reported that as adults, one brother was an alcoholic and the other had a history of drug abuse and drug dealing. However, both of them had established their own families and their independence, away from home. The patient was the only one who still lived and worked with his parents. He hated his job in the family shop and his dependency on his parents. Nevertheless, he remained afflicted with inertia, unable to change the status quo, as if he was locked in an adverse but paradoxically safe relationship with his parents.

Biography of Social Development

During the psychohormonal visits when he was eighteen years old, the patient described himself as a "shy dreamer." He recalled: "When I was in the first and second grade, the teachers used to keep me after school and that's because I used to daydream instead of doing the work. And I guess that it's always been like that." In fact, since early years, daydreaming was, and continued to be one of his favorite experiences. It was as if he lived in two different worlds—the mundane world, and the fantasy world.

In the mundane world he was a lonely, obese, slow, and clumsy boy with a tiny penis, ridiculed and teased by his two older brothers and peers. School became an arena of his social and intellectual defeat. His failing grades led the teachers and his mother to a suspicion that he was brain-damaged.

In the fantasy world, he was never lonely, for he created an imaginary "invisible friend" with whom he shared his thoughts. This invisible friend was later replaced by a dog which became his close companion. In fantasy, the clumsy boy turned into either a jazz band soloist applauded by admirers, or into a renowned writer. Another of his fantasies was of himself being a hero overpowering the monsters from his favorite movies. In his post-pubertal years, sexuoerotic fantasies substituted for live encounters. The common theme of both the mundane and the fantasy worlds was his pre-occupation with his own physical, social, intellectual, and erotosexual status.

The onset of behavioral difficulties was simultaneous with his recognition, sometime before age seven, of his genital abnormality. It was then that he suddenly started gaining weight to the extent that he became grossly obese. It was his obesity that soon made him a target of cruel teasing at school.

Between the ages of nine and eighteen, he tended to belittle the impact of teasing by peers and brothers. He admitted on several occasions that he had been teased "a bit" because of his obesity, but it was not "that bad." When he was nine, during one of his psychohormonal visits he drew a picture of a boy without clothes and without arms. His comment was that "the boy is unhappy because he has no clothes on." For many years of follow-up he did not mention his small penis as being a target of his peers' teasing. He talked about his relations with schoolmates in a tone of resignation: "They are nice only when they are alone, though. They like to pick on younger boys. They throw croquet balls at my legs." At twelve, he commented ironically on his relationship with peers, saying that it was "Normal. Rotten. They call me fatsy." His relations with his two brothers were not any better: "They never want me around," he complained. "I'm not good enough for them because I'm too fat. They call me 'slow poke' or 'fatso.' " His brothers avoided parental reprimand by bribing their victim with small amounts of money to keep his mouth shut.

It was not until he was twenty-six years old that he spoke of how happy he was when in the ninth grade an injured knee excluded him from gym class. The locker room, showers, and school bathroom were virtually torture chambers for him. "I never really used the bathroom in school," he said. "I usually waited until I got home. I would use stand-up urinals when no one else was around, if possible. That might have caused my being a more private person than what I might have been normally." He wished he had known that he could have been medically excused from gym class on the basis of his genital condition.

He occupied his leisure time with activities that did not require the company of other participants: watching TV, listening to music, and writing. He was only ten years old when he proudly announced that he had written several short horror stories. In the tenth grade he took a journalism class and worked for the school gazette, writing cartoon captions. He dreamed of a career as a professional writer or actor. Sometimes he bought the script of a theater play and then performed it all alone in his room, playing all the characters himself.

His enthusiasm for writing did not cease even though, in his mid-twenties, he no longer believed that he could become a professional writer. The major obstacle in his path for a writing career was, he rationalized, that he had no place to write. He often had to drive to the town's pizza parlor for the privacy that he lacked at home. Being an author, sitting alone writing in a booth at the pizza parlor, was the next best thing to being in a Left Bank cafe in Paris.

Throughout his school years his highest level was that of a C student. He failed the third grade, having lost many school days owing to the hospital admission for penile repair surgery. His IQ, tested at the age of 8 yrs 9 mos on the Wechsler Intelligence Scale for Children, was normal (Verbal IQ, 108; Performance IQ, 96; Full Scale IQ, 102). The analysis of subtests did not indicate any specific deficits. On the Wechsler Adult Intelligence Scale at the age 18 yrs 1 mo, the Verbal IQ was 114, the Performance IQ was 113, and the Full Scale IQ was 114. School underachievement could not be attributed to intellectual deficit, but rather to other impediments.

After graduating from high school and commencing his work as a serviceman in the family-owned repair shop, he continued to cherish his childhood and teenage dreams. At age twenty-six, he said: "I can probably do anything, if I want to put my mind to it. But I don't, because not a lot interests me that much." He had many ideas on how to improve his life and even become a millionaire. He remained a dreamer living in his two worlds, one of which offered unlimited opportunities to counterweigh the burdens and restrictions of the other. The same applied to his sexuality (see Lovemap Biography).

A short story he wrote at age twenty-six was about an old man who journeys to the social security office to inquire about his eligibility for benefits. There, he is confronted by "an average guy." Everything about Mr. Average's life is average: his name is John Smith. He has an average family: a wife, a daughter, and a son. When the statistics report that the size of an average family decreased, Mr. Average loses a child. When statistical size of the family is reported to have increased, his wife becomes pregnant again.

The story is significant insofar as its two main characters symbolize the themes familiar in the author's own biography, the theme of eligibility and normalcy. His was the lonely struggle of a child growing up stigmatized by a deformity that threatened his social, romantic, and sexual eligibility as a male. He was doomed to be different from other, average people. The story epitomized, like his childhood fantasies, his longing for the unattainable.

Lovemap Biography

At the age 8 yrs 9 mos, when he was for the first time seen in the PRU, this boy had no basic knowledge regarding sexuality, reproduction, or his own clinical condition. In preparation for upcoming penile repair surgery, he was given the necessary information together with basic sex education. The same information was then repeated a year later.

There were no reports of childhood sexual rehearsal play in the pre-pubertal years, nor of masturbation. He was twenty-one when he retro-spectively referred to that subject in these words: "No, there weren't really any little girls in the neighborhood to play with. As far as little boys go, I wouldn't do that." With the knowledge of hindsight it was more likely that it was not the absence of little girls in the neighborhood, but his self-diagnosed genital defect that kept him from joining any group activities that might threaten his privacy. Referring to masturbation, he stated that he did not do it until he was about thirteen.

Before age twelve, he consistently hated girls "because they scratch too much and kick." At twelve, his report differed: he now stated that he did like girls, but they did not like him. He could not further explain how he felt about it until fourteen years later. Then he said that a girl, knowing of his defect, might have publicly humiliated him at school. "That might have done me in," he commented, "as far as dating is concerned."

When at age eighteen he returned after five years to the PRU, he had a negative report with regard to dating, sex life and falling in love. He reflected upon his sexual loneliness in these words: "I think I'm sensitive about some subjects, like my penis, of course. Well, I don't get around a lot and I'm mostly alone."

His only sexual activity was masturbation, which, he said, he was "uptight" about. He anxiously asked whether masturbation can be harmful if as frequent as once or twice a week. For masturbation imagery, he occa-sionally used soft core pornography magazines like *Playboy* or *Penthouse*, which he kept hidden from his mother. "She would kill me if she'd catch me," he commented. Ordinary porno stories were, in his judgment, "just bad." He did not find them sexually stimulating. They depicted just ordinary heterosexual intercourse, while his real sexual turn-on were images of bondage and coercive sex.

He remembered having bondage fantasies ever since he was about thirteen. His description of a daydreaming session was as follows: "I start daydreaming and just all of a sudden it turns out to be one of the bondage fantasies. For example, a girl ties me up and seduces me and stuff like that. Usually it's in some secluded field or something like that. There is one woman usually, sometimes two. They are tying me up and they kiss me all over. I don't know what happens to my penis. I don't think about it that much." He also had fantasies in which the roles were reversed, and he was tying up a woman and having sex with her.

During one of his visits at age eighteen, the theme of coercion and death appeared in his responses to Thematic Apperception Test cards. Card 13MF presents a young man standing with downcast head buried in his arm. Behind him is the figure of a woman lying in bed. The story the patient narrated for this card was as follows: "A lady was walking into her bedroom to get undressed to take a shower. In the shadows was a man who was waiting for her. As she undressed he got more tense. The more she undressed the tenser he got. Then suddenly, as she finished undressing, he jumped on her. Slashing her throat, he raped her, then got up and wondered why he did that, then jumped out the window, falling to his death."

The blank TAT card evoked the following response: "It'll be a fantasy about a man who traveled on the Amazon to find out if the city of the Amazons existed. The Amazons were a race of superior females. The females were war-like, at least in the myths, and are totally brutal to men. He went through the woods until he came upon a village. Suddenly, he heard a noise from behind. It was too late. The Amazons grabbed him. He did not get away. They tied him to a stake and started dancing around him and kissed him in various parts of his body. As each one kissed him, the farther down they went. After they had gotten through regular type fucking, and got their sexual pleasures out of him, enough to keep the Amazons supplied with pregnancies, they burned him at the stake."

A paraphilic fantasy became also the theme of a short story about a strangling ivy vine, written by the patient when he was eighteen. He considered the story as well as his fantasies to be "deranged in the sense that people don't think that anybody sane would think of stuff like that." Having narrated the story, he gave a précis of it in the taped summary interview: "The kid likes horticulture, growing plants. His father brings home the girl he is going to marry. The kid and his almost step-mother go out on a picnic. And he plants ivy vines around her and they grow on her. In a few hours she is completely entwined."

When asked if the ivy vine story was in any sense related to his bondage and coercion fantasies, his response was affirmative: "Yes, I guess. Like, as I told you in the story, he takes off her clothes, tears her clothes off, so there wouldn't be any trace of where they had been picnicking. And, of course, he'd have to tie her to the tree or else he wouldn't be able to keep her there."

The written version of the same story included a detailed description of the victim: "She seemed to be quite nice, she was a bit tall, her hair was completely straight and fell about the middle of her back, it was a dusty blonde." About the motif for the planned murder of her, the pertinent paragraph in the story read: "I never let it slip to what degree I loathed her. I realized it was not against her, but against what she was going to do to father and me." In the narrated version, what he loathed her for was that he forced her to rape him and she stole the secret of the size of his penis. To recapture the secret, the ivy vine had to dispose of her, and leave no trace.

The patient said he did not spontaneously ascribe personal significance to stories he wrote: "I don't think much when I write something. I just go ahead and write it. Maybe after I write it I think what it's about. I think that's just something that popped in my head. I can't really place it anywhere as what it would be like in my life."

The ratio of paraphilic and normophilic fantasies was, in the patient's estimation, about 50:50. He said that when he had pictures of attractive women from *Playboy,* they would trigger fantasies of normal intercourse. In the absence of appropriate erotic pictures, the paraphilic fantasies of sadomasochistic bondage, rape, and death were more likely to prevail.

At twenty-six, he was more explicit in reporting the details of his masochistic fantasies: "The kinkiest one, I guess, is possibly some female domination. I get tied on the bed spread eagle with both legs and arms tied. I won't be allowed to come for a while, that's the biggest thing. She is playing around with my cock orally and with her cunt and fingers. Just when I get to the point of orgasm, she backs off." There was also some "pinching or squeezing around the nipples, and some biting which makes it even more spicy."

In his estimate, the strongest arousing component of his fantasies was the depiction of himself in the submissive role of a sexual victim. He found himself aroused by domination stories from *Playboy,* while remaining unaffected by the ordinary, straight erotic stories.

Lack of any sexual experience with a live partner made it impossible for him to judge whether he would be able to act out these fantasies: "Thinking of it and doing it," he said, "are two different things."

In retrospect, the patient was not sure whether he had or had not had homosexual or bisexual imagery. He was sure that he had not engaged in sexual activity of any type with a partner of either sex. He could only recall vaguely that there was perhaps a short period of time in his early teenage when he might have had "some thoughts about wanting to be a girl." He was uncertain whether these thoughts appeared in his sleep dreams or day dreams. It was typical for him, he commented, to have sleep dreams so vivid that he would confuse them later with actuality.

Throughout teenage and early adulthood, he remained too shy and inhibited to take the initiative in establishing closer contact with a woman. He was twenty-five when, finally, for the first time in his life, he made an attempt to start a relationship with a woman, but "it didn't even materialize into much." Recounting this experience was so painful to him, he said, that he was unable to disclose anything more pertaining to this short-lived relationship except that the woman was five years his senior and had four children. Right after their first date she unexpectedly moved out of town.

At the time of his last follow-up visit at the age of twenty-six, he was seeing another woman, the divorced mother of a nine-year-old son. He had not had sex with her, and was pessimistic about the future of their relationship. He assumed that the woman was probably seeing three or four other guys, and was "on her way to alcoholism."

With regard to marriage and parenting, he was undecided. He did not exclude a possibility of marrying "if the right girl came along." It would be a marriage of "obligatory fidelity." He leaned toward the concept of a childless marriage. "I'm not the parenting type, I guess," he concluded.

Significance of the Case

Prenatal Precursors of Paraphilia. With respect to the future development of paraphilia, in this case the significance of the chromosomal sex is that it was, as expected in a male, 46,XY, and concordant with the gonadal sex (testicular) and the prenatal hormonal sex (masculinizing). Though concordant among themselves, these three variables were discordant with the appearance of the external genitalia, insofar as the penis developed prenatally as a micropenis. It was extremely deficient in size for an otherwise normal child. On the basis of the evidence of pelvic morphology, one may conjecture that the sexual dimorphism of the brain was more masculine than feminine. However, there is no proof that this conjecture is correct, especially in view of the mother's barbiturate overdose while pregnant.

Postnatal Precursors of Paraphilia: Prepuberty. Ostensibly, the baby's neonatal assignment as a male was not questioned. From the child's viewpoint, there was no explanation of why his micropenis defect was treated as nonexistent by his parents and pediatrician until he was 8 yrs 4 mos old, so that he had to endure in lonely secrecy the mortification of being abnormal, avoiding exposure in sexual rehearsal play. Stigmatized by obesity under which his retracted micropenis became virtually invisible, he became even more a loner. In his own family he was like an unwelcome intruder with no allies and no close friends. He lived in a fantasy world that eventually encompassed sadomasochistic imagery.

Postnatal Precursors of Paraphilia: Postpuberty. Convinced of his erotosexual ineligibility, he had no adolescent sexual or romantic experience except for solitary masturbation. In his masturbation fantasies, females were paraphilically transformed into those who either longed for his sexual favors or raped him, and those whom he overpowered and conquered erotically. In some fantasies they became victims of erotic death.

Adulthood Paraphilic Outcome. In adulthood, he remained socially and romantically isolated. Heterosexual sadomasochistic fantasies persisted. His role in them was sometimes sadistic, but more prevalently masochistic. There were supplementary normophilic fantasies. Neither they nor the sadomasochistic fantasies were put into practice with a partner.

Paraphilic Stratagem. The noxious primary and secondary consequences of being a victim of micropenis were transposed, according to the principle of opponent-process, from tragedy into triumph by becoming erotized into masochism and sadism—masochism for the self, and sadism for others. Paraphilic sadomasochism coexisted with normophilic fantasy. Both were heterosexual. Bisexualism failed to persist beyond a shadowy recollection of early teenaged thoughts of being, maybe, a girl.

CHAPTER 6

Biography 4: Autassassinophilia in a Bisexual Male with a History of Congenital Ambiguity of the Sex Organs

Diagnostic and Clinical Biography

Biography 4 is that of a chromosomal male born with hermaphroditically ambiguous genitalia. He was designated male until fifteen months of age, and then reared by his grandmother as a girl for a year, after which he lived again as a boy. Multiple surgical admissions ensued and were experienced as nosocomial abuse. His lovemap in adulthood was bisexual. Its homosexual component was masochistic and directed toward self-arranged assassination. His adult life was punctuated by severely morbid binge alcoholism.

Information regarding the patient's birth was obtained retrospectively from the mother when she first brought him to Johns Hopkins for genital surgery at age five. She had had a miscarriage prior to the birth of her first child, a girl. Twelve months later the patient was born, followed within the next two years by a brother and a sister.

The mother was twenty-three years old at the time of the patient's birth, which was one month premature. The delivery was at home. Though a young physician had been in attendance, the mother did not know where the obstetrical record could be retrieved. She recalled having been told that the baby was a boy, and that she should seek a consultation at a nearby hospital. She had immediately recognized that the baby's genitalia did not look normal and that there were no testicles in evidence.

Neighbors, she said, told her that the child was a "morphodite." The term was unfamiliar to her. They said he was a freak whom she should put in a circus, for a side show. She recalled, though there are no records to confirm it, that she had taken the baby to the hospital because of swelling in the genital area, and had been instructed to give warm baths, which did reduce the swelling. There is a hospital record of two pediatric outpatient visits at age three, for tonsillitis and impetigo, respectively, with no mention of the genital defect.

At the age of three months, the baby and his mother went to live out-of-state with the maternal grandmother. The medical opinion that the mother recalled having received in her mother's home town was that "it looks like he is both, a girl, and a boy," and that she should return with the child to Baltimore and take him to Johns Hopkins. After about a year, she herself returned to Baltimore, but left the child with her mother. The child was 2 yrs 3 mos old when she returned a year later, and was "wearing little dresses and ribbons tied on long, brown hair, all fixed up like a little girl." Dismayed at what the grandmother had done, the mother immediately arranged for a haircut, put the child into boy's clothes, and brought him back to Baltimore as a boy. A quarter of a century later, the patient's only memory of this change was that, for the winter train ride north, he wore a new, blue snowsuit—being blue, of course, for a boy.

By school age, the child's behavior at home was like that of "any other boy," except that sometimes he cried and asked his mother why he couldn't stand up, as his brother did, to urinate. She told him that he would have to have surgery. At school, his age mates would ask why he had to sit to urinate. He responded with elective mutism, social distancing, and self-isolation. A school medical officer initiated the Johns Hopkins referral and the first evaluation for treatment of the birth defect of the sex organs. The child was 5 yrs 8 mos old. For eleven weeks he was admitted for exploratory laparotomy and the first stage of hypospadiac repair.

The genital examination showed a hypospadiac micropenis, bound down with chordee. Insofar as it could be stretched, its stretched length measured 5 cm and the width 1.5 cm. The urinary meatus opened, slit-like, onto the perineum, without a urogenital sinus. There was a bifid labioscrotal structure, with "very mobile oval bodies" in the region of the inguinal canals. Rectally, neither uterus nor prostate was palpable. Urethroscopy showed a vestigial vaginal pouch entering the urethra near the neck of the bladder. The exploratory laparotomy confirmed the absence of mullerian organs internally. Surgery was not extended to include the inguinal gonads which, therefore, were not biopsied.

The progress of hypospadiac repair was not as expeditious as originally projected. There were postsurgical complications of severe keloid scar formation, recurrent urethral strictures, and urinary fistulas. Because of these complications, there were six different surgical admissions and eleven different surgical procedures in the two and a half years between the first admission and age eight. At the end of this period, standing to urinate still was impossible. Worse yet, there was continuous urinary dribbling that created a social problem and prevented school attendance for a year at age eight. Because of sloughing of the left nipple and the skin-graft donor site below it, this region required its own graft from the left thigh, leaving the torso disfigured in two places.

The fifth operation, done at the time the boy had his seventh birthday, was a reconstructive urethroplasty. Three months later, there was a right-sided infection with epididymitis. This necessitated removal of the right testis. Four months and two operations later, the boy was again admitted, this time with acute urinary obstruction secondary to urethral stricture. After a suprapubic cystostomy had been performed, the urinary drainage tube became blocked one night. In the morning, urine had extravasated through the abdominal wall. The boy's calls for help had been ignored by the night staff. Two further operations during this admission corrected the urinary obstruction, but required that the boy sit to urinate from an opening in the perineum. The surgical correction of this defect required five more admissions and five more operations between the ages of eight and thirteen. The final operation was the fifteenth.

Upon discharge three weeks before his fourteenth birthday, the patient was at last able to stand to urinate, though not very well. At present, the urinary orifice opens into a ragged, funnel-shaped sinus on the shaft of the penis. From the glans penis to the urinary orifice, the skin of the constructed urethral tube has separated in the midline, thus forming an open gutter for a distance of 3.2 cm. After the cessation of urination, urine has apparently backed up internally so that it then slowly leaks out through the funnel. There is a second source of leakage in the perineum, between the scrotum and the anus, where the former site of a postoperative, indwelling urinary catheter has failed to seal completely.

The patient did not tell anyone about his hygienic problem of urinary leakage for fifteen years, until he was twenty-six years old. At that time he opted against a surgical referral. His explanation was: "I didn't mention it until today because I don't want to go back in the hospital, not for that." On the same basis—"no more cutting"—he had at age nineteen opted against the implantation of a prosthetic right testis.

In the fifteen years between ages eleven and twenty-six, there had been three surgical admissions: at fourteen for severe urethral infection; at sixteen for tonsillectomy; and at twenty-four for repair of a left inguinal hernia. In addition to these three admissions, there began at age eighteen a long-continuing series of outpatient and emergency room visits, punctuated by psychiatric and alcohol detoxification admissions.

The presenting problem at age eighteen was premature ejaculation and copulatory erectile failure. Another problem was the onset, then recent, of acute asthmatic attacks requiring emergency-room treatment. They have persisted until the present, with an annual average of three emergency-room treatments.

An additional problem was brought to the fore at age eighteen, namely, increasingly severe and painful osteoarthritic contractures of the third, fourth, and fifth fingers of each hand, representing a worsening of a congenital phalangeal deformity. The knees also were subject to arthritic pain. The upshot of a surgical consultation was to postpone intervention so long as the contractures did not become grossly incapacitating.

The first emergency room admission was an overnight for depression and suicidal thoughts, and the second for exposure, frostbite, and facial contusions. The patient was twenty-six years old. Over the next nine years, in at least ten different emergency rooms, psychiatric hospitals, and alcohol detoxification centers within the Baltimore metropolitan area, the count of ascertained admissions totaled twenty-five, and a higher actual count is likely.

The typical sequence was that the patient would be brought to an emergency room, in several instances unconscious, suffering from wounds incurred either by accident or attack, while inebriated. After an overnight in an emergency room, he would be discharged either to outpatient or residential rehabilitative care, or to a psychiatric admission. There were six different psychiatric admissions of two to four weeks' duration, and two longer ones ordered by the court as a sequel to arrest and imprisonment for drunk and disorderly conduct.

Presently, at the age of thirty-six, the patient is again enrolled in a rehabilitation program, and again is on treatment with Antabuse for alcoholism. He is also on prednisone for asthma. From the latter he has a mildly cushingoid facies. He has also a problem of hypertension (blood pressure 140/94).

During a psychiatric admission at age twenty-eight, hormonal levels were ascertained as tabulated in Table 6.1.

From a skin biopsy, the level of 5-alpha reductase was found to be only minimally subnormal. Intracellular androgen-binding receptors were normal in number, but subnormal in level of androgen-binding. The elevated levels of FSH (follicle stimulating hormone) and LH (luteinizing hormone) could not readily be accounted for, except in terms of an unidentified partial deficiency in gonadal function.

Karyotyping with the Giemsa and quinacrine banding technique was read as normal 46, XY with a minor polymorphism, namely, a large satellite region on chromosome 14.

The dimensions of the penis at age thirty-five were: stretched length 12.5 cm, and base width 4.5 cm. The one remaining testis, on the left, measured 3 × 3.5 cm. The distribution of pubic, axillary, body, and facial hair was sparse, with shaving required once or twice per week. The voice was properly masculinized. The overall manner and appearance were unremarkably that of a male, except for an unsightly scar, the site of a skin graft, that partially obliterated the left areola and nipple. The scar on the left thigh was not so unsightly.

TABLE 6.1

Endocrine Test Results

Hormone	Level ng/dl	Norm ng/dl
Testosterone	456	575 ± 150
Androstenedione	104	109 ± 20
Serum FSH	711	187 ± 89
Serum LH	158	50 ± 14

Recently, at the patient's own request, a sperm count was done elsewhere, and reported to him as prognostic of infertility because of sperms that were too few and malformed.

Family Pathology

The patient was born into a socially disadvantaged family living in an urban black ghetto. He was the only one of four siblings affected with a congenital birth defect. Since his defect was visible and urination was possible only in the sitting position, the members of the family were aware that he was different from other children. However, there was no recall on the patient's part of traumatic teasing or ridiculing by family members.

The marriage of his parents survived no longer than the birth of the fourth child. The father was a heavy drinker with poor control over his behavior when intoxicated. He left the family when the patient was about three years old. Thereafter, there was no adult male in the boy's immediate surrounding, except for occasional visits of his mother's boyfriend. She did not formally divorce her husband and did not remarry.

Deprived of any financial support from her husband, and unable to work, she struggled trying to make do with welfare checks, her only source of income. Her husband was jailed for nonsupport, to no avail. He never resumed regular support payments. He moved to another city where he worked for a contractor. There were only a few occasions when he returned to visit with his family, but never long enough to reestablish the broken bonds of fatherhood.

The patient, in his ninth year, once told one of his doctors that he missed his dad but immediately added: "But he is mean. He beat at us. He beat all of us except my mother." He said that he did not know a man he would really like. He could not recall the name of his mother's boyfriend who visited them weekly but, he added, "He doesn't treat me like a father." Soon after that interview the arrangements were made for the boy to be placed under care of the Big Brother organization. For the next five years he had a Big Brother, who partially replaced the absent father.

In spite of the adversities of life in welfare poverty, he pursued with impressive persistence a commitment to make his way out of the ghetto. He found himself more and more distanced from his family, caught between two worlds, the one he wanted to leave behind, and the one he was heading for, the world of "nice-middle class neighborhoods and steady income."

Paradoxically, the success of enrollment in a college program marked the beginning of the deterioration of his ties with his family. At family gatherings, he said, he felt "ignored, and rejected as some kind of disease." There was no substantiating evidence that he was correct.

In desperate attempts to find an explanation for his uncontrollable binge drinking and recurring depression in his mid-twenties, he focused on his family as the presumed origin of his behavioral difficulties.

The father became a target in his search for an explanation of his own pathology. He recalled meeting his father after fifteen years of no contact with him. It was at the wedding reception of his younger sister, who had invited their father to attend. The confrontation left a strong impression: "Well, at the wedding reception," he started his story, "when I was drinking some beverages, he said I inherited drinking from him, so I guess that was his way of saying, just like, you know, father and son, you know. He got a little inebriated and he called me. I didn't answer him, and he said 'I'm your father,' and I said 'What father?' I think it kinda hurt him. . . . I think he saw something in me when I said that, and I don't think he will ever forget it as long as he lives, but neither will I." The patient claimed having gained "a little of relief" resulting from that clash.

The relief, if any, did not last long. Two years later, his resentment toward his father was bitter: "When I was born and I was about six weeks old, and they kept taking me to the hospital, he told my mother that he didn't want that. If I remember her words, she said, 'He don't want this thing.' " He continued his story with: "I think my rage started with my father before I was born. I guess from the incident before I was born to this world, when he kicked my mother when she was five or six months pregnant, and I blame this kick for my physical handicap."

He had no critical comments with regard to sibling relations during childhood. The children, he said, protected and looked out for one another. They were especially drawn together when his younger unmarried sister had a baby. After all of them had gone their own ways, he missed the closeness. Then tragedy brought them together for a while when his younger brother was seriously wounded in Vietnam. After that, he realized that "something was missing" and "no one gave a damn about anyone else."

His own attitude to his kin was that they felt, "Okay, asshole, since you want to go to college, and be better than us, go ahead." He spoke of his brother as a "typical ghetto guy" with whom he had nothing in common.

In adulthood, he established his own living quarters and lived alone. He had by this time become subject to periodic binge drinking. When drunk he was unpredictably violent, self-destructive, and subject to provoking attack and sustaining injuries for which he required emergency hospitalization. At such times, his family felt victimized and helpless. By contrast, during his periods of sobriety, they found him amicable and cooperative.

Biography of Social Development

As a boy of four in nursery school, before his first hospital evaluation for hypospadias, the patient already was known for keeping to himself and not talking very much either to his teacher or other children. Some of the other children would ask the teacher why he was so quiet. They had probably watched him when he went to the bathroom, the mother speculated, because they had also asked why he had to sit down to urinate.

During the eleven weeks of the child's first hospital admission, the phenomenon of not talking became recognized as so extreme in degree as to qualify as elective mutism. The surgical house staff were nonplussed by his failure to communicate and respond, except, it was noted, to have "a psychogenic fit of monotonous moaning and wild screaming" when he was subjected to a needle puncture or injection, or had a dressing removed. They wrongly inferred that he was mentally defective, and this stigma was perpetuated in the medical chart for several years.

One psychiatric consultant interpreted the reaction rather as apathetic listlessness, and another as a quasi-catatonic inhibition of social responsiveness, possibly related to disillusionment regarding surgery. He had expected repair of his penis, but had received only an exploratory laparotomy. Prior to discharge from this same admission, the first surgical stage of hypospadiac repair, namely, a release of chordee, was performed. Subsequently, beginning at age 5 yrs 10 mos, there began a progressive lifting of elective mutism.

Ten months later, even though further surgery would be needed before standing to urinate would be possible, the boy surprised his pediatric endocrinologist by being able to talk to him. He explained that formerly he hadn't been sure what he was, a boy or a girl, whereas "I'm going to be all right now that I've had my operation." At home he told his brother the same thing. He was not modest when undressing or bathing with his siblings around. His sex educators were the PRU staff.

The extent to which, at this stage of his life, he may have known about the year he had spent as a girl is not on record. However, he did recall, at age twenty-six, that his cousins had told him that his grandmother had considered him a girl and called him "my little sweetheart."

From age seven onward, he did not ever again experience elective mutism globally, only episodically. There were some residual unspeakable things in his life. The persistence of urinary leakage was one of them, for to speak of it would risk additional surgery. Also, early in adolescence, at age fourteen, he was not able to talk about what he knew or needed to know about sexual development either in general, or in reference to his own status as a genitally imperfect male.

One of the side effects of postsurgical problems with urinary leakage, already mentioned, was that the boy lost a year of schooling at age eight. Having the surgical confirmation of his sexual status as a male, however, he was no longer afflicted with elective mutism in the classroom. When he was able to attend school, he was academically an achiever. Concurrent with this change, there was an upward shift in scores on the Wechsler Intelligence Scale for Children. The comparative IQs at age 5 yrs 11 mos and 7 yrs 7 mos were Verbal IQ: 68, 94; Performance IQ: 74, 106; Full Scale IQ: 68, 99.

It was not until many years later that, as a young man of nineteen, the patient explicitly formulated his academic ambition. In the context of talking about transcending ghetto poverty, and comparing himself with others, he said: "With me, I've always been different. I've always said, even as a child, that if I ever get, if I ever live to get older, I'm going to try to outstrive the conditions I'm in. I've always said that. No matter how much it takes, if it doesn't kill me, I'm going to try to better my conditions— better myself. It's rough for any child who grows up in the ghetto. If you have a broken family, too, it's not easy; and I've had a lot of disappointments.

I've had a lot of them."

He had been only three years old when his parents separated and his father moved out of state, and he was nine when he got a Big Brother. This man worked in the administration of a local college and thus, by example, endorsed the boy's ambition to educate himself beyond the ghetto.

The course of his progress was interrupted when he began his sophomore year in high school. He changed from full-time schooling to working part-time, at night. This change meant that his mother would lose family assistance funds if he lived at home as a wage earner. So he left home to live with an aunt and uncle.

It was around this time that his high school girlfriend broke up with him because her sex life with him was, in his opinion, unsatisfactory. Also at this time he had a severely acute asthmatic crisis for the first time, and the onset of arthritic joint pain. "Physically," he said, "I feel like I'm falling apart, but I'm trying to keep it all together, mentally."

Despite these challenges to his academic ambition, he continued working and studying. He was twenty-one when he obtained a high school diploma. In the fall of that same year, having just turned twenty-two, he enrolled as a freshman in a local college. He took courses on a full-time basis. He worked part-time, evenings and weekends, to support himself. The campus was within commuting distance of the home of his aunt and uncle, with whom he continued to reside. Lacking a family of their own, they had taken him in permanently so that he would have privacy and the quiet needed for studying, which he would not have had in his mother's house.

He began his freshman year "on a high note, enthusiastic and confident," he said, and made the Dean's List for the first two semesters. Then he began to procrastinate on assignments in favor of drinking and partying with uneducated and unemployed off-campus friends. Progressively, his ambition and achievement disintegrated. Those who stood by him became alienated, and his provocation of personal catastrophe and destruction became a way of life. This change did not prevent graduation with the bachelor's degree, but it did delay it for a year.

The patient revealed a sign of self-sabotage for the first time when, at the age of twenty-four, and after an absence of fifteen months, he requested a psychoendocrine clinic appointment "because I didn't like the idea of being locked in the dark and doing something I didn't have any control over." His loss of control occurred when he came home drunk and unruly, foul-mouthed, and violent toward his aunt and uncle who had shared their home with him. Once, late at night, when he became drunkenly torpid, he had left food to incinerate in the oven, thus endangering the dwelling.

Though, on this occasion, he effected a reconciliation with his aunt and uncle, the binges of drinking and drunken rage alternating with binges of remorseful repentance continued. After almost two years, there was a particularly violent blowup, after which he was homeless. "I want to destroy that rage in me," he said, "and I want to destroy me at the same time." His strategy was to get drunk enough to go out and rob someone, in the hope that the police would beat and arrest him, or better still, put a bullet through the back of his head as he tried to escape. "The idea of getting killed is a very potential thing, very strong," he said.

Four years later, while once again in the clinic, and still showing the effects of a hangover, he reverted to the same theme: "I'm scared I'm going to go out there and buy me a gun, and just go somewhere, and start shooting people, and just let, let the police, just let the police end all this turmoil. I'm scared of that. I really am. I don't really want to hurt nobody, but at the same time I want somebody to hurt me. . . . I guess I'm talking a little foolish, but it's not foolishness. I can't find no happiness. I can't get nowhere. I can't, you know—I'm just tired. . . . I keep losing all the battles. And all the wars."

In the ten years of his life between the ages of twenty-five and thirty-five, there were literally dozens of times when the patient did get high enough to go out on the street, or into a gay bar or adult bookstore, and stage-manage an assault on himself. This pathological reaction required only the amount of alcohol that would make many people mellow. Rarely, he also would smoke a little marijuana or swallow a Valium or other sedative pill. Frequently he would pass out and be amnesic for how he had been injured, whether by assault, walking into a moving vehicle, or falling. He would also not recall how he had been rescued and transported to the nearest hospital emergency room.

Time after time, his pathetic plight would galvanize those who tended him into mobilizing all the resources of rehabilitation at their command. Dozens of people spent many hundreds of unpaid therapeutic and rehabilitative hours on his behalf. There were four occasions in particular when success was within his grasp, and he was placed in a salaried public-service job, teaching or providing social service for the underprivileged. In each instance he lost everything when he went on another binge of drinking and self-injury, and omitted to register for sick leave within the specified time limit. Reduced to penury, he would seek shelter in one of two inner-city rescue missions, or else live on the streets, until embarking on the next cycle of rehabilitative effort and its collapse.

Lovemap Biography

At the age of seventeen, following a hiatus of three years, the patient initiated a return to the Psychohormonal Research Unit (PRU) as he had begun his sex life and was having a problem with the functioning of his penis. Earlier in boyhood, there had been, at age five or six, an episode of kissing his sister's girlfriend, and lying on top of her, both with their clothes on; and at age ten, with another girl, kissing and genital fondling. At age seventeen, he and his high school girlfriend decided to have sexual intercourse.

It was his first attempt, and he felt inferior as she had begun her sex life at age fourteen with another boyfriend nine years her senior. In the patient's opinion, she knew what to expect of a partner with a penis much larger than his own. His inferiority intensified with repeated failures to get a good erection, or having got one, to maintain it. If he was able to put his penis in her vagina, it would ejaculate immediately. Then it would not erect again. "What makes me feel so afraid," he said, "is because we've been going together for nine months, and doing it for nine months, and she only actually climaxed with me once. . . . She don't never get no satisfaction from it." With variation in foreplay and afterplay, they tried accommodating to one another for little over a year, "and then me and her broke up. . . . It was too much strain and too much worry and too much frustration—too much embarrassment. I mean all we just had to scream about was about our sex life. That's all. . . . If I didn't satisfy her, and me knowing it—she'd probably go to somebody else and get it, that would make me feel even worse."

Seventeen years later, recalling this girlfriend, he said, "That was the only true love, young love, of my life. I couldn't satisfy her. I think that had a great impact, even to this day, on my life."

After the breakup, he began "playing around" with two other girls, "but I'm not getting involved," he said. With these partners, the problem of impotence "just went away. . . . Perhaps I was too much emotionally involved with the other girl," he speculated, by way of explanation. Subsequently, there was a recurrence of impotence in relationships of a casual nature, including two in which the partner was, ostensibly, a virgin.

The issue of deficiency in sexual performance faded in prominence, however, and was replaced by the agonies of adversarial fighting and reconciliation in two other long-term relationships. In neither of these relationships did the imperfection of the patient's genitalia evoke complaints from the partner. In each instance, the woman was older than the patient, by approximately five and twenty years, respectively.

The younger of the women had known the patient since they both were young children. She and her husband had become close friends with him when he was in college. A couple of years after graduating, upon release from a month of psychiatric hospitalization, he lived for a time in a rented room in their house. They needed the money, according to the patient. The husband had sickle-cell disease. Periodically, he had acute attacks, one of which killed him in his mid-thirties.

The relationship between the three of them was one of pathological interdependency, punctuated by episodes of violent quarreling associated with drinking that began sociably. It was one of those relationships in which each of the participants has a different version of what happened. The patient's own version was that the husband's disease rendered him impotent, so that his sexually impoverished wife would, possibly with her husband's collusion when all three of them were loosened up with alcohol, signal a sexual advance to the patient, and he would respond. The couple's version was that the patient ranted and raved in a quite irresponsible and crazy way when he drank too much. He also became, at times, unpredictably threatening and violent, which he himself confirmed. After the husband died, the widow and the patient kept up a social, but not sexual, friendship.

The older of the two women with whom the patient maintained a long-term relationship was also a widow, an attractive woman who looked younger than her years. To earn a living, she took in lodgers, including one or two who were elderly or infirm and needed daily care. In his final student year, the patient became a lodger in her house, having first met her daughter, who dated him and had sex with him on a few occasions. He recalled having been "completely flabbergasted when Bernice [the mother] wanted to fuck." He was a student, and his reaction was "What the hell! If she wants some dick, okay, here's a good way to get some spending money." She was good-hearted in helping him financially. About a year later, their relationship began to change. It became "more than just sexual," he said. They enjoyed each other's company, helped each other, and began to like each other. "You could call it love," he concluded. In a PRU interview, his partner allowed that his penis was small: "It's like a baby's," she said, "but then it's not how long it is, it's how you do with it."

When his status as a lodger terminated, presumably because of the irregularity of his rent payments, the relationship did not. It was sometimes harmonious, and sometimes fractious. Like all of his close relationships, including those with members of his family, this one was contentious and strife-ridden whenever he was on a drinking binge.

Despite the turmoil of their relationship, Bernice was genuine in being drawn to him with a combination of protective care, erotic affection, and her own loneliness, as was evident in her contacts with the psychohormonal staff. She visited him when he was psychiatrically hospitalized. During the year when he was twenty-nine years old, there were three such admissions. Because he had nowhere else to go, she took him in upon discharge from the third admission. Her daughter revolted against having him once more as a lodger in the house. The all-too-familiar pattern repeated itself: disruptive drinking, violent arguments, and emergency-room treatment for beatings

ation, his fifth, followed by transfer to a residential alcoholic rehabilitation program and thence to a halfway house.

In subsequent years, Bernice continued to care about his welfare, and to see him once in a while as a friend, but fewer times as a lover. He did not again share a dwelling with her. He continued to be residentially unstable, and disputatious with other occupants of the places where he lived.

He did not mention the homosexual component of his erotic life until, at the age of twenty-two, he reported having been picked up in a gay bar by a man twice his age. This man was a business executive who made periodic business visits to the city. The two established a friendship that lasted until the man died of a heart attack six years later. As a young black college student, the patient particularly appreciated being on equal terms with this older, wealthy white man socially, as well as in the privacy of their infrequent sexual activity. Ten years later he established a similar friendship with another older man. It also ended prematurely, when, after a year, the friend had a stroke and died.

After the initial meeting with the first of these two older men, the patient said, "I felt guilty—like it's all right to experience that, but I got this feeling that maybe I'm homosexually inclined. . . . One thing I would have in my mind is that it's not really me. I would always be wanting or wondering how it would be to have a heterosexual relationship, the same kind of ingredients, the compassion and the understanding, so I think I'll stick to women. I want to be with a woman and be able to like, express myself through copulation or through emotions."

These statements disregarded a five-year, prior history of homosexual street cruising that had began at age seventeen, and that the patient first disclosed only when he was twenty-six. "It happened the first time quite by accident," he said. "I was walking—as a matter of fact, I was going with this girl when I was seventeen, and it was late. It was in the summertime. So, she said, 'You're going to walk home this late at night?' It was only about one o'clock. So I was coming down to the Circle. . . . This real big tall guy was coming toward me. I was young, you know, but I guess I was attractive. I was dressed pretty flashy and neat. He said, 'Hi!' Then he took a cigarette out of his pocket, and say, 'You have a match?' I said I don't smoke. . . . He say, um, 'Would you like to take a walk for a minute? My car is right there. We can take a little drive.' I said, 'A little drive for what?' So that's the first time I heard the term, blow job. . . . He asked me where I was coming from. I said from my girlfriend's house.

He say 'Did you fuck her?' I say, 'Yeah.' He say, 'Did she really satisfy you? Would you want me to give you another way of having it? I'll give you a blow job.' Then I had to ask him what the hell was a blow job. I didn't know what a blow job was. So he say, um, 'I want to suck you off, you know.' So I say, 'Sure. What the hell if you give me some money.' "

In the urban culture familiar to the patient since boyhood, he was able to classify himself as a heterosexual who engaged in hustling, especially if he received money, provided his role was to pick up men whose turn-on was to perform oral sex on him or, much less to his liking, have him perform anal penetration on them. In his subsequent history, he became familiar with the section of town known to be a gay cruising area, and he would go there whenever he had the inclination to be approached by a homosexual seeking a partner. When he became old enough, he would hang out in a gay bar and also in the peep-show section of an adult bookstore where pickups could be transacted.

By the time he was twenty-six, the already mentioned ominous component of some of his homosexual ventures became evident, when, primed with alcohol, they progressed to traumatic personal injury that would neccesitate treatment in a hospital emergency room. In some instances the patient had no subsequent recall of the detail of what had happened, and in others his explanations were less than plausible. A likely formulation is that, after he became partially inebriated, ideas of being himself homosexually subjugated and raped engendered in him an acute attack of panicky belligerence. He would insult, rob, or threaten a would-be partner. Then he himself would be beaten-up, wounded, and possibly left unconscious.

At age twenty-eight, there was one example of a panic attack which the patient did recall in detail, perhaps because it occurred one night in a city rescue mission where, because alcohol was forbidden, he could not have continued drinking until he blacked out. He was there because he had had a fight with Candy and Jimmy, his married friends in whose house he rented a room. He had accused them of stealing his money.

In the mission that night, he said, there were about forty young men whom he believed to have just been released from jail. "They were constantly masturbating," he said. "It was sort of like the raw bestial-like animal behavior of man in his sexual attitudes. . . . It was sort of like they had a code message, like this is their time to start, like to run a contest, you know. . . . It's as if they were in a training session, you know. They just kept on going, and all the slurping noise and, you know, whistling and moaning, continuously on and on and on. . . . Well, they gave this up, and I tried to go to sleep. So I put my pillow over my head, because the noise was bothering me and annoying me. I was curled up, and I kept hearing this one guy over in the corner saying, 'That guy over there sleeps like a faggie.'

And, of course, I didn't pay him no mind, you know. Then this one guy kept on, persistent. So the guys that were in the place said, 'No man, he's been coming here before. No, he's no faggie. Leave him alone. Let him sleep.' So anyway, he kept on insisting, saying the same thing. And finally, by him hammering on the same thing, they all, you know, began. I guess it's their mentality. All of them are beginning to say, 'Hell, this is a piece of ass.' And they're all mixed up. They want their penis in a hole. They didn't care if it was a female or a male, you know. . . . They were ready to sort of like attack, you know. So they, one of them, a couple of them started for my bed. And I jumped up, you know, and I told the guy who was in front that if he came near me I would try to pulverize him. So he got back in bed laughing, and said he was only joking.

"And I laid back down, and the same guy started it all up again masturbating, and they started doing it dangerously, you know. And several of them started howling about how much they wanted a piece of ass, you know, and I became more frightened. And they kept this up all night. Two of them tried to push me again. So I put a little blade [fashioned from the cap of his asthma atomizer] between my fingers, because the first one that touched me, I was going to use it, you know, before they hurt me. . . . One guy over in the top bunk said, 'I got something for that,' and he pulled out a switch blade and opened it up. And I became more frightened. . . . The night guard came with a flashlight, and wondered what all the commotion was about, and everybody jumped back in bed, just any bed, and made out like they was asleep."

He was not reassured when the night guard told him, "Not anybody there going to bother you; they're all gentle." Trying to go to sleep, he was sure he heard "one guy sitting on a bottom bunk say, as he held up a gun, 'Hey, you're not going to get out of here alive today.' He was putting bullets in the gun. I was really scared, so, I, you know, my water broke. I went back to tell the guard again that they're threatening my life. He still ignored me. So finally he got angry with me and told me to get my coat and just get out. It was about quarter to five in the morning. I told him I wasn't going anywhere unless he was going with me. So he went to the door with his flashlight, and I grabbed my coat, and he told me 'Go get your coat and get out.' "

Running four blocks to a hospital, he fell and slit his leg, he said. In the emergency room, the people thought he was drunk, and the policeman on duty did not respond to his complaint about being threatened in the mission. He was being given treatment for an asthma attack when he thought he saw one of the men from the mission come in. So he rushed out of that hospital and to another one, nearby, where the emergency room people knew him and had previously treated his asthma attacks. There he rested until, later in the morning, he went to his sister's house.

A couple of months later, the patient had another similar experience. On this occasion, though he was at a different rescue mission, the men whom he feared would rape and beat him were, he believed, the same as before. He escaped to book in at a hotel. From there he went out drinking. His next recall was of being taken, cut and bruised, to an alcoholic treatment center, where he refused admission. On this occasion, he once again did not report for work, nor call in sick. So, once more, he lost his job. His married friends, Jimmy and Candy, whom he had reviled only a few months earlier, decided to give him another chance. They took him back to live in their house.

The next known episode of alcoholic hallucinosis, half a year later, involved his friend Jimmy. As the patient reported the incident on the phone, he got drunk and started messing around with Jimmy. "Jimmy doesn't like me to go down on him in front of company," he said. "He started to beat me up." After returning to his mother's house, the patient tried to leave with a screwdriver, saying that he wanted to kill Jimmy. His sister persuaded him not to take the screwdriver.

In the course of a long interview four days later, the patient disclosed that he had been having a recurrent dream of fighting with Jimmy and stabbing him with a butcher's knife: "I'm in there with Jimmy, and I'm just, I'm stabbin' him, and someone tryin' to pull me off him, and he's already dead. And I just kept stabbin' him. That's bad, bad, bad. I wanted— and I don't like that kind of feelin'. But in the same sense of dreamin' about that, at the same time I'm dreamin' of spendin' time in prison for killin' Jimmy. And I dream about Candy hating me. . . . And the part that gets to me, when the judge said so many years, I keep thinkin' 'bout livin'—life in prison. I thought about what could happen to me. And by me bein' so, the kind of person I am, I end up bein' a, a homosexual. Somebody gonna rape me and, you know, use me any kinda way you want to. And I, and in that dream also I, I figured that I couldn't take that. So I, I was, I probably end up killing myself."

Upon further inquiry, he said that he thought about this dream during the daytime, while not asleep. "I can feel it," he said. "It's gonna happen." When he was told that his friends had to be told about the jeopardy in which this dream placed them, his first reaction was indignant mistrust. Eventually, he felt relieved to have it out in the open.

Jimmy and his wife came to the PRU together for an interview. "When he's not drinking, he don't say nothing to nobody," Jimmy said. "All right. When he does drink, he curses me out, curses my wife out. He goes upstairs. He pulls his private out. He exposes his self. . . . I feel the man is very depressed when he's drinking. I'm going to tell you, he goes into a female bag. And he tells me he loves me, and he does things, uh, like homosexuals would do. He try to kiss me. And he does all this while he's drinking. He even tried to feel my penis. And this, this has been going on for about I guess in the last six years. . . . Oh, he even told me that—he said, uh, 'I'm getting ready to come on my period.' He talk words like that. He said, 'You got, uh, a Tampax or a Kotex? Because my period getting ready to come on.' Man, we looks at him, you know." His wife finished for him, "And say, uhm, what's the matter with him?"

There was no recurrence of violence between the three friends in the few remaining months of Jimmy's life before he died in a sickle-cell crisis.

In the ensuing six years the patient has mentioned only one other episode of alcoholic hallucinosis. It was not so dramatic as the three foregoing episodes. The risks of binge drinking continue, however. For example, after a very recent resolve to undergo surgical repair of the two persisting bodily stigmas of deficient masculinity, namely, the meatal defect on the shaft of the penis, and the perineal fistula, the patient succumbed to drinking again. Thus, he circumvented a surgical consultation and interrupted several months of abstinence as a member of Alcoholics Anonymous.

There was one occasion, only a week before Jimmy died, when the patient's behavior added an additional clue as to the character change that he underwent when embarking on a drinking binge. It began at around ten o'clock one evening when his woman friend, Bernice, telephoned, desperate to know what to do to restrain him from another bout of drunken injury. Only a few hours earlier he had had stitches removed from facial injuries suffered a week earlier. Now he was being abusive and demanding more money for alcohol.

He himself talked on the telephone. His manner was jaunty and defiant, and at the same time narcissistically wayward. He was about to go out on the town, and there was no stopping him. He'd had a pint of wine at 6 P.M. and now he needed two more good strong drinks. He would get them from Jimmy, or on the street. He needed "some happiness, not all this sadness around here—and dancin'. Jimmy always has some music."

He spoke as an addict on a euphoric high who was not about to be cheated out of his claim to a moment of joy by a warning about getting himself homosexually assaulted. "Never underestimate the human mind," he said, claiming Freud as his authority. He'd been preached at for twenty-nine years, and wanted no more of it.

In the content of the conversation, there was no evidence of vivid eidetic imagery or hallucinosis, but rather of an altered state of consciousness. The patient may very well have been in a dissociative, fugue-like condition, such as is characteristic of the paraphilias. If so, it would explain the chasm between the nonsexual side of his life as a college graduate, on the one hand, and on the other, the pathologically sexual side as a paraphilically compulsive and self-destructive danger to himself and others.

He was dissociatively indifferent to the possible injuries consequent on his paraphilic approaches to men as though he were an insistent harlot. In the euphoric state of embarking on a sexual adventure, he disregarded not only the injuries that would be inflicted on him, but also the possibility of their bringing about his death. There is something more here than ordinary masochism. It is a paraphilia of stage-managing one's own erotic death, the name for which is autassassinophilia.

The masochistic component of his lovemap was explicitly manifested in self-injurious masturbation. "I've discovered masturbation as a form of punishment," he said in an interview in his late twenties. "I guess the discovery was through trial and error, a new angle in trying to find other ways of relieving my anger than drinking and getting myself in trouble. I figured that now when I'm full of anger and frustration that I resort to masturbation, vigorous masturbation—even to the point of hurting myself in my pelvic region, and also around my abdomen. I do this practically all night long. It don't have to be night. I do it whenever I'm alone by myself, whenever I get the feeling of frustration of anger; and I do it forcibly and sometimes continuously all night, off and on, to the point that the next day I'm sore, sore not in the penis area but around my joints and my pelvis area— also to the point where I think I strained myself, sometimes. To me it's a form of relief and a feeling, too, at the same time. Because, when I do it, I like the feeling I get from it. Not just the—it's a feeling of ejaculation, but also the alternate feeling, like a feeling that now you've done it to relieve that anger. It's just the fact of doing it and getting it over with.

"Maybe I'll start with thinking about the last time Candy and I had a relationship. That's the initial thought. And I get an erection on, and then I start masturbating. But right in the midst of masturbation, thinking of sex is starting to fade out; and I don't think about anything in particular. But I may have in the back of my mind that I'm thinking about, you know, punishment for letting myself get into the predicament (of having no employment) that I am in. And to the extent that I can't do anything about it, you know, this is my way of saying it's what you expect from a child. . . . I think I use my penis because my penis is the only extension of me that—after all the operating I've been through, it's still ever present in my mind about the agonies I went through."

Significance of the Case

Prenatal Precursors of Paraphilia. With respect to the future development of paraphilia, in this case the significance of the chromosomal sex is that it was 46, XY, as for a male, and concordant with the gonadal sex (testicular). The prenatal hormonal sex could not be unequivocally established. The chromosomal and gonadal sex were discordant with genital sex insofar as external genitalia were only partially masculinized and had sexually ambiguous morphology. The evidence of ambiguous morphology of the external genitalia suggests that there was an error in prenatal gonadal function or in prenatal utilization of gonadal steroids. Thus, it cannot be excluded that the sexual morphology of the fetal brain was, like the external genitalia, partially demasculinized.

Postnatal Precursors of Paraphilia: Prepuberty. At birth the ambiguity of external genitalia led to ambivalence regarding the sex of assignment which was not finally resolved until the age of 2 yrs 3 mos. From then until age five, the child was left in a limbo of procrastination and neglect, with nothing done to correct the stigma of his very unmasculine-appearing genitals and his inability to stand to urinate. Finally, when after age five surgical correction was begun, he became traumatized by what he experienced as severe nosocomial stress and abuse, to which his initial response was phobic aloofness and elective mutism, both of which increased nosocomial stress and abuse. The promise of an early and complete genital repair proved false. By age eleven he had had ten operations for penile repair and for corrections of postsurgical complications. The final outcome was that he had lost one testis to infection, and had a penis that was too small, was deformed by scarring, and that leaked urine from a chronic urethral fistula.

Postnatal Precursors of Paraphilia: Postpuberty. After a nosocomially traumatizing childhood, puberty was spontaneous and masculinizing. Post-pubertally, the boy continued to be stigmatized by his defective genital appearance and urinary leakage. His first heterosexual affair ended in a traumatic fiasco. After graduating from college, he underwent a pathological personality change and became a binge-drinking alcoholic and on-and-off derelict.

Adulthood Paraphilic Outcome. When inebriated, he embarked on masochistically dangerous homosexual adventures during which he acted like a harlot putting the make on a man. The hidden agenda was to arrange for the erotic death (autassassinophilia) of the female whom he suspected lurked within him, about whom he talked only when he was intoxicated, in which state this woman within sporadically threatened erotic homicide. When he was not intoxicated, he had friendships with both women and men, some of whom had a history of being sexually attracted to him. He was unable to reciprocate and sustain such a relationship on the basis of both affectionate love and sexual lust, and would break away into yet another episode of intoxication and paraphilic lust.

Paraphilic Stratagem. In this case, the chronic nosocomial traumatization, abuse, and victimization experienced as aversive became paraphilically eroticized, by means of opponent-process transformation. Diagnostically, it took the form of autassassinophilia, that is, conspiring to have oneself assassinated. In this case, the paraphilia of self-arranged assassination was superimposed on the homosexual component of bisexuality. The strategy was to approach men, including those who repudiated homosexuals, and to provoke them to violence by soliciting, insulting, attacking, or robbing them. This strategy was incompatible with long-term, lover-lover pairbonding in a self-accepted homosexual partnership. It was incompatible also with long-term pairbonding with a heterosexual partner.

CHAPTER 7

Biography 5: Masochism in a 46,XY Female with Androgen-Insensitivity Syndrome

Diagnostic and Clinical Biography

Biography 5 is that of a girl who, despite the female appearance of the external genitalia, had a form of male hermaphroditism. The diagnosis was made at age five, on the basis of anomalous internal reproductive organs. The case was one of androgen insensitivity, so that puberty was feminizing. The lovemap differentiated as bisexual. Homosexuality was ambivalently repudiated. Heterosexuality was fused with masochism which existed during young adulthood in fantasy only.

The patient was referred for an evaluation in the Johns Hopkins Psychohormonal Research Unit (PRU) at the age of 9 yrs 1 mo, at which time she had returned to the Pediatric Endocrine Clinic (PEC) for routine follow-up. She needed to be informed about her condition, prognosis, and treatment plan in preparation for upcoming hormonal replacement therapy.

During her first psychohormonal visit, all she was able to say about her condition was that she had had an operation for a hernia when she was about six years old. It was done in a hospital in her hometown. Because she had had "pain in her side" after the operation, she had had to come to The Johns Hopkins Hospital to have her appendix removed.

What she had not been told, but what could be found in her hospital record, was that immediately after the operation, performed when she was actually 5 yrs 4 mos old, the pediatrician and the surgeon told her parents that the hernia contained an undescended testicle and that their child was a male who should be raised as a boy. She was then referred to the PEC, which specialized in birth defects of sex organs, with the view to confirming the diagnosis, prognosis, and treatment especially with regard to the sex of rearing.

At the time of her initial endocrine evaluation at the age of 5 yrs 6 mos, the diagnosis was already known to be an unspecified variety of a male hermaphroditism (also known as male pseudohermaphroditism). The differential diagnosis turned out to be either the testicular-feminizing syndrome of androgen-insensitivity, or male hermaphroditism secondary to prolonged gestational exposure to diethylstilbestrol (DES) taken by the mother. In their extreme form, both syndromes are characterized by extensive demasculinization. The external genitalia appear female, though the internal genitalia do not.

The androgen-insensitivity syndrome (AIS) is genetically transmitted through the maternal pedigree as an X-linked recessive. The cells of target organs that are normally dependent on androgen for their development are unable to bind the hormone, or else are enzyme deficient and unable to use it. Without androgen, a fetus that is chromosomally male and has two testes is unable to differentiate the wolffian ducts into the internal reproductive organs of the male. Masculine differentiation of the external genitalia also fails, and normal female external genitalia differentiate instead. Female internal reproductive organs are absent, however, as the fetal testes do not fail to secrete antimullerian hormone, which suppresses the differentiation of a uterus and fallopian tubes from the mullerian ducts.

The DES syndrome is iatrogenic in origin. Its history dates back to the second third of the 20th century, when newly synthesized sex hormones became popular because of their alleged benefit in preserving pregnancies threatened by miscarriage. Only gradually did it become recognized that DES is able to have a demasculinizing effect on male fetuses. Dependent on the degree of demasculinization, the outcome may be morphologically the same as in AIS. It is not known whether the demasculinizing effect is limited to the prenatal life only, or whether it may, even rarely, leave a permanent cellular effect that will impair or prevent the hormonal masculinization of puberty.

In both syndromes, because of the morphology and future sexuoerotic function of the vulva, babies with either syndrome are assigned and reared as female. Both syndromes may be diagnosed in infancy or childhood if the gonads, attempting to descend from their abdominal position, produce inguinal hernias or labial masses. In AIS, it is not uncommon for the diagnosis

to have been delayed until adolescence and then made as a sequel to amenorrhea, secondary to absence of the uterus.

In AIS, apart from amenorrhea, puberty is feminizing, as testicular
estrogen is unopposed by androgen. In the postpubertal period, gonadectomy
is usually performed to prevent possible development of a gonadal tumor
(Migeon et al., 1981).

In the DES syndrome, in cases in which demasculinization is complete,
if the testes have been preventively removed in advance of puberty, estrogen
replacement therapy is necessary to induce pubertal feminization.

In the present instance there was no ascertainable family pedigree of
AIS. Thus, the diagnosis of AIS could not be confirmed on the basis of
genetic transmission within a pedigree. It was also not possible to confirm
a DES diagnosis with certainty, as there is insufficient knowledge of the
dosage, timing, and duration of exposure to DES required to bring about
a degree of demasculinization so complete as in this case. Because the mother
had had two previous miscarriages, she thought that she might have begun
to take the hormone preventively, even before getting pregnant. She also
thought that she took the hormone throughout the pregnancy, but could
not specify the dosage.

Findings from the initial endocrine evaluation and subsequent exploratory surgery showed that, morphologically, both external and internal sex
organs were compatible with AIS. The external genitals had a female
appearance. On close inspection the size of the clitoris was at the upper
limit of normal, and there was a slight posterior labioscrotal fusion. The
vagina, 2.5 cm deep, had a small introitus. No uterus or fallopian tubes
were found. The buccal smear showed a male chromatin pattern. To prevent
the possibility that the testes might become malignant, and that they might
produce androgen at puberty and increase the size of the clitoris, they were
removed. An additional rationale for gonadectomy was the parents' extreme
anxiety about having a daughter with testicles which, for them, meant that
she was not a girl.

At the time of initial endocrine evaluation the parents were informed
about their daughter's diagnosis, prognosis, and future endocrine treatment
plan. However, it was extremely difficult for them to absorb and adequately
understand the prognosis. Having been previously told that their daughter
was actually a male with testicles turned out to be a trauma of great magnitude. It would prove to have devastating long-term psychopathological
implications affecting all members of the family.

By the time the patient was first referred to the PRU, aged 9 yrs
1 mo, it was obvious that it was too difficult for the parents to give the
child information necessary for her to understand the plan of her treatment.
The constraints of travel time and distance precluded an extension of the

psychohormonal visit, on this first occasion, so as to allow sufficient time for the girl to obtain an age-appropriate explanation of her syndrome and plan of treatment. The proposed follow-up appointment was not kept, but was delayed until the girl was 11 yrs 4 mos old. It was then that one of the psychohormonal staff explained to her the rationale of upcoming hormone therapy. She was told that the hernia repair she had had in childhood had been necessitated by misplacement of the internal sex glands, which were malformed. They had been removed because they did not make eggs, and might possibly be incapable of producing the body's own female sex hormone at puberty. She would be able to achieve motherhood by adoption, or by "instant motherhood," as a step-mother. The doctor who gave her that information noted: "I deliberately left things understated, especially in the matter of sterility, because I recalled the history of emotional instability not only in the child, but in the family also. She absorbed the information with understanding and apparent equanimity."

That same day, the girl was seen also in the PEC, and was started on methyltestosterone (5 mg daily) in order to test whether her body would respond to androgen in a feminizing manner. Two months later, the only significant change noted was the growth of a small amount of pubic hair and some acne. The breasts had not developed. The girl was very disturbed about pubic hair which, she said, "other girls of my age don't have." Therefore, further hormone administration was postponed for six months.

During her next PEC follow-up at the age of 12 yrs 5 mos, the girl expressed no concern about lack of sexual development, so that hormonal replacement therapy was postponed again. It was a year later that estrogen treatment was finally begun (Premarin, 0.65 mg daily), with the patient's begrudging consent. From this time onward, she demonstrated an increasingly aversive reaction to physical, and in particular, genital examinations. Rebellion against feminization of her body, covert initially, became overt (see Lovemap Biography). It transpired that she took her estrogen pill only occasionally. She often resorted to spitting it down the toilet. Years later, she gave her rationale for this behavior, namely, that by not feminizing she would have the strength to retaliate when her father beat her. She declined to be physically examined. The treatment plan had to be redesigned so that it would not aggravate her already severe behavioral problems.

Noncompliance with estrogen treatment resulted in development of eunuchoid body features. At the age of 16 yrs 3 mos the patient was offered, as an alternative, the option of taking a nonfeminizing, androgenic hormone (Delatestryl, 300 mg intramuscularly once a month). Since she had previously showed a partial response (growth of pubic hair) to testosterone treatment, it was possible that androgen would promote a fusion of epiphyses necessary to arrest further bone growth. At the same time it would serve as a test of androgen insensitivity.

Aware of the adverse effects of further delay in the onset of puberty, the patient agreed to take the hormone. However, after three injections of a high dose of the hormone, her bone age remained unchanged, and there was no evidence of hormonal puberty, either masculinizing or feminizing. Under the circumstances, she finally resigned herself to being treated with estrogen, despite continuing reluctance to undergo its feminizing effects.

A year later she appeared to have accepted her new, feminine body appearance and spontaneously asked for an increase in estrogen dose. She said that she wanted to have "a little bigger breasts." After that she continued taking Depo-Estradiol cypionate (5 mg intramuscularly, every other week) until the age of nineteen, when she started taking oral Premarin (2.5 mg daily) with Provera (10 mg daily).

During her last endocrine follow-up at age 23 yrs 8 mos, she was 5 ft 9 ins (174.3 cm) tall, and had well-developed breasts and typically feminine body features. Her vagina had normal secretory function. She was informed that the vaginal introitus was small and that vaginoplasty might be needed if dilation proved inadequate. She postponed the possibility of surgery. She was referred to an endocrinologist in her hometown, and has been lost to further follow-up.

Family Pathology

From the time of the patient's first PEC visit at age 5 yrs 6 mos, the parents made it abundantly evident to the psychiatric consultant that their relationship was one of married adversaries. In the ensuing years, the pathology of their relationship together, and with their children, used up an inordinate amount of interview time that would otherwise have been directed toward the enhancement of their capability to meet the special challenge of rearing a child with a birth defect of the sex organs. This challenge was so taxing for the mother that, by the time her daughter was 11 yrs 6 mos old, she fictionally changed her diagnosis. For a parents' magazine, she wrote and published a mother's tragic story of her flawlessly beautiful daughter on the threshold of a womanhood marred by the invisible handicap not of hermaphroditism but of minimal brain damage and learning disability—for the study of which the mother had enrolled herself in special courses.

Both parents were good-looking, urbane and highly intelligent, as were their children. Together, they could effortlessly convey the impression of the American dream materialized. The father was a successful entrepreneur whose business dealings betrayed nothing of the pathology of his domestic dealings. By contrast, his wife's long-standing psychopathological problems affected all of her daily life.

The wife characterized her husband as short-tempered, violent, explosive, and verbally as well physically abusive. She illustrated his alleged lack of impulse control by retrospective recall of an incident in which he reportedly had hit her while she was holding her six-month-old daughter. She assumed that the marital conflicts were a result of sexual incompatibility. "I think," she said, "I always felt my own abnormalities. There was sex that I felt very guilty for all my life, even when I was a youngster. My feeling was that I would never be able to respond to a man, and because of this, and conflict between my husband and I, and because of my own sexual problems, it actually came to pass that I was right." Her own upbringing led her to believe that "sex is unpleasant and all men are hateful about sex, but a wife should never refuse it." Besides, it was impossible for her to let herself go in "enjoyment of sex with a man with whom she did not have a spiritual relationship." On another occasion, she said that she probably had never been in love with her husband but married him for "his mind and New York sophistication."

After the couple's first joint session in the PRU, the interviewer noted: "The amount of hatred that circulated back and forth was really quite unpleasant. Of the two people, the husband was the one who seemed to have the most human animation about him, in this struggle. The wife had more the appearance of a talking mask. My impression was that of the two, the wife is the one who is the most severely disturbed neurotically." Believing that it would be of greater benefit to the children to have both parents together, the parents postponed divorce for the next thirteen years.

Despite their many years of mutually antagonistic litigation, blackmail, physical assault, and verbal abuse, the couple did not totally give up on sex. After fifteen years of marriage, the wife said that she had had to learn how to separate sex from sentiment, and had done so successfully. She considered her husband a good lover who, like herself, could "enjoy sex without expecting any sentiment." That statement was made in the wife's long story of a recent legal fight over her husband's financial support of the family. For a leverage in that fight, she had threatened her husband with exposure of alleged income tax evasion. She added that she had also collected samples of her husband's favorite "pornographic" pictures in case she would be able to use them against him legally.

The husband's actual contribution to the family pathology remained an open question. The reliability of the wife's and the daughter's reports concerning his behavior at home could not be validated. It was known, however, that both wife and daughter considered themselves victims of his alleged verbal and physical attacks. According to the patient, he "just strikes me or rams my head against the side of the door. Once he gets going he just doesn't stop. Even if what I do is so terrible—which it isn't, I feel—but even if it is, the least he could do is hit me like a human being. A smack across the face or a strike on the arm, even that is okay, but not the way he kicks and just gets on me like a horse."

By the time the parents finalized their divorce, the patient's image of the father was revealed in her recall of an episode when she was in her early teens and the whole family were guests of the owner of a summer camp. As she recalled it, she had learned from some of the girl campers that her father had been taking photographs in the vicinity of their dormitory washrooms, allegedly trying to get pictures of them dressing and undressing. She adduced this evidence, plus that of a "pornography" magazine she had found in his office, to support her outrage at his being "a brute, bully, old horny bastard and a sadist" in the way he treated her. She blamed him for having "ruined her for life." After the divorce, she refused to maintain any contact with him. However, she was similarly critical of, and resentful toward her mother, whom she described as an "insensitive, emotionally cold bitch."

It was obvious that the patient was caught up in the family's adversarial relationships, both as a victim and an instigator, as is evident in the Biography of Social Development, below. She considered herself to be the scapegoat of her family, and that her parents favored her two siblings, a brother, three years younger, and a sister, six years younger. The mother described the two siblings in a favorable manner in contrast to the patient, whom she considered to have been a difficult child since infancy. Though the evidence available was somewhat tenuous, it appeared that the parents did indulge and favor the two siblings. For example, the eight-year-old son had set a series of fires in his mother's clothes closet, once with his five-year-old sister crouching in fear nearby. The mother was almost benignly tolerant in euphemizing this sign of psychopathological disturbance. By contrast, she was intolerant of the patient and reported even trivial disobedience as an example of the girl's behavioral pathology.

Apart from the son's fire-setting, there was no reporting of gross psychopathology in either of the two younger siblings during the juvenile years, after which they were lost to follow-up.

Biography of Social Development

The information on the patient's early life was supplied chiefly by the mother at the time of the girl's initial PEC evaluation at the age of 5 yrs 6 mos. Pathological behavior that she attributed to the child could not be differentiated from pathological distortions of it in her own perception.

The diagnosis of male hermaphroditism had so traumatized the mother that a psychiatric consultation was arranged. Professional assurances of a favorable prognosis were in vain. The mother misconstrued the diagnosis and prognosis throughout whole period of follow-up. She watched her daughter constantly, in search of behavioral noncomformities which to her were evidence of psychopathology. In her retrospective report of her daughter's early infancy and childhood, she presented the facts selectively, so that they would substantiate her opinion that the girl was an unusually difficult child right from the cradle.

The daughter was reportedly a "demanding and unsociable" child since early infancy. In the nursery school she would always play alone and have temper tantrums if unable to solve a simple task. At age five, the child was in individual psychotherapy with a local psychologist. According to the mother, the only effect of therapy was that her daughter learned to play with her therapist, but remained socially inept with peers. She repeated the last year of kindergarten. It was the teachers' opinion that she was emotionally immature and not ready for first grade. That failure had an adverse effect on the child. The mother said that she often referred to it with resentment. Coinciding with this failure in the kindergarten, the two hospital admissions (see Diagnostic and Clinical Biography) turned out to have an additional adverse effect on the child.

The mother perceived her daughter as being very tomboyish, which she thought could be an effect of her encouraging the girl to be athletic and "praising her for things she accomplished rather than the way she looked when dressed up." She said: "I would not want my child anything but normal, but I admit, I didn't want to see certain—well, unbearable aspects of female in her, such as lack of initiative, lack of aggressiveness, too much prissiness about her dress. I'm very pleased with the fact that she started developing muscularly." However, after the mother found out about her daughter's medical condition, she became paradoxically anxious and oversensitive to her tomboyish traits. The girl's behavior began to look abnormal to her. She described her, then 5 yrs 6 mos old, in these words: "She is ungraceful. She doesn't look like a girl, the way she walks. The things she is interested in—when we buy trucks for her brother she wants trucks, and has never been interested in dolls." To the clinical staff the patient appeared to look and behave like a girl. Her tomboyish interests appeared to be within normal limits.

In the PEC it was repeatedly noted that she was "extremely shy of doctors," resistant to physical examinations, and fearful. The mother continued to report that she had difficulty in integrating into her peer group. Because of the teacher's complaints about her inattentiveness and disruptive behavior in the second grade, her mother took her to a local psychiatrist.

Treatment with a tranquilizer, the name of which was not recorded, presumably brought some improvement in the girl's behavior and school achievement. In the third grade she was taken off medication. She still had no close friends, disliked school, and in spite of her IQ (WISC Verbal IQ, 120; Nonverbal IQ, 96; Full Scale IQ, 109), she remained an underachiever.

At home, the mother said, the girl was either withdrawn, spending long hours alone in front of the TV screen, or overtly antagonistic and defiant in her relations with both parents and siblings. When she was 11 yrs 4 mos old, according to the mother's report, she abused herself when angry by scratching herself or banging her foot into a door, injuring her toes. The mother was concerned with her daughter's apparent low self-esteem, as she often referred to herself with words such as "dummy" and "unattractive" and tended to belittle her own accomplishments.

At age twelve, on the mother's initiative, the girl was again treated by a local psychiatrist who prescribed promazine (Sparine, 25 mg four times a day). At the same age, during her psychohormonal follow-up visit, her behavior did not betray gross signs of pathology. However, the bad dream which she made up during the structured doll play test was indicative of difficulty at home. The dream was about a girl who was suddenly on a strange floor of a house. She could not find her way back. She tried another way. Then she came back and her house was broken down. She did not know where to go. She was calling her mother and father but nobody answered. As it later turned out, the dream reflected the situation in the patient's home.

The parents were unable to communicate with the girl in a straightforward manner on the issue of her medical status. The inadequately explained hospital admissions and outpatient visits left her with distrust and resentment toward her parents, and with phobic aversion toward anesthesia, doctors, and physical examinations. At seventeen, she still resented genital examinations: "Examinations above the belt are bad, but below is the worst part," she once said. "It's undecent. I know that the people I associate with would never put up with such a thing. I don't feel like a person. It just makes me feel subhuman, like a prostitute."

According to her retrospective report at the age of seventeen, her only close social bonds had been two consecutive eroticized friendships, each with a neighborhood girl (see Lovemap Biography). Her social handicap was made worse by the discrepancy between chronological age and physique age secondary to her repudiation of estrogen substitution therapy so as to be better able to strike back at her parents. "It's much easier," she said, "to act like a boy, and let them beat you, than it is a girl. I just do not want to be feminine around my parents."

She was teased at school and considered a "weirdo" because of her flat chest, boyish appearance, and awkward gait. Her own interpretation was: "I don't think they tease me because they don't like me. It's because they just want to see me suffer, because people like to see other people unhappy. When they see it doesn't get me upset, it's like they can't believe . . . So they try again and again."

At age 17½, she reflected on her earlier teenage school experiences: "I didn't exactly want to be a boy but I didn't want to be a girl either. I wanted to beat my father up. Teasing at school became a big problem. People were always feeling on my back for the bra fastener. So then I was upset because I didn't have breasts. I wanted to be a girl at that minute, but then, like three or four hours later, I'd be at home with my family and then I wanted to be a boy. Like in twenty-four hours I'd want to be one way, half the day, and the other half, the other way."

Her teenaged perception of her peers as nearly sadistic corresponded with her image of her parents' attitude toward her. She once said: "My parents enjoy making me miserable. Real sadists. They won't give two cents for my happiness." For her, the worst offender was her father. She dreamed of getting away from home.

Unable to develop satisfactory bonds with either peers, parents, or siblings, she became enthusiastically involved in horseback riding. Her horse, and later her dog, became her exclusive companions. The animals, in her own perception, constituted her only source of affection. She said once: "In many cases horses and dogs are superior to humans because you never see a horse or a dog turn against other beings of their own breed." At fifteen, in one of her school compositions she referred to people as "this stupid humanity." In her teenage daydreams she depicted herself as an owner of a farm "with horses and dogs and maybe one partner, a girl who doesn't want to get married. It wouldn't be so lonely." She planned to go to a college with a program specializing in animals, especially horses.

In the meantime, her mother, fixated in her conviction, virtually a delusion, that the girl was afflicted with minimal brain damage, placed her in a private boarding school with a special education program. There she failed. So, at age fifteen, she was transferred to a small private Catholic school near her hometown. There she was happy to be among gentiles, repudiating her Jewish parents. She made friends with a couple of girls, and was very fond of her teachers, Catholic nuns. Her school grades improved slightly. She became very interested in Catholicism and had outstanding grades in religion, whereas in other subjects she was doing poorly. At that time she was in the midst of rebelling against the feminization of her body. The school requirement was that all girls had to wear dresses only. That became a major problem. Within a few months she wanted desperately to go back to a public school, where she could wear slacks. The mother's refusal to let her transfer back to a public school aggravated the already poor relations between the daughter and her parents. The next maneuver, to get back at her parents, was to convert from Judaism to Catholicism, and to repudiate the family faith with overtly antisemitic remarks and exaggerated fascination with Hitler.

The battle between mother and daughter over school ended in a truce when, with the supportive recommendation of the psychohormonal staff, the girl was transferred to a public school at age sixteen. She was happier at school, but her relationship with her parents worsened. She seriously considered moving away from home. During one of her psychohormonal visits she said: "My parents, particularly my father, have ruined me for life. You can tell by the way I talk, by the way I am. I don't see how a basically violent person like myself can really change after living for fifteen years with parents who are violent." Later, at the age of 18 yrs 6 mos, she referred back to that issue in these words: "In the beginning I felt that this is the pattern that I'm shown at home. As much as I hated it then, and as much as I hate it now, being beaten and all of that, it was sort of conditioned in my mind that this is the only way that parents show caring." She was ready to move out of her home, which she considered "absolute hell." Her mother did not object any longer. The patient, then in the eleventh grade, moved out of state to live in a half-way house for young adults. While there, she had weekly counseling sessions in the PRU. She enrolled in a local public high school. She limited her contacts with her parents to occasional letters and short visits. After a few months in the half-way house, her sense of well-being improved. She said: "I am learning to live with people. I've learned to be not so uptight when other people are around. I wondered why people hate me, but I notice now that if I'm not so overly courteous, I begin to feel more at ease, and they feel more at ease."

She now wanted to be "a beautiful blonde girl with make-up and a little bigger breasts." She asked for more estrogen to promote her breast growth. Her growing acceptance of femininity was paralleled by her growing alienation from her family and their ethnic origin and religion. For several months she refused to use her family name, and even tried to convince herself and her therapist that she had been cheated out of her grandparents' Christian heritage by parents who had converted to Judaism. She became pathologically concerned about her facial appearance and contemplated cosmetic surgery on her face, which she referred to as "that ugly glob," and "too Jewish looking." To hide her ethnicity, she covered her nose with a thick coat of make-up. Achieving the exact antithesis, she kept one appointment with a covering of peppermint-striped toothpaste on her nose, because her supply of make-up had run out. At this same time she struggled with a handwashing compulsion that left her hands raw.

In the course of weekly counseling, her severely disturbed self-image gradually improved. She referred to her past failures in making friends in these words: "I guess, because I don't accept myself, I can't accept other people for what they are. I used to look at myself in the mirror and get sick. Now I look at myself and I think I see the reason for that ugliness. I see the years of crying out for somebody and nobody answers. I can see it. Right on my face. People look the way they feel. One day the ugliness that comes from not being loved will disappear."

In search of a more home-like atmosphere she moved to another, smaller, half-way house, but even there she felt lonely. Despite her efforts, she failed to establish either a sexual and/or romantic partnership, or a close friendship. She became infatuated with her new therapist, a good-looking gentile, a postdoctoral fellow from Germany. She considered him to be the only person who enabled her to "discover love and friendship with a human."

At age 18 yrs 7 mos she graduated from high school and was accepted by a college where she could pursue her plan to become a veterinarian. In the subsequent two years, her ability to live on her own in a new environment proved to be insufficient to guarantee success. Academically and socially, she failed the first year of college and went back home, where her parents were in the midst of a fight over their divorce settlement. Under the circumstances, her psychohormonal counselor supported her plan to move back to the half-way house and resume her regular counseling sessions, which she did. With a new counselor, also youthful, gentile, and German, she sought the role of a special friend and/or lover (see Lovemap Biography). Failure prompted her to discontinue counseling. At the age of twenty-one she terminated her contacts with the psychohormonal staff.

The last follow-up information was obtained from the mother when the patient was twenty-seven years old. They shared an apartment. After a long history of being a college dropout, she was attending a college again. Her major problem was still the same—lack of social contacts. She maintained no contact with her father. She had, as the mother put it, a good relationship with her "as long as they did not see each other."

Lovemap Biography

The story of sexuoerotic development begins with the mother's statement that her daughter started masturbating early in her life, probably before the kindergarten age: "She'll go, and if one of the girls, neighbor playmates or cousins, is sitting there watching TV with her legs apart, she'll sort of lie on her legs—it's a way of masturbation. She's done it with a doll. We are actually trying not to be strong about it, but we have tried to discourage it." This report turned out to be concordant with that given by the patient, retrospectively, at age 17½, after eight years of psychohormonal follow-up.

Between the ages of nine and seventeen, the patient was unable to reveal personal sexual information. She claimed ignorance of sexual matters. At eleven, asked about romantic daydreaming, she responded: "I can understand that some girls of my age might do it, but I don't do it, not yet." At twelve, she said: "If there are any boys, I like them because they are nice, not as any sexual affair." Two years later, she disclaimed all love with the exception that: "All I love are horses." At fifteen, she admitted to having been the only one in her class who was not interested in boys.

As a sixteen year old, when she was asked about her attitude toward marriage, her reply was: "No, I'd rather live alone—animals are nicer. The only thing I could ever fall in love with is a dog or a horse. I am positive about that. Not with a person, I am almost positive. I will have babies but not the human kind. I am going to take care of my animals." Her problem was not of being erotically attracted to animals, but of being unable to form an intimate relationship with a person of either sex. The closest she came to intimacy, companionship, and trust was with her horse and her dog. Her interviewer made a notation in her history that she might have discovered herself to be erotically attracted to girls, and was unable to disclose it. That assumption was confirmed a year later, when the patient was 17 yrs 4 mos old. She said then that she was sexually interested in girls, "just as boys feel about girls," and added that it made her feel dirty and disgusted with herself. After she found out that her counselor did not condemn her, as she had expected, self-disclosure was progressively expanded in the course of her weekly psychohormonal visits.

A month later, she referred to her rejection of femininity in these words: "Well, I think it was my parents' doing—being beaten like a boy, I didn't even feel like looking like a girl. If I'd come from a normal family, I would not have homosexual fantasies and contacts. The homosexual thing with me, it was sick and dumb, and I like to think it's over now—and forget about it."

She was ready to disclose the facts of her early childhood and teenage sexual fantasies and experiences. She said: "I used to masturbate all the time when I was younger. The first time I did it I masturbated on my brother, on his leg or arm. He woke up right after I did it. I don't remember what he said. I couldn't have been more than six years old. So I know I am not in the normal category. It might be normal for me to masturbate now, but it wasn't then. I didn't know it was masturbation, and I didn't have heterosexual feelings when I started out. I used to have homosexual desires for my fantasies."

She recalled her kindergarten-age "touching games" with a neighbor girl, and having been caught by her father: "It's like we really didn't do anything, just touching, that's all. My father walked in the room one day. I don't know whether my mother was with him or not. And he got very angry, and he told her to go home. Christ, it was terrible! And that was the end of the touching game."

About two years later, she experienced a similar bad experience related to the touching games. She recalled waiting for her friend "in bed, in her room, and her father walks by, and it was terrible. As soon as I saw him I stood up straight. Oh, I hate myself like this. Later, from age ten onward, we used to get on the bed and do it undressed, and I would lay on top of her and she would lay on top of me. I think it stopped when I was fifteen." She reported having had orgasms from the touching games, and also from solo masturbation. She did not recall any heterosexual contacts other than the incident, aforesaid, involving her younger brother.

In the same period of life, she had what she called homosexual fantasies which she described as follows: "Oh, I would fantasize something terrible. Like an imaginary girl partner—she was a little powerful and I was just a piece of nothing. I was like a piece of dirt. It was great, and she took me and threw me over the edge of the cliff or something. I used to have these fantasies about the people who represented my sexual objects, as just massaging me, and turning me into this big blob of yuck, and putting me on a bed. Gross!" It was the idea of getting into a fight with a girl-partner and being a loser that was sometimes a strong sexual turn-on. She referred to her erotosexual fantasies and past experiences with disgust and aversion. She considered herself dirty, sexually abnormal, and a "freak."

At age 17 yrs 8 mos, three months after having moved away from home, for the first time she reported having been interested in a boy. He was from the half-way house where she lived. She thought that she "could have sex with him if he wanted, but he doesn't want it, and he can't have it because he has a girlfriend." Her only reported sexual activity was daily masturbation, which she called "a morning cup of coffee."

At this same age, in the context of masturbation fantasies, identified by the patient as "wicked fantasies," the theme of heterosexual masochism first was disclosed. A favorite one was as follows: "Recently, I had a feeling I was in some sort of concentration camp. This was a heterosexual fantasy. I was tied to a bed and somebody came and started rubbing me because he had nothing better to do for ten minutes. And I enjoyed it. It's a wicked fantasy, but at least it's heterosexual. It was in Cuba and there are a lot of women's concentration camps there. One of the attendants was a big gorgeous, sunburned Mexican, dark guy, and he came over, and he had this ten-year-old boy with him. And it was this ten-year-old boy who did it while he went off." She reported the same fantasy again four years later, in a version in which the concentration camp was run by Germans, and the boy was a blond German Hitler Youth member. This German version was more in keeping with her obsessive repudiation of Jewishness. The earlier version had been reported to her counselor, the young and attractive postdoctoral fellow from Germany. The change of location of the concentration camp to Cuba was perhaps an act of courtesy toward him.

In an attempt to erase the homosexual components of her erotic attraction, she pursued a self-initiated plan to establish a heterosexual relationship as a cure for homosexuality. Her first heterosexual contact, at age 17 yrs 8 mos, was with a boy whom she solicited by "bugging him" to touch her breasts. She described that experience in these words: "I could like him as a person, but I don't like him as a boyfriend and he doesn't like me very much. He went off to California. He was very detached. He had a lot of power over me. I'd say: 'Oh, Steve, please let me just touch you,' and he'd make a joke of it. He'd threaten to kick his shoe all the way up my hole once. That's annoying, I know it is, but I don't consider myself inconsiderate. Because I have these horrible homosexual feelings, I just wanted his arms and his chest. And that's why I wanted him to touch me." After a period of obnoxious rebuffing, the boy finally responded to her explicit seduction. They had a one time contact, in which he masturbated her to orgasm. She then did not get together with him again.

Three months later, she reflected upon her confusion over her own sexuality: "I can see now, not wanting to be a girl, and not wanting to be homosexual—it's like either way you couldn't win."

After nearly a year of weekly sessions between ages seventeen and eighteen, she told her counselor of her wish that he would respond to her erotically. In the course of subsequent therapy sessions, she was able to recognize that "wanting somebody that I can't have" was a guarantee of love unrequited. In this context, she recalled her infatuation with her teacher at thirteen, with her priest at fifteen, and then with her first postdoctoral counselor from Germany. "I'm just not interested in any boy that I can get," she once said. "It hasn't worked out with anybody that I can have. There is more to it. I know that consummation is not possible." She was referring to constriction of her vaginal orifice. She neglected the possibility of either vaginal dilation or of minor surgical vaginoplasty, as gynecologically recommended.

Subsequently, she got involved with two other young men with whom she wanted to have sex, but in both cases she escaped at the last minute, avoiding intercourse. At nineteen, during her first year of college, she reported a heterosexual encounter with a student whom she had invited to her room after a party. She said: "I gave him a hand job, and I had a good feeling afterwards, because at least for once I satisfied him." She did not consider a hand job as a way to avoid penovaginal penetration. Once again, she appeared confused about her actual erotosexual status: "I try", she said, "and fight one way, homosexual, by just concentrating on the other way— with the pills and all, and developing myself in a more heterosexual direction. But you know, the homosexual is still there. I look at my desires, and I am reading about other people who share those desires, and I don't feel like I am totally left out. It's like a constant reminder that, well, I am perverted, but I'm not the only one, and there are the other people who do it."

It was not only bisexuality that jeopardized the establishment of a heterosexual relationship. There was also the handicap of being socially inept, alienated, and incapable of either romantic or friendship bonding with anyone. Her self-image, although considerably improved in terms of the overall attractiveness of her bodily feminization, was hampered by her continued postponement of vaginal dilation to ensure the copulatory adequacy of her vagina. In addition, there was the adverse effect of paraphilic self-martyrdom in inviting masochistic abuse and in engineering erotosexual rejection.

From college she wrote: "I have been to the point where I have a boy up in my room, and one step after another, until he finally takes his organ out, and then I have a fit. I guess I am afraid that he probably wouldn't even get in." Once she got as far as "a dry fuck type of thing," with her on top of the partner. She commented on that experience in these words: "I felt sort of cheap after I'd done it, which is what made things so difficult. But I certainly reached a climax." She had no further contact with this boy.

A month later she met another boy at a students' party and invited him to her room. There, for the first time, at the age of 19½ she allowed a partner to penetrate her vagina. She described that experience as "sort of crude," devoid of affection and foreplay. The boy attempted intromission but "could only get in an inch and half." After he had an orgasm, she "got on top of him" and masturbated by rubbing her vulva against his leg as she had done with her brother at age six. In her fantasy, she said, "It was like bang! The race was on. I've fantasized so many times about lining up with a lot of other people, male or female, and then a guy shoots the gun and the race is on, and everybody is riding their pillows like some kind of a hypothetical horse. And whoever reaches climax, wins the race." By contrast, the actual experience, was bad: "It wasn't a long thing, which is why I was so disappointed. I wanted somebody to stay with me, a warmth, a body. After we reached our peak, he got up and left. I was so sick, I didn't want to see him again. I think the feeling was mutual. We both sort of ran away from each other." There were no further reports of either hetero- or homosexual encounters.

When at the age of twenty, she resumed regular counseling in the PRU, she had twice failed college, her parents had just finalized their divorce, and her long and enthusiastically planned trip to Germany had turned out to be a disaster.

The ostensible agenda of her trip was a summer job for three months in Europe as an exchange student. The hidden agenda was a visit to her erstwhile counselor, the first of the two from Germany, who had returned home. As soon as her flight landed in Germany, she inexplicably discovered herself to be in a state of "uncontrollable panic." She fled from her summer job before the first day of work was over. She did not even phone her erstwhile counselor. Instead, she contacted the airline and booked a return flight. She had been in Germany only three days. Back home, she was confused and overcome with a terrible sense of self-defeat.

A year later, she reevaluated her European experience. She now saw it as a replay of the eroticized suffering she had experienced previously in the relationship with her counselor before he had returned to Germany. He was again close, geographically, but at the same time unattainable as a sexual partner. Her panic state had resulted from her old dilemma of whether to renew this unrequited relationship in which he would never respond in the manner depicted in her sexual fantasy, or to suffer through the final termination of the relationship. Both alternatives were unacceptable. Escape was the only solution, but even escape was only temporary. Her self-martyring pattern of sexual attraction left her trapped and powerless.

There was no effective solution to her dilemma, as she now perceived it, other than to become "an asexual, intellectual being," who only studied instead of "being plagued" by her own body. As to be expected, her resolution to be sexually ascetic did not hold up. Soon, she spontaneously reported her sexual attraction toward her new German counselor. To his supervisor, she explained: "I was being very frustrated over my present relationship with him in terms of some of the masochistic patterns of reacting. Well, I don't call it genuine orgasm, because it was absolutely zero touching. But it was so real, and the emotions and the feelings were so vivid and so genuine. And yet not to be able to touch. To look but not to touch— it's a feeling of such deprivation, it just increases the torture and makes it all the more exquisite, and all the more horrendous at the same time. I see beginnings of it recurring in the past few weeks in my relationship with Dr. C."

She spoke of her clearly masochistic fantasies. The favorite one was the concentration camp fantasy reported previously, but with some elements redesigned as follows: "Well, this particular fantasy is contingent upon my being tied up to a bed, stark naked, in a concentration camp. Laying down with nothing on, not even panties. Nothing. And there was a school boy, a ten-year-old German blond-haired school boy. Not that I usually consider myself attracted to somebody in that age category, but as the fantasy went, the school boy had the characteristics of what you might consider a typical German. He came from school in his Hitler Youth uniform. The scene took place during World War II. He was in the Hitler Youth uniform waiting for his father. His father in the fantasy is the camp commandant, and here this boy comes along, sees me tied to the bed and compliments me by putting his hand in my vagina, and is rubbing it and allowing me to derive the utmost excitement from it. I think the fantasy I just related here is important from the standpoint that it personifies this psychosexual submissive image that I feel, which antagonizes my relationship towards anybody, if they happen to be German or whatever, or to fit that pattern. I feel that the only way I can relate sexually is to relate to somebody who is dominant and elderly, sexually superior—a German master of some sort. It's the only thing that can really excite me."

In her perception, Dr. C. represented all the attributes which she considered attractive: He was a German male, he travelled a lot, and he owned a car. His lack of response to her erotic yearnings, and his lack of aggression, she later admitted, aroused her anger and frustration. She assumed that he did not take her seriously, and did not care about her enough. She was rebellious and manipulative, as if provoking abuse, at least verbally, from the one she cared about.

A few months later, she again contemplated the possibility of "leading a totally ascetic life devoid of any sexual interacting." She said that one of the major reasons for her being in favor of ascetism was the fact that she could not accept her bisexuality. She was convinced that she would never find anyone who could accept her the way she was. She had perceived her counselors as the only potential partners available to her, because they "could understand her problems."

That was the final formulation the patient came up with before she withdrew from treatment at age twenty-one. Six years later, according to the short progress report from her mother, by phone, she remained a loner, still without any close romantic or erotic ties.

Significance of the Case

Prenatal Precursors of Paraphilia. With respect to the future development of paraphilia, in this case the significance of the chromosomal sex is that it was 46,XY, as for a male, and that it was concordant with the embryonic differentiation of testes. By contrast, it was discordant with the morphological differentiation of the genitalia, which were demasculinized by reason of cellular insensitivity to androgen (if not of genetic origin, then possibly DES-induced) secreted presumably in normal masculine fashion by the fetal testes.

On the basis of laboratory and clinical tests at the time of puberty, it was established that, even after the administration of exogenous masculinizing steroidal hormones, there was an absence of cellular response to them. Thus, one may infer that prenatal brain cells had been subject to hormonal demasculinization to the same degree as those of the external genitalia had been.

Postnatal Precursors of Paraphilia: Prepuberty. The error in fetal sexual differentiation led to discordancy between male chromosomal and gonadal sex, on the one hand, and the female sex of the external genitalia, on the other. Years later, it was the clinical disclosure of this discordancy that proved to have a traumatic effect first on the parents, and derivatively, on the patient, so as to affect her sexuoerotic development. Her mother falsely cast her diagnostically in the role of a brain-damaged, learning-disabled child, thus repudiating male hermaphroditism.

Apart from victimization within the family, the girl felt victimized also by multiple genital examinations in early childhood. Uninformed of their rationale, she perceived the examinations as nosocomial abuse performed repeatedly with her parents' consent. She developed an image of herself as a sexual freak as well as a victim of parental abuse. Her childhood sexual rehearsal play with a neighborhood girl was associated with the· humiliation and abuse of being caught and punished by her father.

The victimization theme became incorporated into her prepubertal masturbation fantasies. In sexual imagery, the noxious experiences in her medical and family life became erotically transformed so that they served as a stimulus of sexual arousal.

Postnatal Precursors of Paraphilia: Postpuberty. The girl's self-discovery of being erotically more attracted to girls than to boys contributed to a gender-identity conflict with noncompliancy, from age thirteen to nearly eighteen, with respect to estrogen substitution therapy for the induction of puberty. In teenage, eunuchoid appearance and behavior became an additional source of stigmatization and victimization by peers. She was socially and romantically isolated. Ultimately, she resigned herself to feminizing hormonal therapy, and gradually accepted her appearance as a female.

Adulthood Paraphilic Outcome. In young adulthood the bisexual pendulum swung further in the heterosexual direction than had been the case earlier. The ideal partners were older males whose own lovemaps failed to reciprocate the explicit masochism and submissiveness of the patient's own lovemap. The same lack of reciprocity characterized also the lesbian side of the bisexual pendulum, the side which the patient experienced as being erotically more exciting and more repugnant simultaneously. The resolution was to have no partner, except in fantasies of masochistic bondage and discipline.

Paraphilic Stratagem. The traumatizing sequelae of the diagnosis of hermaphroditism were added to an already pathological family life. The reiterated abusive victimization and humiliation that ensued were erotized, even before puberty, according to the principle of opponent-process. Abusive victimization, specifically bondage and coercion, then became transmuted into paraphilic masochism, erotically manifested in imagery and ideation, though not in live performance. The paraphilia was bisexual. That is, it was superimposed on both the lesbian and the heterosexual alternatives of the bisexual lovemap. In the heterosexual version of the paraphilic fantasy, masochism was fused with gerontophilia insofar as the idealized lover was an older dominant man who represented an opponent-process transmutation of the abusing father of childhood. In paraphilic fantasy, the younger brother, on whose leg she had rubbed in masturbatory coital rehearsal play in childhood, was transmuted, also by opponent-process, into his father's sexually abusing apprentice.

CHAPTER 8

Biography 6: Bondage and Discipline in a Female with a History of Genital Ambiguity and Early Childhood Sex Reassignment

Diagnostic and Clinical Biography

Biography 6 is that of a woman with a hermaphroditic birth defect of the sex organs, and a mixed or mosaic chromosomal karyotype of 45,X/46,XY, who at birth was declared a boy and at age 4½ reassigned by edict as a girl. She was very short-statured as is typical for the 45,X/46,XY syndrome. Her lovemap in adulthood was that of a masochist and a bisexual. Hypothetically, it had its biographical origin in the way the early sex reassignment was imposed and managed surgically in the hospital and socially at home.

At the time when the girl was first seen in The Johns Hopkins Hospital for endocrine and psychohormonal evaluation at the age of thirteen, the family policy had been to conceal information from her pertaining to her clinical history, including the history of sex reassignment at age 4½ yrs. Within the family, the sex reassignment from boy to girl existed for the child herself as a non-event, on the pretext that she would have no memory of it.

The mother's retrospective account of the neonatal and subsequent history was as follows: "The doctor that delivered her said we had a boy. But he wouldn't give us any details after we felt as though something was wrong. When he did say something, it was that nothing could be done about it. So we tried a pediatrician. He felt as though it was a girl. When she was three weeks old, we went to Dr. G., the urologist. He felt differently— that it was a boy. So we changed back again. He checked on her each year until she was four. Then he did the first operation, trying to enlarge the clitoris that actually looked like a penis. And then at the second operation, when they did an abdominal, they discovered that she had all the female intestines. So then they changed her back to a little girl." Within the half year following the change of sex at age 4½, the child underwent surgery for resection of the penoclitoris and first-stage vaginoplasty.

There were three siblings, a brother, aged twelve, a sister, thirteen, and a brother, fifteen, at the time when they had to reorient themselves to having, as the baby of the family, a sister instead of a brother. They were left to understand the change as best they could, with no guidance as to its social repercussions on their own lives. The mother's policy was one of cover-up. She said that, until they moved from a city house to live on a farm, she protected them from neighborhood inquisitiveness and teasing: "I kept her [the patient] inside at home, and drew the drapes. We kept her to ourselves, and we changed ourselves. We were there only two weeks. We moved and went straight to the farm to live. I got her fancy nightgowns, and a few dresses. She just thought she was playing dress-up—just switched over gradually and changed to frills and baby dolls. I let her hair grow. She just looked like a boy that needed a haircut. As soon as I got to the farm, I stopped right away and put a permanent into her hair. It didn't take much to change it over. And she went right on from there and accepted the whole thing and never questioned it anymore. One time, when she was little, she said, 'Some people used to call me Jerry.' And I said that it was just short for Geraldine. And she never asked anymore. You see, we had kept it Jerry, in case. Once you've been switched back and forth, you don't know for sure, until the last minute. So we weren't taking any chances."

For many subsequent years the mother lived in fear of the girl's questions about her childhood operations: "Just the way she asks me things sometimes, it makes me wonder if she has ever heard anything. Like she wants to ask me something, but it just won't come out, and she doesn't know how to put it in words. Sometimes she would go into a fit of temper tantrums and she'd say: 'You're not telling me the truth. What is it? What's the matter with me?' " The mother told her daughter no more than that she'd had to have abdominal surgery because her "stomach wasn't properly developed."

When the girl was thirteen, and physically prepubertal, she was referred to the Pediatric Endocrine Clinic (PEC) by a local physician because of short stature, excessive hair on the arms and legs, and the history of genital ambiguity at birth. The physical examination revealed female-looking external genitalia with a scar where the phallic organ had been completely extirpated. There were no labia minora. There was a vaginal opening measuring 4–5 mm in diameter. The buccal smear was chromatin negative, and thus excluded a diagnosis of female hermaphroditism. A diagnosis of male hermaphroditism was ruled out after the chromosomal karyotype proved to be a mosaic, 45,X/46,XY, and after exploratory laparotomy revealed not testes but bilateral streak gonads, which were excised. The exploratory operation also revealed a normally formed uterus and fallopian tubes.

The pathology report indicated that the bilateral gonadal streaks contained some tubular structures of wollfian origin, as in a testis, but no sperm cells, and no hormone-secreting interstitial (Leydig) cells. The ultimate risk of malignancy in such malformed gonadal tissue made its surgical removal imperative.

Because the patient had no internal source of pubertal hormones, it was necessary to induce and maintain feminization with exogenous estrogen. Treatment was begun with Premarin 1.25 mg daily, two weeks postsurgically. The patient was 13 yrs 2 mos old. There was no recorded explanation of why feminine maturation was at this time given precedence over growing taller. Increase in height would have required postponement of the induction of puberty, as the hormonally induced pubertal growth spurt signals the cessation of bone growth and increase in height. The bone age at the onset of estrogen replacement therapy was 11 to 12 years. Whereas the average height age for the female at age thirteen is 5 feet (151 cm), the patient's height was only 3 ft 11 ins (119 cm). It was, in fact, short stature that made the girl vulnerable to social stigmatization (see Biography of Social Development).

Postsurgically, in addition to being started on hormonal replacement therapy, the patient was also referred for psychohormonal evaluation and follow-up. On the topic of her own clinical history, she knew she had had three earlier operations, of which her only understanding was: "When I was born, well, my organs weren't exactly straight the way they should be. My intestines weren't straight, in their proper position." To illustrate the recent operation, she drew a picture of intestines first closely coiled, and then correctively uncoiled like an S. "I don't know anything about the other operations," she said, "but I'm pretty sure all four were right in the same spot. I would like to know about my three operations. I have the right to know what they were about. They were performed on me."

Her ignorance of sexual anatomy and physiology was extensive.

Therefore, basic sex education and an explanation of the future endocrine treatment plan became the two main topics of her first psychohormonal visit. The policy of progressively building up her knowledge of the clinical history and prognosis of her condition in the successive visits could not be implemented, as the mother was embittered. The referral to Johns Hopkins had, in her estimation, culminated in "guinea-pig surgery." So she took her daughter back to her much-trusted referring urologist. He discontinued estrogen replacement therapy at the mother's request. She suspected that hormone treatment would make the girl "oversexed."

Mother and daughter returned to the psychohormonal clinic four years later, following the urologist's death. Then seventeen years old, the patient was still uninformed regarding her condition. She had no recall concerning her early years, before the sex reassignment (see Lovemap Biography). While her search for the lost biography had been going on, she had formulated an explanation for her condition on the basis of high school biology: "I feel that it is due either to genetics or to my glands." As if to pursue more information, she developed an ambition to become a histologist, though in fact she eventually trained for computer programing.

In counseling, she obtained an adequate working knowledge of her clinical history. This knowledge covered the function of hormonal substitution therapy, hormonal regulation of menstrual cyclicity, and in the absence of some unforeseen obstetrical breakthrough, parenthood by fostering or adoption. By itself alone, this information did not counteract the forces of noncompliancy, thanks especially to a phobia of hypodermic needles (but not of self-pricking her own finger for a blood sample). There was an additional complication also, in that at age 17½ a trial period of treatment with a growth-promoting anabolic steroid (Halotestin 2.5 mg daily) was instituted, with a view to increasing height. This hormone is technically an androgen, but very weakly virilizing. The patient's height at the onset of Halotestin treatment was 4 ft 3 ins (129.5 cm). Even though during six months of therapy her height increased by ¼ in (0.6 cm), identification of Halotestin as a "male hormone" made it suspect to both mother and daughter. They did not keep further endocrine appointments.

When two years later, at age twenty, the patient returned to Johns Hopkins to see a gynecologist, she reported having been off hormone therapy for nearly a year. She was started on 1.5 mg of Premarin to be taken cyclically for the first 20 days of each month. Three months later she had some breast enlargement but no menstrual bleeding. Premarin was increased to 2.5 mg daily. Its effect could not be ascertained, as the patient did not return for a follow-up visit. As it later turned out, she had moved out of town. At the age of twenty-three, she made contact with another hospital where, according to the gynecology report, she underwent vaginoplasty at the age of twenty-nine, prior to marriage. Postoperatively, her vagina was coitally adequate. She had normally developed breasts. Her ultimate height was only 4 ft 4 ins (132 cm). At age thirty-two, she reported taking Premarin plus Provera, cyclically, and having regular menstrual periods.

At the age of thirty-nine, on the occasion of a telephone follow-up, she reported having been off hormone therapy for about six months. Her periods, she said, had become very uncomfortable, with severe cramps and bloating. She discontinued medication so as to avoid these unpleasant symptoms. For the past several years she had taken Premarin and Provera periodically, usually for about three months followed by three to four months without medication. Whether on or off hormone therapy, she had not noticed any differences in her physical or mental status, except for the presence or absence of menstrual periods.

Family Pathology

When the patient was thirteen, the psychohormonal interviewer's impression after his first encounter with her mother was that the lady "told her story with the relentless self-control of a refugee or disaster victim, resigned and habituated to suffering." Her account of her martyrdom dominated the picture in the ensuing seven years of her contact with the psychohormonal unit. First, it was the story of her lonely struggle through the adversities of her daughter's medical condition. Her husband, she said, was not the type of man to lean on. He did not accompany his wife and daughter to the hospital. He left the care of the children to his wife. His priority was to take care of a small contracting business which he owned in partnership with his brother. Financially, he was not successful enough to support his family, as he and his brother gambled away the profits of their business. The wife had to work full-time as a waitress, as well as take care of the four children and a disabled, elderly aunt living in the household. Her burden of responsibilities at home and work became unbearable when she started experiencing menopause-related health problems. She was, she said, "on the verge of a nervous break-down. I got to the point where I could just cry for no reason. The doctor suggested that I take nerve medicine. It did help a great deal." She finally decided to place her aunt in a convalescent home, but that did not bring an end to her misery. Subsequently, there were some unspecified "troubles with her husband's business" that further contributed to her chronic distress.

All the foregoing pertains to the period before the patient was first seen in the psychohormonal clinic at age thirteen, by which time the mother scapegoated her daughter as the major source of her woes. She blamed her for precipitating marital conflict, which progressively worsened until divorce ended it. The mother and daughter existed in an adversarial state of mutual incrimination and suffering. The mother did not recognize her role as a victimizer, only as a martyr.

By the time the girl had reached age seventeen, the mother described her as "a difficult child, impossible to get close to." She expected her husband to take her side in her battles with the daughter, and when he failed to do so, she blamed the girl for "driving a wedge" between her and her husband. "She dotes on creating friction between my husband and I," the mother once sobbed in the patient's presence. "I can't make my husband understand that she's enjoying it." The girl was then nearly eighteen years old and trying to cope with her newly rediscovered knowledge of her childhood sex reassignment.

The mother's long-standing feud with her daughter reached its peak when she went so far as to state that, during a recent conflict, her daughter grabbed a gun in order to shoot her. Her husband stayed out of the scene, she said, and was glad to be watching her being attacked. The girl confirmed that she did get the gun, but only to leave the house and go out hunting with her older brother so as to avoid further escalation of the conflict.

This gun scene had taken place at the time when the wife was negotiating marital separation procedures with her attorney, and after she had reported her husband to the states attorney's office because of alleged nonsupport. She suspected him of having "outside interests" because of his lack of interest in sex.

It was when she was nineteen that the patient presented her own interpretation of the impending break-up of her parents' marriage. She said that they had married because her mother was pregnant. Her mother's family, she said, "took my dad's side over her, and he went over to them. Instead of going to mom to talk something over, he talked to them, then talked it over with mom afterwards." Her mother suffered under family criticism, mainly about how to handle the baby.

For as long as the patient could remember, her mother had been talking about leaving her husband. A major issue was his gambling. All four of the children would advise their mother to stop talking about the separation and do something about it. Her timetable, however, was to leave her husband only after the patient, their youngest child, graduated from high school. She implemented that plan, on schedule, but not before throwing a party to celebrate her daughter's graduation from high school, two months before her nineteenth birthday.

Retrospectively, at the age of thirty-nine, the patient commented on that earlier period of her life: "At the time when my parents' marriage was breaking-up I was kind of used in the middle. That caused a number of problems. Even after the separation they had me running back and forth between them. They were constantly asking me what the other one was up to, whether either was seeing anybody else, asking me to spy on the other one, and getting mad at me when I refused to do that." Neither parent truly welcomed her. She spent the first year with her father and became "disgusted with his company of drunks invading the house every evening." So she moved in with her mother, whose sarcastic verdict was: "She found out that living with him is not all roses." When she was twenty-two, she and her mother moved to another state. The mother opened a small business in which they both worked together.

In the daughter's words, retrospectively, "The move pretty much resolved things between mom and dad." By contrast, the period of rebellion against her mother's excessive restrictions on her attempts to establish independence and autonomy continued: "I had to start growing up," she recalled, "and it was tough. I got involved with drugs, taking just about anything there was that didn't require a needle: hash, LSD, uppers, downers, just about anything I could get hold of." After a year, she was able to quit drugs on her own, without any treatment.

Four years after her parents' divorce, she managed to free herself from the pathological mother-daughter relationship. She established an independent career for herself and got married. She maintained family ties, but loosely. By age thirty-nine, she had practically no contact with her younger brother. "He lives somewhere on the West Coast," she said. "He keeps himself pretty separate from the family. I am not sure exactly what the problem was. Apparently, he had a fight with my father and was keeping it to himself." Her older brother had died of cancer when she was thirty-four. She visited her older sister and her parents only occasionally. Both parents had remarried. She was able to get along with both of them and with her step-parents because, she explained: "I made a lot of changes on my part—mainly just to grow up to be more tolerant."

Biography of Social Development

Developmentally, everything about this girl's social life was dominated not only by her sexual anomaly, but also by the discrepancy of five or six years between her chronological age and physique age. Thus, when she was thirteen, she had the appearance of being seven or eight, and when eighteen, of being at most a very short prepubertal twelve or thirteen. In accordance with the principle of the "tyranny of the eyes," other people, at home, school, and hospital invariably juvenilized her. The predictable reaction was that her social responses were too juvenile relative to her chronological age. Her mother epitomized her daughter's resultant social isolation at age eighteen, by saying: "It's like watching someone that life is passing by."

Quite apart from the dilemma of physique age, the patient had in teenage a progressively more nagging suspicion that something about her history was being withheld by the mother. At thirteen, she recalled: "Mainly after I was about six or seven I started wondering what was wrong with me. I asked my mother and she said she didn't know and she didn't understand it anyway. I think she did know." The girl's mistrust of her mother laid the foundation for the long-standing conflict between the two. The mother's secretiveness was compounded by her restrictive supervision which she attributed to her daughter's immature appearance, not to her history of sexual ambiguity.

The mother limited her daughter's autonomy, protests notwithstanding. At age thirteen, the girl was forbidden to ride her bicycle on the street with her age mates, or to cross the railroad tracks to go alone to the nearby store. Her mother treated her as if she were about eight years old, she recalled. She tried her best to learn to "act thirteen." She watched her classmates and tried to imitate their gestures and habits. Nonetheless, at that time her psychohormonal interviewer noted: "Taking my cues from size alone, I would react to her as a young child, about eight years old. She was prepubertal not only in appearance but also in all her demeanor."

When the patient was nineteen, her position in her family was still that of an eternal child. She had her first job, in a small display-model business, after graduation from high school. Her mother insisted on driving her to and from work, even though it was only a few blocks from home. The mother argued that it was "unsafe for a person so small to walk alone. Even though she is nineteen, she is emotionally nowhere that old. She is still a child." The patient quit her job after three weeks, one of the reasons being that she was ashamed of being treated like a child in front of her coworkers.

According to her own retrospective account of her history, her short stature did not cause her particular concern until she went to school: "I really didn't notice it that much until about second grade. That was really when I started getting peeved about my height." By the time she reached the fifth grade, her relations with schoolmates were already severely disturbed. She was teased and ridiculed at school. "In the fifth grade," she said, "I had one friend and they teased both of us. We wouldn't even take our tennis racquets to school because they would throw the ball on the roof or in the mud. After one child started the others would join in." When she reported the offenders to the teacher, they would become even more aggressive. In revenge for her complaint, one of her schoolmates, a particularly malicious girl, spat right into her face in front of other children. The girl tried another strategy: to join with her tormentors when they laughed and joked about her size. In the long run, however, even that did not protect her from being stigmatized by her age mates. In the fifth grade she quit dancing lessons, "because I didn't get along with the girls in grade school, and they were the main ones who went to the dancing classes."

She passed beyond the usual age of first adolescent romantic attachments without any romantic experience (see Lovemap Biography). Her social life was nearly nil. She had no friends. She stayed at home watching TV or crocheting. Confrontation with a group was particularly threatening to her: "It seems as if I get along okay with any of the girls as long as there are just one or two around, but whenever they get together in a group then I begin to have trouble." Concerned about her growing isolation, she tried to establish some social contacts outside of her school environment. At seventeen, she joined the Ladies Auxilliary Fire Club. Her mother's disapproval coerced her to resign. The mother was irreconcilably ambivalent about her daughter's social isolation, as well as of her choice of people with whom to associate without too much risk of further stigmatization. For the daughter, it was a no-win dilemma.

From the grade school years onward, growing difficulties in social relationships were paralleled by progressive deterioration in academic achievement. The mother recalled that when her daughter's IQ was first tested at the age about four, prior to sex reassignment, the results had indicated an accelerated intellectual development. By the time the girl reached fourth grade, she reportedly "didn't seem to comprehend things right." The test for IQ performed in the Psychohormonal Research Unit at the age 13 yrs 3 mos (WISC Verbal IQ, 110; Nonverbal IQ, 94; Full Scale IQ, 103) failed to indicate an intellectual deficit that might explain the deficit in school achievement. There were, however, multiple indices of mental blockage. The girl complained of inability to concentrate in class. She had a behavioral history that included irritability and explosiveness; phobic fear of darkness; and nightmares and bed-wetting until the age of about nine.

Conflicts at home made everything worse. They intensified after she had, at age eighteen, retrieved the lost early years of her biography and embarked on achieving more adolescent autonomy. School grades further deteriorated, and she failed the ninth grade. The mother reported that one of the reasons for that failure was that the school was attended predominantly by "clannish children" (by which she meant Jewish) who rejected the patient "because of her religion and short stature." She was transferred to a Catholic school. Though she continued to underachieve, she graduated at the age of nineteen without further failure to pass from one grade to another.

In her mid-twenties the patient accomplished college management training, which led to in-service training and a career in computer programing. At work she met her future husband, a computer systems analyst. They lived together before they got married when she was thirty-two. She was "successful at work," she said, "and had lots of friends."

Lovemap Biography

Postnatally, insofar as the declared sex was male and the early rearing that of a boy, the early postnatal phase of lovemap development may be presumed to have been more that of a boy than a girl. Recall of living as a boy, and of sex reassignment imposed at age 4½ was subsequently blocked out from the child's memory. Subsequent upbringing was consistently female. For nineteen years of follow-up between ages thirteen and thirty-two, the patient's lovemap development, insofar as it was observably manifested, appeared to be female. However, self-disclosure at age thirty-two revealed it to have been, by history, bisexual, with a mild degree of paraphilic masochism.

When the patient was thirteen, the mother's retrospective story was that during the 4½ years that she had reared her child as a boy, the child had acted and looked like a little girl: "She was a beautiful little boy," she said, using the female pronoun. "Really, I mean, people would actually say that she looked like a little girl. She just had the features. Of course they didn't know how much apprehension they were giving us, but she was very dainty with everything when she was small. She had always liked to play with dolls, so always in the back of my mind I had had doubts. Now, since she's gotten older, she's gotten more tomboyish despite her tiny size. It's not, in the strongest sort of sense, like boys' play. She just likes to play those boyish games. I was a typical tomboy myself."

When, after the child's sex reassignment, the parents had moved to a farm and transferred their three older children to a new school, the older sister and two brothers "came through [the sex reassignment] wonderfully well," the mother recalled. "When I went home from the hospital and asked them what they would think if we had to change Jerry, they said that the only thing we want you to do is bring her back."

The newspapers and national magazines were, at the time, carrying sensational reports of the first publicized American case of transexual reassignment, that of Christine Jorgensen (Jorgensen, 1967). The mother thought that the news coverage of this case helped her three older children to accept easily their brother's reassignment as a girl. The husband, she said, "took it the same as the children. He takes everything in his stride. Very few things trouble him at all." From then onward, the family kept their secret from everyone, the patient included, on the false assumption that a child would not have any memory of the first four and a half years of life.

As a thirteen year old, the patient had no recall of her early years as a boy, nor of what had been done surgically to her genitalia when as a boy, at age 4½, she had undergone surgical demasculinization and reconstructive feminization as a girl. This memory blockage had been paralleled by a complete inability to specify the basis of genital sex difference. At age thirteen, even after having been shown diagrams of male and female genital anatomy, she maintained with wide-eyed naivety that she had not been able to observe genital sex difference even by observing tiny babies being diapered.

It was not until age thirty-nine that the patient recollected juvenile show-and-tell play: "Well, I do remember," she said in a follow-up telephone interview, "that I was about five or six and we were living out in the country. We used to all go back into the woods and play games of 'you show me yours and I'll show you mine.' The patient's older sister's intervention put a stop to such games: "We were about five of us playing back in the woods and my sister came walking by. She scolded us rather thoroughly and then spanked me all the way home. We didn't go back there and do it anymore. It was pretty much the end of these games."

When the patient was thirteen, her mother admitted that she had not talked about sex with her daughter. "She's so small," she said. "When they have parties, they only invite girls. She's still to that stage. When they want boys and all like that, then I think that's more or less time to talk." This statement was made while the girl herself, in an adjacent room, was telling another interviewer: "Yes, sir, I have one. I have one at school. There isn't much to tell about him. He has blond hair, and, uhm, he has kind of dark complexion, and he's real cute." The boy knew he was her boyfriend, because "one of the girls told him. I don't think I could have kept it from him too long. I have his name written all over—he saw his name written all over my binder. Of course, I found out he has my name written all over his binder, anyway."

When, at age seventeen, she returned to the psychohormonal clinic to resume treatment, she had had no further romantic or sexual experiences to report. The adversities of being only 4 ft 3 ins (129.5 cm) in height, even though her breasts were adequately developed, had contributed to the constricted development of her romantic life. She herself was interested in boys, she said, but "most of them tease me, and the others won't date me because their friends would tease them if they did." One exception occurred when, at a friend's house, she met and became friendly with two mentally retarded boys on leave from the local institution where they lived. Her mother put a stop to that. "We already have enough of a problem with her condition," the mother said. Her daughter's response, given in a joint interview with her mother at that time was, while crying: "I hate my mother sometimes. I don't know why. I just can't understand it. I love my mother and all, but sometimes I simply can't stand her."

The girl's resentment toward her mother was augmented by her suspicion that a secret was being withheld concerning her sexual biography. Though seventeen years of age, she still had no explicit recollection of her early years, prior to the sex reassignment at 4½: "I don't remember too much until when I was about four," she said, "but then I remember everything from that time on." In dreams, however, there had recently been intimations of the earlier years. She had dreamed of "playing in a big back yard; getting a souvenir Peter-Pan hat at a movie; being given china plaques of elephants to put on a wall near my bed; and being in a crib, with my parents coming in and giving me a toy car."

Her search for her own lost biography manifested itself not only in dreams, but also in poetic expression. One of the poems written at this time was given to the counselor two sessions later:

Lonely Search

I walk a long and lonely path
With not a soul to guide me
I travel alone, without a friend
And my life is dull and empty.

I wander forever, a searching soul
Watching always for what I seek
A wanderer without a goal
Searching every hour of every week.

My life is but a constant search
Only my soul knows what I search for
While it sits on a lofty perch
And I search forever more.

Only when I find my quest
Can my restless soul be at peace
But till that time my soul cannot rest
And my wandering cannot cease.

The discovery of the lost biography had actually been foreshadowed in a dream, dating from age seven. It was recalled, but not reported until the present age of seventeen: "I had gone to see Dr. G. [the urologist who had operated on her genitalia]. He was examining my arms, and he made some remark about 'they were definitely feminine.' And that night I had a real wild dream about when I was born, that I was born a boy; and for some reason I'd started turning into a girl. I woke up in the middle of the night. I was shaking. My sister [then aged 16] was sleeping in the same room. She sat with me for a few minutes, and I went back to sleep. But, I thought quite a bit about it the next day, and I kept trying to piece things together, things that would point to—different things that were said to me, the fact that I had so much hair on my arms, and everything. And I tried to find facts to discredit the idea. I thought it was impossible for that to happen—that a boy could change into a girl, or a girl change into a boy." She did not discuss the topic with anyone: "I just decided that it couldn't have happened, and that it wasn't worth bothering with, or even thinking about."

A month later, when she had her next counseling session, she was told the story of the embryology of ambiguous differentiation of the genitalia, illustrated with diagrams, and of how a baby could be born "genitally unfinished."

"I started then to feel," she later commented, "that maybe the dream—maybe I had been raised as one sex, and then they found out I was more of the other sex, and had assigned me the other sex. It wasn't very upsetting, except that I wanted to know just what had happened." Upon having the historical accuracy of her dream confirmed by her counselor, she wanted to inform her parents of what she knew, "to ease the burden of what they've been living with for quite a few years."

On the night following this counseling session, she dreamed again the dream of when she had lived as a boy. "Previously," she said, "I saw myself—I saw what was happening [in the dream] through the eyes of the person. The night after our last session, the dream was the same, only this time I saw the person—I saw myself, and I realized that it was myself, and I was dressed as a boy. It was almost like looking at a photograph. The next day, after I came home from school, my mother showed me quite a few photographs that had been taken at that time. One of these was the scene that I had seen the night before—the same toys, the same clothes. Everything was exactly the same. I was kind of shocked, and then I grabbed the picture, and told my mother that this was the dream that I had had. She told me I had just turned three when the photo was taken."

The revealed secret temporarily eased the tension between the girl and her mother, though not for long, as there would be two more years of family feuding until at age nineteen she graduated from high school and her parents separated. Before the separation, the patient established an alliance with her older brother (see Family Pathology). With him she went on hunting trips, and it was through him that she met Hank, who was twenty-six when she was nineteen. They got into "kissing and hugging, but nothing genital. I have to fight him off, a little," she said. Their partnership was short-lived, and broke up in a dispute related to antagonisms within her family.

In the ensuing decade, there were eventually other romantic attachments. In a follow-up telephone interview at age thirty-two, she said: "I dated quite a few people and had a few serious relationships, both with men and women. Before I was thirty, when I had vaginal surgery, there was no way I could have a normal sexual relationship with the men. With the women, there was a perfectly normal relationship." She first disclosed that she had become aware of a bisexual potential at high school, but had not talked about it, nor acted on it for ten years or more, until her heterosexual life had come into bloom.

Just as there had been a delay between the discovery of bisexuality and its disclosure, so also was there a delay between the discovery of autoeroticism and its disclosure—which was as recent as during the contemporary follow-up at age thirty-nine. The newly reported information was that masturbation had been first discovered at about age fifteen. Looking back over nearly twenty-five years, the woman recalled having had good feelings from digital self-stimulation in the region of the vulva, but without the climax of orgasm. Retrospectively, she dated her first experience of orgasm to the age of twenty-one. She rated an autoerotically induced orgasm as much less intensely pleasurable than one induced while her husband would be orally or manually stimulating her nipples in synchrony with reciprocal, penovaginal thrusting.

The consummation of penovaginal intercourse with intromission had, of necessity, been delayed for financial reasons. "I'd been denied health insurance all along," the patient said. Thus she was nearly thirty before being able to afford to undergo second-stage vaginoplasty to release constriction of the vaginal orifice that had been present since the first-stage surgery at age 4½ years.

She and the man who became her husband had met at work. They were a complete contrast in height, he being over 6 ft (183 cm) tall and heavily built, and she being 4 ft 4 ins (132 cm) tall and not heavy. "We started dating," she said, "and after about eight months, he moved in. We decided to live together for a while to make sure the past medical history was not going to hinder a normal marital life." Three months later, they married: "It's working out very well. I couldn't be happier."

On the subject of orgasm, her estimate at the time of inquiry, when she was thirty-two, was that she achieved it 95% of the time. "As far as I can relate it to anything else, it seems to be perfectly normal. I really don't know how I would describe it other than very enjoyable." It was more diffused than focused, "but very intense. When we first start, breasts are more stimulating than genitals" (the clitoridean structure had been excised as part of the feminizing surgery at age 4½). As self-estimated, her sex drive was average. She could not rate any particular stimulus, or any one of the senses as being specially likely to induce a romantic and sexy mood. "But I'm rather a touchy-feely type person," she said, "hugging and such."

Despite the intervening ten years of hiatus in follow-up, the patient was able to give information in a long-distance interview, without being inhibited or evasive. The interviewer systematically covered a list of topics on a standard schedule of inquiry. It was in this context that "kinky sex" became a topic of inquiry. "I do tend to fantasize a lot," was the response, "and my husband and I do get into some light bondage and things like that. We do experiment with this. He'll come into the room dressed in full leather, or something like that—leather cuffs and thongs; tying me to the posts of the bed, or I'll tie him. It's not necessary, but we find it makes it much more enjoyable. We have gotten together with friends and done bondage scenes together. We have tried various costumes as well as the leather—various uniforms, like a military uniform, pith helmet, or a motorcycle-type person wearing leather. And we'll act out the scene with me as a villager, and things like that. We make it up as we go along. Our fantasies do match quite well. I feel a lot of satisfaction, a lot of closeness, knowing I've brought enjoyment to him, as well as being well satisfied myself."

The schedule of inquiry included the topic of open marriage and group sex. "We do, somewhat, have an open marriage," she responded, "but we mainly have one basic agreement—he doesn't go to bed with any other women, and I don't go to bed with any other men. Other than that, it's free, because that [bisexuality] is one part of our sexuality that the other can't fulfill."

During the telephone interview at age thirty-nine, the patient again talked openly about her marital and sex life. She estimated her sex drive as "mild," which meant that, ideally, she would like to have sex with her husband once or twice a week. In practice, however, they had sexual intercourse about once every six months: "The biggest problem is my weight and his—it becomes quite exhausting," she said. "He winds up quite short of breath afterwards." At the time of the interview the husband was about 100 pounds (45 kg) overweight. The patient said that she only recently managed to reduce her weight from 145 pounds (65 kg) to 110 pounds (50 kg), which is 14 pounds (6.5 kg) above the upper limit of normal weight for her height of 52 inches (132 cm) (according to the Body Mass Index; see Wilson and Foster, 1985). The deficiency in the sexual relationship did not void, in toto, her relationship with her husband, she said, "because he does show a lot of affection, and there is a lot of closeness, which helps."

She had no qualms about masturbation with sexual fantasies and hard core porno magazines, which she used to enhance sexual arousal. She said that she had no specific preferences as to the type of porno materials. Both heterosexual, homosexual, and bisexual themes of sexually explicit images of men and women were equally stimulating. She no longer had extramarital sexual contacts. Ostensibly, the marriage was still an open one, she confirmed, "but with the AIDS problem there isn't that much of an activity, not at all." When queried about the content of sexual fantasies, she became reluctant as compared with formerly: "This is one area I do have trouble talking about. I always consider fantasies the one thing that is really personal and you can keep locked up. It's like handing somebody my diary. When I agreed to that phone call I thought I could; but now I am having a hard time." She said only that there was a wide gap between the content of her fantasies and her sexual practice—her fantasies could not be acted out in sexual encounters with her husband. She thought it would be easier to write her fantasies down, or talk about them when she appeared for an appointment, in person, which she planned to do sometime in the future (but did not).

The possibility of parenthood by adoption was first introduced during the long-distance interview that took place during the first year of the patient's marriage. She and her husband were both positively inclined toward adopting. Her preference was for a child at the toddler age, since a child at that age would tie her less to the home and interfere less with her outside, salaried career. "Actually, we'd run into quite a lot of difficulty, trying to adopt," she said, "considering our past histories of bisexuality." After the first three years of marriage, the prospect of adoption changed, as the couple moved in with the husband's elderly parents to take care of them. Years later, they still considered adopting an older, five- to ten-year-old child, but they postponed a decision until circumstances would allow them to live on their own again.

Significance of the Case

Prenatal Precursors of Paraphilia. With respect to the future development of paraphilia, in this case the significance of the chromosomal sex is that it was neither XX (female) nor XY (male). Instead it showed a highly atypical mosaic pattern in which some cells were chromosomally 45,X, and some were 46,XY with the Y chromosome itself atypical.

This chromosomal combination was apparently so deficient in testicular-determining genes, that the gonads were unable to differentiate as testes. Without the second X chromosome, they were also unable to differentiate as ovaries. The end result was that, instead of testes or ovaries, there were only streak gonads.

Prenatally, streak gonads are usually hormonally inert and, therefore, compatible with fetal morphological differentiation as a female. In this case the internal differentiation was as for a female. In the absence of MIH (mullerian inhibiting hormone) normally secreted by fetal testes, the mullerian ducts proliferated and formed the uterus and fallopian tubes. In the absence of testosterone or its metabolites, the proliferation of the wolffian ducts failed. There was not, however, a total demasculinization of the external genitalia. They differentiated not exactly as for a female, but so as to be mildly ambiguous in appearance. Considering the evidence of sexual morphology, one assumes that the fetal brain was, like the external genitals, incompletely demasculinized.

On the basis of this one case alone, it is not possible to ascertain whether chromosomal sex or gonadal sex were or were not direct precursors of the subsequent genesis of paraphilia. Together, however, they were indirect precursors insofar as they did influence the neonatal appearance of the genitalia, and it was the genital appearance that triggered a sequence of traumatizing events in the lives of the parents, and then in the life of the child.

Postnatal Precursors of Paraphilia: Prepuberty. At birth, the child was erroneously assigned as a male, and subsequently, at the age 4 yrs 6 mos, reassigned from male to female. For the family, the trauma of reassignment was intensified by what appeared to be a medical miscalculation that had required it. With the knowledge of hindsight, it is evident that, for the family, the social ramifications of the sex reassignment were also miscalculated. It was professional mismanagement, which would today be regarded as malpractice, to require the family to relocate and, in effect, sever itself from its own history. Social relationships within the family became progressively more pathological. The primary victim of the family pathology was the patient. In addition to being victimized within the family, and later on within the school, she was also nosocomially victimized by the medical and surgical procedures that, despite the best of intentions, were from the child's point of view, if not downrightly abusive, then extremely traumatizing.

Postnatal Precursors of Paraphilia: Postpuberty. The hormonally inert streak gonads were potentially malignant, and thus surgically removed at age 13 yrs 2 mos. The patient's noncompliancy with hormonal (estrogen) treatment delayed the onset of puberty, until at age twenty, it was clinically induced and, in accordance with her social status as a girl, regulated so as to be feminizing.

By this point the history of progressive traumatization and victimization had reached a climax in personal sexual and interpersonal pathology, which for several years remained unresolved. During this period, there was no manifest evidence of either normophilia or paraphilia in the patient's sexuoerotic development. The crisis did not begin to resolve until she was in her mid-twenties.

Adulthood Paraphilic Outcome. Not until adulthood was she able explicitly to admit to herself that her sexuoerotic orientation was bisexual, and masochistic as well. She was not able to give full expression to the masochistic aspect of her lovemap until after meeting and eventually marrying a bisexual man whose predominantly sadistic lovemap reciprocally matched her own predominantly masochistic one.

Paraphilic Stratagem. In this case, the experience of nosocomial traumatic victimization became paraphilically transformed, according to the opponent-process principle, and manifested itself erotically as paraphilic masochism which was attached primarily to the heterosexual component of a bisexual lovemap.

CHAPTER 9

Biography 7: Bondage and Discipline
in a Girl with Congenital Vaginal Atresia

Diagnostic and Clinical Biography

Biography 7 tells the story of a girl who discovered in childhood, and confirmed in adolescence, that there was no depth to her vagina. Only when she had failed to menstruate by age sixteen did she have the nerve to ask her mother to take her to a gynecologist. At puberty, her lovemap included a masochistic fantasy based on a veterinary analogy of a pelvic procedure performed "for its own good" on a restrained animal. Following successful corrective surgery, there was a transition from bisexuality to exclusive heterosexuality, and masochism was maintained only in erotic arousal narratives.

The first contact that this patient had with Johns Hopkins was via a phone call made to the psychohormonal research unit by her father on the recommendation of his own surgeon. The surgeon had recognized not only the condition of atresia of the vagina, but also that the girl would benefit from a referral where psychological evaluation could be combined with the establishment of a differential diagnosis, an endocrine evaluation, and a program of surgical treatment.

The history antecedent to this referral was that, since the age of eleven, and probably at a much younger age, the girl herself had known that the depth of her vagina was deficient. She had not said anything about it, until, at the age of 16 yrs 6 mos, she told her mother that she would need to see a gynecologist. She knew that late onset of menstruation was not viewed with alarm in the family, insofar as her mother had not menstruated until age seventeen. Even though her three sisters, then aged twenty, fourteen, and thirteen, had all begun to menstruate at age thirteen, her own primary concern was not menstruation, but the fact that, eight months earlier, intromission had proven absolutely impossible when she had resolutely tried to have sexual intercourse.

An appointment with the family physician yielded the advice that there was nothing wrong and nothing to worry about. Dissatisfied, the mother took her daughter to a gynecologist whose examination demonstrated the depth of the vagina to be only two inches. She advised an endocrine evaluation, which was bypassed in favor of a surgical evaluation. Because of the possibility of "a misplaced bladder in the midline," the surgeon recommended an exploratory laparotomy. The father sought a second surgical opinion, the upshot of which was the referral to Johns Hopkins. At this time the patient's age was 17 yrs 2 mos.

After the gynecological examination at Johns Hopkins, the diagnosis was given as a "classic example of the Rokitansky syndrome" of vaginal atresia, amenorrhea, and agenesis of the uterus in association with normal ovaries, normal female hormonal function, and a normal 46,XX chromosomal karyotype. The developmental history included onset of puberty at age eleven, normal-sized breasts slightly larger than those of her two sisters, and no menstrual cramps as well as no menses. Pubic and axillary hair were normal. The height at age 17 yrs 2 mos was 5 ft 1 in (155 cm) and weight 110 pounds (50 kg). Although no uterus had been palpated rectally, at the age of 17 yrs 5 mos, in the course of surgical vaginoplasty, "a soft, cystic enlargement, probably one of the ovaries, about 5 cm in diameter, was felt in the midline." It was elected not to take action other than to keep track of this soft enlargement, in the expectation that it would, if a functional cyst of the ovary, be self-reducing.

The vaginoplasty was done according to the standard McIndoe procedure, with a split-thickness skin graft, taken from the right buttock, used to line the extension of the cavity of the vagina. When the form that held the grafted skin in place was removed after eight days, the graft was seen to have taken quite well.

Nineteen days later there was an unexpected postsurgical complication in the form of a fluid-filled cavity bulging into the anterior vaginal wall. The fluid proved to be blood and mucus. It was released, and a surgical drain was put in place so that any further discharge could leak out. A foul-smelling discharge failed to clear up until, nine months later, an exploratory laparotomy revealed the source of the problem to be the soft mass which was formerly thought to be a cystic ovary, but which was actually a small uterus. It had no vaginal outlet. By a coincidence of timing, the first menstrual period had commenced shortly after the operation for vaginoplasty. The necessary surgical correction was made, so that the menstrual outflow could escape through the surgically constructed vagina. After healing was complete, there was no further recurrence of symptoms. The vagina was, according to a gynecological report, of very adequate dimensions, with a length of 8 cm. In the ensuing years, menstruation was "pretty normal" but at irregular intervals, sometimes two to three months apart.

Family Pathology

This is a case in which the term "family pathology" does not apply. The disagreements between the parents and their daughter were serious insofar as they derived from the girl's undisclosed concerns about her sexual adequacy. Nonetheless, they were not added to from unrelated sources of behavioral pathology within the family, nor did they become a source of such pathology.

On a written questionnaire at age nineteen, the patient rated her relationship with her parents in childhood as good, in teenage as bad, with many fights, and in young adulthood as much better. She experienced early teenage as a period in which there was a discrepancy between her value of independence and her parents' value of protectiveness, but she did not consider that her parents were intentionally unfair. Of her father she said: "I know he likes me a lot. As a matter of fact, I've been, like, his favorite. And so we fight—more than any of my sisters fight with him." On the Sacks Sentence Completion Test she wrote: "I feel that my father seldom understands my way of thinking. My mother and I have different points of view." Counterbalancing these criticisms, she wrote, "Compared with most families, mine is bearable." The latter appeared to be a realistic appraisal, for her family of three sisters and two parents did seem, by and large, to accommodate to each other without acrimonious excess.

It was the patient's father who made all the necessary arrangements for the Johns Hopkins evaluation. The interviewer's impression after talking with him was that he behaved as a concerned father with a normal degree of empathy and pity for his daughter. He respected her right to psychohormonal counseling sessions in private, without subsequent quizzing. There was a hint of paternal pride in his statement that his daughter is "a bright girl who is quiet about her private life and makes her own decisions."

There was some degree of parent-child discord when the daughter was in late teenage. She was verbally rebellious. She expected her parents to endorse her right to spend her free time her own way, without asking their permission. Her parents adhered to relatively orthodox upper-middle-class standards in rearing a teenager. By the girl's own account, they were not overtly religious or moralistic but were reluctant to let her always have her own way. She thought that the reason she was being watched by them more closely than her sisters was that she presented herself to them as an independent and liberal mind. "I don't know," she said, "how much they'll respect my opinion. They like to hear what I have to say but still stick to their own ways, you know."

At 17½, she decided to hire a lawyer to represent her in court after she was summoned for sunbathing topless on the beach. The overt agenda of her action was to defend her civil rights as a feminist activist. The hidden agenda was to declare, in public, that the upper part of her femininity was normal, and to do so independently of her parents. She later commented on it: "My parents know about the lawyer. They know they have little control now. Actually I'm getting along better with my father. They are finally beginning to accept my independence. They know they have little control of me now but I'm courteous to them. I like my father. He has a head on his shoulders and he is using it now. I'm afraid there is no hope for my mother, though. Well, what the hell?"

By the time she reached the age of legal adulthood, eighteen in her state, the situation between her and her parents had improved. She now could go out at night simply by telling her parents where she would be and when she would be back. When her anger about parental restrictions ceased, she said that she felt guilty about having too little feeling for her mother, whom she described as "terribly straight."

Her misunderstanding with her parents had been secondary to her inchoate and unspeakable concerns regarding the significance of her secret discoveries about her vagina, to which was added failure to menstruate. The error of her parents had been that they were too naive to be seriously concerned soon enough.

Biography of Social Development

If left to her own devices, the girl was the go-it-alone kind of teenager who could meet adversity by dismissing it with a shrug of "so what?" and a blend of resilience, daring, and maybe a bit of defiance in making the best of what can't be changed. "When the odds are against me," she wrote on the Sacks Sentence Completion Test, "I never give up." And, "When luck turns against me, I don't let it get to me." These were not idle boasts. They accurately represented the way in which she had coped with her sexual anomaly.

The sexual mores of her time required that as a sexually active teenager she not disclose to her parents the intimate history of how she had discovered that she had an imperfect vagina which would not function in sexual intercourse. "She is quiet about her private life," her father said, "and makes her own decisions." She did not establish the logic of connection between the teenaged strife that existed between her and her parents and the self-imposed isolation that the very nature of her inability to copulate as a teenager imposed on her. "I was basically a loner," she wrote, "but socially outgoing, also." There was only one friend, a girl, whom she rated as a best friend. They had known each other since the age of three. "We understand each other pretty well," she said, "and are open with each other." At high school, her friendships were mostly casual, and with boys. She did not get seriously involved with a male friend until age eighteen. With him, she was "very close and had a very good sex life."

When there is a discontinuity of philosophy or understanding between the members of two generations or, alternatively, of two cultures, one of the contingencies of the formulation of a new code of values and a new meaning of existence may be the visionary experience of a pharmacologically altered state of consciousness. This concept may well have applied to the high school generation of the affluent middle-class culture of which the present patient was a member. In her case, the discontinuity of values between her and her parents pertained specifically to sexuality and eroticism. She did, in fact, define new perspectives for herself while high on one or another of the drugs that were in fashion among the high school crowd of the era. She did not have money to buy her own. When friends offered them, she tried them, but "only when I'm in a good partying mood, and only at night." She did not become drug dependent. Her educational achievement did not deteriorate.

Her academic level and her IQ were consistent. On the WAIS (Wechsler Adult Intelligence Scale) administered at age 17 yrs 2 mos, the scores were: Verbal IQ, 124; Performance IQ, 108; Full Scale IQ, 118. The Verbal-Performance discrepancy was attributable to specific superiority of verbal reasoning (Specific Factor IQ equivalent, 141), not to specific inferiority of either praxic or numerical reasoning, both of which were average.

As a senior in high school, she had an ambition to teach karate and to pursue her early childhood affinity for animals by becoming an exercise girl for horses. She took karate lessons and enrolled in a vocational school class on race horses. Her recreation included swimming, motorcycling, camping, boating, and waterskiing. Though she wore blue jeans predominantly, and always while working with horses, she had a more varied wardrobe to select from, as the occasion demanded.

"I definitely get along with guys a lot better than I get along with girls," she said in one interview, "but I always thought that sometimes a girl and a guy can be more alike than two girls, so I was glad when

I found in my reading that someone else thought the same. When I—I mean there's no way I want to be a guy, and I definitely know I'm a girl. But I definitely get along better with guys." She found the level of psychosexual and psychosocial development in other girls of her own age to be younger than her own, especially when she was a college freshman.

After graduating from high school at age 18 yrs 5 mos, she enrolled at the local campus of the state university, taking courses in chemistry, calculus, psychology, and contemporary morality. Predictably, on the criterion of the IQ differential, she did poorly in chemistry and calculus, and so changed her major from biology to psychology. The most prevalent grade was B.

During the academic week, she lived in the college women's dormitory, and went home on weekends. She did volunteer work at the student gynecology clinic, counseling women on the use of birth control. She had never before realized that "so many people are up-tight about sex." On weekends she went home, where on Saturdays she was employed in the local pet store, in charge of the exotic animal room.

Her future plans at age 17 yrs 5 mos included marriage, but not at the expense of forfeiting a professional career. About housekeeping, her comment was, "I'm pretty lazy, but clean," and about motherhood and childcare, "not too swift." She characterized marriage as "an extremely close relationship where you don't have to be constantly with each other. You don't have to push each other, and you do separate things, but you have a good sex life together. And there are maybe things like major goals and everything, the same, so that you could strive together for them. And also you can't just be lovers. You also have to be good friends—be able to talk together, be best friends."

Pondering the issue of the possibility of future infertility, at the age of 18 yrs 3 mos, she said: "A lot of people, little girls, are trained that they're going to be a mother and have children. They play house all the time. And that's what their life is all about. I just never thought that way. I never played too much of those games and anything like that. I was usually off to myself, anyway, so I guess I never received that type of training."

Here may be represented the coping strategy of finding the redeeming feature. There had been another, though different, manifestation of the same strategy a year earlier in which the black cloud, as then declared, was infertility contingent on absence of a uterus, and an imperfect vagina that was not healing well, postsurgically. The silver lining was the feminine perfection of the breasts and body contours.

"Do you remember," she wrote in a letter asking for advice, "when I told you that I felt really strong about females not being able to go topless? Well, I started going topless on the beach—not too close to other people, and not acting lewd or anything. At first it was just me, then my girl friend, then a few other friends. We met a few other guys without suits and got into some really good conversations . . . . Further down there's a gay beach where there are more people with my ideas. . . . Some people gawked. Some thought it was disgusting. Most thought it was cool. Some even came up and complimented us on our guts. I felt really good and comfortable. But yesterday the cops got us, me and Pam. 'It's just a $5 or $10 summons; just go and pay it, and your parents won't know about it,' said the sweet pigs. I'm so fuckin' pissed. I feel like I've been arrested for picking my nose. . . . I feel like telling them I am genetically XY and I got too much female hormone in puberty, and so I developed breasts. I have to go to court. The easiest thing to do would be just to pay them. But I would feel like I was giving money to the 'Be ashamed of your bodies and go back to Victorian times league'. . . . I think if someone took it to the Supreme Court, they might make it legal."

She and Pam succeeded in retaining an ACLU (American Civil Liberties Union) attorney to make a test case of their summons. Afraid of publicity, her friend dropped out, leaving her to take time off from school only to find that the court date had been put forward several times. In the end, the judge dismissed the charge, and she let it go at that.

After the postsurgical vaginal complications were cleared up, there was a period of ten years of no further psychohormonal contact until a long-distance audiotaped interview by telephone at age thirty. By then she had been married for seven years to a fellow college student of her own age. They had lived together for three years prior to marriage. He was employed as a metropolitan police officer. She was in her third year of nursing school, maintaining a straight-A average. She financed her education and simultaneously sustained her lifelong close relationship with pets by working as a veterinary technician and private dog trainer, and by breeding and training dogs to sell.

At the time of marriage, she had wanted no pregnancies, and her husband had agreed, even though "he is a lot more family-minded than I am. He really loves kids. I'm not really a kid lover." She had, at the age of nineteen, required emergency treatment for what proved to be an ectopic, unplanned pregnancy. That left her with only one fallopian tube, which was apparently blocked. When she and her husband had changed their minds in favor of pregnancy, it had proved to be necessary to induce ovulation. There were two attempts at in vitro fertilization, but no pregnancy. After graduation from nursing school, she planned another attempt at in vitro fertilization. If it failed, she did not favor adoption. Rather she would pursue an advanced degree in nursing or medicine.

Lovemap Biography

As a young adult of 17½, this patient reconstructed the kind of sex life she had had as a child between the ages of five and eleven. "When I was really young, we'd have the typical 'I'll look at yours, and you look at mine' type of thing. Me and my friend would get into playing veterinarian a lot, and we'd always be having kittens. . . . We even got to the point where we'd actually mount each other like an animal would—not undressed or anything. We'd try to do it as close as we could as animals would be doing it. We never tried it as people." She estimated her age as eight or nine when she first learned that human beings have sexual intercourse. At that age the idea of "having intercourse scared me, but I was really curious and everything."

As a seventeen-year-old with a serious interest in the science of ethology, she had a history of always having a deep attachment to animals. "As a child I was always pretending to be an animal," she said. "Even now, with wild animals . . . I'd make them feel that I'm part of them, instead of part of the human world, and if other human beings were to come by, I'd think of them as being intruders on us." She attributed her sexual philosophy to her attitude toward animals. "I relate everything to animals, and it seems to me that just about anything that's open and free and natural with animals should be the same with people."

She considered that more of her sex education had derived from animal behavior than from printed or spoken information. However, with the advent of puberty at around age eleven, there had been some quasi-furtive reading of erotic stories. She recalled that she and her closest girl friend would "each have a book to read and be really getting hot over the book, and somebody would come downstairs. We'd throw it behind the couch and whip out *National Geographics.*" Her parents' policy had been to answer questions, but not to volunteer sexual information. When she was thirteen, her mother provided her with a book about menstruation, but did not discuss it.

At around this same age she went through what she called "seventh grade bullshit which I never believed in, in the first place. . . . You go into the woods with anyone you can, and they feel you up and they feel you down. You don't really enjoy it, but you do it just to find out what it is. . . . And he was so glad to go and tell his friend, 'Wow, I did it!' you know. I guess the guys got something out of it, but I never did." As she got older, she hated "anything that's going to cause a rush job— definitely not. If it comes to back seats of cars and junk like that, I hate it. Absolutely not."

While other seventh graders were perfecting the dimensions of their newly adolescent sexuality, the girl already knew, no matter how inchoately, that something about the depth of her vagina was imperfect. Five years later, when she was a senior in high school, it continued to be a virtually unspeakable monstrosity in her life, even when she gave an otherwise remarkably open-minded sex history in the course of her initial psychohormonal evaluation. The monstrosity was declared not in an interview, but in a letter written after she had returned home from the second surgical admission, the one necessitated by postsurgical complications following the first admission.

"Before I had this operation," she wrote, "I did a lot of suffering. I can easily remember how I felt. I knew there was something wrong, but I hoped there wasn't. I was always trying to find my damn hole, first when I was eleven I tried so often to insert a tampax, then trying to get my fingers in, and then in final desperation, when I had first met Dan and knew I'd try balling him soon, I spent some horrible times clawing at myself until I was bleeding, hoping I was ripping a tough hymen, and clawing even more when I could still not get in. It was really painful, but I was so very badly determined. And there was no one to talk to about it. Later on I used to dream and fantasize about balling, and it would be so great, and I'd have nothing to worry about, because I had a nice big juicy hole!"

Her letter went on to express her distress and to give a graphic description of the unremitting, foul-smelling, greenish discharge leaking from where a surgical drain was in place inside the vagina. "But in spite of it," she continued, "I have been even happier so far than I knew I would be since I have acquired a hole. I thought I was happy with my life and living it good before, but now it is twice as intense, mentally and physically. I get delight out of such little things now, and my senses seem to be working so intensely, I seem to be much more aware of them, especially smell and touch. Even just to pet a cat, or to come out of the ocean soaking wet and then lay in the sun, I can feel it warm me and I love the goose bumps when a soft, warm breeze passes over my still wet body, hitting the body hairs, making them rise. It is all so intense I can't possibly describe it all. I can't wait to make love, and I hope nothing holds me back."

The postsurgical discharge did hold her back for another eight months, at which time she was readmitted for a third surgical procedure, the exploratory operation that revealed that her internal reproductive organs did indeed include a small uterus without a vaginal outlet. Then, in the recovery room she had a scary, déjà vu experience in which what actually happened seemed to be a fantasy come to life: "I had doctors holding my legs and hands. Then I grabbed one of the doctor's hands and tried to pull him away. Meanwhile, they were pulling some kind of packing out and putting stitches in, and putting a clamp in, and I could feel that, it was really super painful. . . . When I think about it, it seems like a true fantasy." Subsequently she asked a doctor what had happened and he told her: "Oh, you were bleeding a little bit, and we had to put a clamp in and put some stitches in."

This recovery-room episode evoked a very early memory: "I remember when I was about five years old, my friend told me that her sister had a hernia or something like that, an operation, and they had to cut her vagina with a knife, or something like that. She didn't really tell me the details. But I used to sit there and have her tell it to me over and over again. I'd get really horny over it," she laughed, "just for her to tell me about that. I guess she did too, because she kept telling me, you know. . . . I think I base my fantasies of being held down on that story."

The first disclosure of the fantasy of restraint and submission had been audiotaped nine months earlier. "It was not necessarily sexual, but just like when they were trying to help me, or perhaps to get me pregnant, and breed me for some kind of experiment. It was like you had found an animal and tried to hold it down to help it, you know. It wouldn't realize you were helping it. It would bite you. And that's exactly the thing I was relating to." At a later date she added, "I was not usually a human being in the fantasy, I was more an animal. It wasn't specific what type, it just wasn't a human type of thing. And I didn't want it to happen, but I didn't have a choice, and a lot of times I was passive because I was drugged or something. So I didn't fight it that much. Usually I was pretty scared. They'd be doing all different kind of things, just you know basically doing different tests, just handling everything down there, you know touching everything, probing into everything.

"Just thinking about that would get me pretty horny, you know. I never have a fantasy to the point of orgasm unless I'm sleeping, but it's enough to get me really horny. And when I'm actually having sex—I have never really had a fantasy while I'm having sex. When I think of having sex, I think of it as something like I can really let myself go and do whatever I want. So usually it's sort of a crude, animalistic type thing where I just feel I'm having raw sex like an animal is having—unless it would be with somebody I really care for." At this time, at age 18 yrs 3 mos, actually having sex was subject to the constraints of the adverse postsurgical complications.

In the fantasy of being forcibly constrained while struggling, she always saw herself not as an animal but a human. Whereas the fantasy by itself alone did not precipitate orgasm, the two coincided for the first time early in adolescence. "I guess I was about eleven or so at the time," she said. "I was getting in bed. I don't, you know, let my dog sleep on my bed.

But she jumped up on the bed, and I said, 'What the hell, the dog can stay.' Okay, so just as a natural instinct, I guess, she just started nosing around, and I was going to kick her away—you know, tell her no. But it felt pretty good, so I just let her go at it, you know. I can't remember if I had an orgasm from it the first time I let her. It was either the first time or the second. . . . I wouldn't actually think of the dog as a person. I'd be thinking basically of being held down for my own good, and the more I struggled, the better it would be."

". . . When I did get an orgasm from it, it was good, but I had definitely felt it before, I don't know where. That is what really surprised me. So after a while, you know, I just kept it up every night. . . . If she didn't know where to lick at the right time and the right spot, I'd put butter there and that did the trick. . . . I was really nervous, you know—like my mother coming in or something like that. But she'd just come around and sit by the bed and start begging, and I'd say okay, and she'd hop up. After a while, if anyone started walking by the door, the dog would jump down. . . . After a while, since I knew that I couldn't have sexual intercourse, it seemed a lot easier with the dog, because there was no explaining to a dog. Then I just started masturbating [either in bed or with a jet of a water under the shower] by myself, without her, because I'd begun to feel guilty about it. . . ."

At around this same time, she found from her reading that her fantasy of being bound and tied down sexually was not too grossly atypical. She used Alex Comfort's book, *The Joy of Sex* (1973), as a lead-in to talk about bondage fantasies with a friend: "When he came to that part," she recalled, "he said, 'Have you ever done that?' and I said no, but I've thought about it, and he said, well, he had, and it was really good and everything."

It was also around this time that she experienced in actuality not the bondage part of her fantasy, but the struggling and fighting part. The partner was a friend older than herself. "I was in the apartment," she said. "I had waited for him. After he had kissed me, he went into the kitchen and came back, and all of a sudden he started beating me up, you know. And I went along with him. We got into fighting each other, and chasing each other around for, like, fifteen minutes. After that we just started getting into, er, regular sex—oral sex, not intercourse, because I couldn't then. But we did have anal intercourse." Her way of explaining her vaginal incapacity was to say that she had a constricted womb.

The next item on her sexual agenda was to see if intromission could possibly be achieved. She half knew that her partner in this enterprise would be a friend, ten years older than herself, whose younger brother was the boyfriend of her closest friend, Pam. The four of them were together at his apartment. "He asked me if I wanted to come with him to feed the doves. I said alright. I knew what was coming on. We both knew it was coming. . . . I didn't know what to tell him, or anything. I figured I might as well take a crack at it. Maybe I just had a tough hymen. So the next thing you know, we didn't have too much on and we were laying in bed. And I said to him, 'Dan, I'm a virgin,' and he said, 'I don't care.' I knew it was going to be a tough time. After a lot of foreplay, I was pretty calm, but I was still nervous about finally getting it in, you know. And then we got into oral sex. It was really good, and I didn't expect it. Then we tried actual intercourse. And we tried and we tried. It hurt like hell. We kept trying. We stopped for a while and just relaxed, and drank some soda, and talked. I felt really bad, you know. Then after a while we tried it again and it still didn't work, but he came anyway. I didn't have an orgasm because I'd been really worried about it. As long as he came, and got satisfied, I was happy over that. I could have enjoyed it a lot more. I was upset, but I wasn't crying or anything like that. I rarely cry. It takes a real lot to make me cry. . . . Dan helped me feel better. He told me how nice I was, and how pretty, and don't worry about it."

After she returned home from the first vaginal operation, she read "over twenty books and magazines" dealing with sex, and was exuberantly considering ideas of how she could get practice in using her new vagina. For instance, she and her girlfriend Pam thought about the idea of making a group with Dan and his younger brother, Bobby, Pam's boyfriend, but didn't follow through. "I prefer having emotional things there," she said. "I like the loving part that goes with it, and it's not just sex. . . . I would like to find me a guy that I can love, maybe not forever, but it would be a real love relationship."

Now that she was able to envision herself as being Pam's equal in vaginal intercourse, despite the disappointment of postsurgical infection, she was able for the first time to tell her everything regarding the operation. "She was really thrilled that you doctors could do something like that," the patient said in her next taped interview. "So we got to talking about all the things that we used to do when we were little, and everything. . . . And then she told me about the night when she slept over, about two years ago, and made it with the dog, my dog, while I was sleeping. Finally, like, I really wanted to make it with her, and she wanted to make it with me, but neither of us were really going to come out and say it. I was in a kind of messy state with discharge after surgery, and she said, 'Well, where's the dog?' " With butter as an enticement, the dog licked Pam. "I was just really turned on. The dog was still licking her, and after a while it was just me. It was, you know, pretty good and all, but it's not that I—I really don't feel like a lesbian or anything like that. . . . I just thought it was something different, you know, and something that I'd probably do again, but not something that I'm really into." Pam was not able to keep going along with it until she had an orgasm, so neither of them had one.

Telling everything about her surgery to Pam broke the ice for her to tell it also to Dan. Even though she knew that she would not "be going out with him forever, because he was a lot older" and already had another girlfriend, she invited him over. "It was really strange," she wrote in her sexual diary. "We blew a few joints, and I told him everything. We were completely open with each other. I found out more about him and related to him better than the whole time I was going out with him two years ago. I told him about how I was not really at ease when I had had sex with him, and he told me he had really enjoyed it, hole or no hole. I wish I'd known then. Anyway, he told me he'd had a hard-on all night thinking about me coming over, and a lot of times he got a hard-on just when I came over. I wasn't surprised, but I thought it was pretty funny. . . . Anyways, we started to get it on, and it was almost really good. We did erotic touching and kissing and oral sex. I had explained to him about the form and the discharge, and that I could not have intercourse yet, and this did not bother him at all. He just licked my thighs, lips, and clitoris. It was really good, because we brought each other to orgasm. But I still did not have intercourse. But we were open and responsive and relaxed. And we also laughed, which I love to do."

The next rendezvous with Dan was delayed because the travel schedule of his regular girlfriend was changed. In the meantime, the patient was alone at home and Pam sometimes slept over. One night, "after everybody left my house at around 1:30," she wrote, continuing her sexual diary, "I said, 'Let's get into some bondage.' Pam said, 'Yeah, far out, what do you want to do?' So I showed her. (Actually this is really easy to tell you when I'm writing it, you know.) I got some string and tied her hands to the head of the bed. She was lying on her back, her legs free. I got some body lotion and my old lady's mink stole (she'd flip if she knew). And then I started talking up a fantasy: that I had her drugged and she had to do what I told her. I treated her as a helpless earthling that I didn't want to hurt, but I had to perform tests on her. I was from another planet, and I had caught her for experimentation. I tried to calm her while she moaned and wriggled. I went over her with my hands, my tongue, the mink, and the lotion. I also went down on her, because I felt I knew just what a chick would like, because I'm a chick myself. We both really got into the whole thing. It was so good. Then we switched places and she did the same thing. I loved it. By the time we were done, it was 4 A.M. Amazing. I have enjoyed this more than anything, not because it was with a chick, but because we felt so free and open about acting out a really good fantasy."

Although there would be another 7½ months before the final vaginal operation and the ultimate cessation of unhygienic vaginal discharge, the two months following the first vaginoplasty procedure had been sufficiently successful that she was able to review them in her sexual diary as follows: "What a fine Labor Day weekend! I'm so sorry the summer must end. I've gone boating, waterskiing and swimming a lot. I got a good job, and I've changed my head quite a bit. There's so much to learn. I also got a hole. And I also used it. I've really missed a lot, you know. Balling is great, but I'm sure I don't have to tell you that. I feel I can get the most feeling in the doggie position. Female on top is really good too. I got Dan into rabbit pelts (furs) and he really digs it. I dig it with guys better than with chicks, probably because they have cocks (I talk like a real lady, don't I?). But I really dig it a lot with Pam because, as Pam puts it, 'We've done everything together, so why not sex?' So I am very close to her. In other words, if I can find a guy and have a love relationship, then sex would be all the better. But it's okay in the meantime." Her age when she made that diary entry was 17 yrs 7 mos. Her sexual odyssey in the preceding six months had covered a long distance.

The end of the year marked the second and final installment of her sexual diary. One entry read thus: "You gotta hear this! Okay, are you ready? I was talking with my friend Cliff (whom I have balled before), and he was telling me that all cunts are located differently, and on different angles, which I already knew. Then he told me that they all feel really different, that some were really nice and comfortable, and some were just all right, and some were uncomfortable and scratchy, which I didn't know. And then (now get this!) he said that I shouldn't worry, that mine was the best he ever felt and, I quote, 'God was really good to you, he gave you some gift and you really know how to use it.' Man, I almost shit in my pants (excuse my French). I mean I was really laughing to myself. That really blew my head off. Now, what do you think of that?"

This final entry in her sexual diary was written also as a letter to the young psychohormonal physician to whom her case had been assigned. She addressed him in the final paragraph. "I can't complain about anything, really. I'm secure. I have good friends, a good outlook on life, and I feel I'm a very stable person. So I'm just riding the bumps a bit, and taking things as they come. Writing to you every so often just helps me smooth the bumps a bit, like shock absorbers. Have a really fine holiday. Tell everyone the same."

After the last gynecology admission and follow-up at age 19 yrs 6 mos, she had no further need of any clinical services, and her sexual diary was discontinued. She had already met the man who would become her husband. In a sex-history questionnaire filled out at this time, she indicated that the most sensitive genital areas were the clitoris and the lips; that arousal induced vaginal lubrication in about one minute (although later in life she would sometimes need to use K-Y jelly); that the best word to describe orgasm was "intense"; that she climaxed most of the time; that she had experienced multiple orgasms; and that the interval between intromission and orgasm could be five minutes or much longer. She rated her sex drive as stronger than that of most women, and her feeling after sexual intercourse as very satisfied and conducive to looking for more sex.

The body parts that were most sexually arousing were listed alphabetically as abdomen, back, buttocks, clitoral region, vagina within, and vaginal opening. On a five-point scale, the maximum enjoyment rating of 5 was assigned to foreplay, oral sex, and satisfying the partner; 4 to intercourse; and 3 to masturbation. To induce a romantic and sexy mood, with 9 as the maximum, her ratings were: seeing the person you love, 9; touch, 9; reading material, 9; smells, 8; seeing some part of the person you love, 7; sounds (talking in whispers and exciting conversation), 7; erotic movies, 7; tastes, 5; and still pictures, 3. She could be aroused by an erotic movie only if she found the male in it attractive. Though she might take a look at a man on the street and say he'd be really nice, she would not get really horny. If she responded to a female pin-up poster, it would be to compare herself with the other female.

After the initial exuberance of having a vagina and learning to appreciate it, her sex life became conventional and, with her husband, monogamous. Their coital frequency varied according to work schedules. Typically it was four or five times a week. Sometimes she would have a sexy dream almost to the point of orgasm and then wake up her husband. "He's a lot more responsive than I am. He'll never say no. Anytime I want sex, he's in the mood, whereas I'm not always." The dream content "seems more like feelings than it does visual," she said. "I can recall the feelings, but I really can't recall any content to them. . . . I'm definitely more oriented to touch than anything else." By contrast, she could get turned on by sexy stories, of which the content would be "bondage. I could be either dominant or submissive, not real heavy, just light. I usually don't care for typical, mushy love things. Just reading straight stuff like that doesn't interest me."

A bondage story would be "more exciting if it's explicit. And if I'm being told the story out loud, I like it explicit. . . . I've trained my husband to do it. It's almost like foreplay. In fact, he can probably turn me on fastest if he does that. It took me a while to teach him that. . . . Whenever we make up a bondage story, it's real short, because I start hearing it and get horny so fast that I just want to get down to it." She gave an example.

"Let me see. I'm alone in the house and somebody, an intruder, comes in. I'm afraid of him, or whatever, and he just sort of makes me submit—either ties me down, or tells me that I'm going to have to stay still, or he's going to do something, you know, actually more telling me what he's going to do to me, if I don't do what he wants me to do. . . . You know, it's funny because it has nothing to do with what's really—I would hate that, if it happened, real. It would drive me crazy. I would be totally the opposite. But sexually I like it. I mean, if my husband were ever to try to push me around in real life, I would just go bananas. But sexually, you know, it's different." Even sexually, the narration of bondage was far more arousing than enacting it, and than being tied even "just lightly. I don't like being tied. It's almost like going through the motions of doing it, but not really doing it. Then when I actually have sex, I'm free."

In the technical terminology of the paraphilias, hers was narratophilia. The theme was bondage and submission, but it was not paraphilically enacted as masochism. As is typical of paraphilia, hers had its origin early in childhood, possibly as early as age five, and represented the solution to the problem of having no vagina. It is probable that the success of vaginoplasty aborted the development of a full-blown masochism which would have dictated clawing, ripping, and bleeding of the vagina as an erotic practice. Likewise, it may well have aborted the evolution of oral sex, either with the dog or a woman partner, as an alternative to failure to be able to use a penis.

The end result, narratophilia, with a theme of submission and bondage, is a typically feminine paraphilic outcome to the challenge of retrieving genital lust from the threat of extinction. In this case it was a playful, not a noxious outcome, and it was compatible with the reconciliation of lust and love in an affectionate and lasting relationship with a partner whose own erotic arousal was not inhibited by the game of being the narrator.

Significance of the Case

Prenatal Precursors of Paraphilia. With respect to the future development of paraphilia, in this case the significance of the chromosomal sex is that it was 46,XX, as for a female. It was concordant with the gonadal sex, the prenatal hormonal sex, and external female morphology, all of which were concordant and normal for a female. The one abnormality was in the morphology of the internal reproductive organs insofar as the uterus was poorly formed. It did not connect with the cavity of the vagina, which was shallow and ended blindly. The external genitalia were normally formed, so that there was no uncertainty regarding the sex of assignment as a female. On the basis of the evidence of sexual morphology, one assumes that the sexual morphology of the fetal brain was subject to the action of the same hormonal feminization.

Postnatal Precursors of Paraphilia: Prepuberty. Insofar as the external genital appearance was normal, it offered no contradiction to the rearing of the child as a normal female. Visibly, she appeared normal to other people as well as to herself. Her discovery that she was abnormal was by reason of digital exploration. This discovery might have been made as early as age eight, and had been quite definitely made by age eleven.

Postnatal Precursors of Paraphilia: Postpuberty. At around age 5, age-appropriate sexual rehearsal play began with a girl friend. From age eleven onwards the girl knew that there was something wrong with her vagina, on the basis of such evidence that a tampon could not be inserted. She suffered in secret but became progressively traumatized as menstruation failed to appear, and four months before her sixteenth birthday desperately arranged an attempt at intercourse which failed. At least four years earlier she had already become aware of masochistic paraphilic imagery and ideation derived from an animal paradigm in which a veterinarian performed injurious procedures on a restrained animal, "for its own good."

Adulthood Paraphilia Outcome. After the surgical construction of a functional vagina was finally successful and the menses unexpectedly began, the effect was detraumatizing. Early adolescent erotic diversification involving a pet, a girlfriend, or a boyfriend, yielded to heterosexual pairbonding and, eventually, a stable marriage. The paraphilic ritual of bondage and discipline was no longer performed. Its residual took the form of narratophilia. In copulatory foreplay, having her husband narrate a story of sexual coercion stimulated her arousal and "horniness" for him, very effectively.

Paraphilic Stratagem. In this case, masturbation fantasies were a metaphor of being an animal restrained and subjected to a painful pelvic procedure, "for its own good." Originally aversive, the procedure became attractive, according to the opponent-process principle, by being paraphilically erotized and conducive to orgasm. In the patient's own case, after the painful pelvic procedure had had a successful outcome, restraint and discipline were transmuted from masochistic ritual to story-telling, that is, to narratophilia, with a theme of bondage and submission.

CHAPTER 10

Developmental Precursors of Paraphilia

Prenatal and Postnatal Precursors of Paraphilia

The findings from the seven biographies pertaining to the prenatal and postnatal developmental periods, respectively, are heuristically subdivided into two categories in Table 10.1.

TABLE 10.1

Precursors of Paraphilia

Prenatal

Chromosomal Status
Gonadal Status
Fetal Gonadal Hormonal Status
External Genital Morphologic Status

Postnatal

Sex of Announcement and Rearing
Juvenile Sexual Rehearsal Play
Stigmatization

The data on the four prenatal precursors are presented in Table 10.2. Comparison of Columns I through IV shows that there is a high degree of correspondence between the four precursors. This correspondence is to be expected on the basis of the principles of normal embryological development. In normal embryonic sexual differentiation, the XY or XX sex chromosome configuration in sexual differentiation is limited to determining the dimorphism of the gonads. In the XY embryo, the gonads typically differentiate as testes, and in the XX embryo, as ovaries. Once the male or female gonads differentiate, sex chromosomes have no known direct influence on subsequent sexually dimorphic differentiation. Dimorphism of the internal and external fetal genitalia differentiates under the influence of gonadal hormones.

In Table 10.2, there are various discrepancies between chromosomal, gonadal, hormonal, and morphologic sex. For example, in Biography 5, despite the male chromosomal karyotype, the external genital morphology is that of a female. What is specially noteworthy about Table 10.2 is that even in a sample as small as seven, three different chromosomal karyotypes

TABLE 10.2

Four Prenatal Precursors of Paraphilia

Biography	Sex Reared	I Chromosomal Status	II Gonadal Status	III Fetal Gonadal Status	IV External Genital Morphologic Status
1. B.O.	Male	46,XY	Testes	Normal Testicular Masculinizing	Male
2. H.E.	Male	46,XY	Imperfect Testes	Defective Testicular Masculinizing	Micropenis
3. M.O.	Male	46,XY	Imperfect Testes	Defective Testicular Masculinizing	Micropenis
4. R.H.	Male	46,XY	Imperfect Testes	Testicular Demasculinizing	Ambiguous Male
5. K.A.	Female	46,XY	Imperfect Testes	Testicular Feminizing	Slightly Defective Female
6. W.E.	Female	45,X/46,XY	Streak Gonads	Sex Steroid Failure	Slightly Defective Female
7. K.O.	Female	46,XX	Ovaries	Normal Ovarian Feminizing	Female

are represented. The preponderance of cases with the Y chromosome, six of the seven, is consistent with the principle of sexual differentiation that is epigrammatically stated as: Eve first, then Adam. In other words, when masculinization fails, nature's contingency plan of demasculinization is for the ensuing stages of differentiation to be as a female.

Chromosomal Sex

Inspection of Table 10.2 shows that five patients had a 46,XY karyotype as in a normal male, one had a 46,XX karyotype as in a normal female, and one had a mosaic 45,X/46,XY karyotype, with the Y being incomplete or a Y fragment.

Traditionally, paraphilias are attributed to males. Despite the prevalence of the XY karyotype in Table 10.2, two other karyotypes in a sample as small as seven indicate that the Y chromosome cannot be considered to be an exclusive site of genetic error (if any) contributing to the development of paraphilia.

Gonadal Status

Table 10.2 shows that only two of the seven patients in the sample had normal gonads, as evidenced by their congruence with the chromosomal, genital, and hormonal sex. In the remaining five cases, the fetal gonads were presumed to be defective, as evidenced by a variety of accompanying genital defects. The gonadal defects were associated with the 46,XY karyotype in four cases, and in one case, with the mosaic 45,X/46,XY karyotype. The present data show that although paraphilia can be associated with either normal female or male gonadal status, is was more often associated with defects in testicular differentiation.

Fetal Gonadal-Hormonal Status

It goes without saying that prenatal clinical assessment of steroids secreted in the human fetus is ethically not possible. Under the circumstances, one must rely on the body of knowledge deriving from clinical investigation of human syndromes and from experimental animal research.

The significant feature of Column III in Table 10.2 is the variability of prenatal hormonalization, which ranges from normal masculinization to normal feminization. The fetal hormonal abnormalities exemplify, on the criterion of the chromosomal status, a variety of defects in fetal masculinization. In this respect, the prenatal hormonal status parallels the gonadal status. Thus, the paraphilic outcome in the present sample was more often associated with fetal demasculinization than with normal masculinization or feminization.

External Genital Morphologic Status

As is well exemplified in the present sample, the external genital morphology is not always a direct derivative of either chromosomal or gonadal sex. Comparison of Columns I and IV in Table 10.2 shows that, in six cases, the external genital morphology was to some degree discordant with chromosomal and/or gonadal sex. The paraphilia was present irrespective of normal or abnormal external genital status. The prevalence of individuals with impaired genital differentiation suggests that the longterm stigmatizing effect of a birth defect of the sex organs exposes an individual to an increased risk of a paraphilic developmental outcome, though it does not, of course, rule out nongenital risk factors in individuals born with normal genitalia.

Sex of Announcement and Rearing

The sex of rearing was consistent with the sex of neonatal assignment in all cases, except that of the one patient who was reassigned to live as a girl at age 4 yrs 6 mos. On the criterion of ultimate sex of assignment and rearing, there were three women and four men (Table 10.2). Therefore, sex of rearing alone cannot be considered to be significant with respect to the paraphilic outcome.

However, in five cases (Biographies 2, 3, 4, 5, and 6), there was some degree of discordancy between the appearance of the birth defective external genital organs on the one hand, and on the other hand, the sex of assignment and rearing. Such discordancy proved to have a detrimental, stigmatizing effect on the sexuoerotic development of these five patients. As children, they became aware that something was wrong with them. The same applied in a sixth case (Biography 7), in which the girl discovered in childhood that her vagina ended blindly.

Juvenile Sexual Rehearsal Play

Mutual genital inspection and manipulation, including rehearsal of coital motions and positioning, are the most common components of juvenile sexual rehearsal play observed in human beings and other primates. The data on juvenile sexual rehearsal play (Table 10.3) derive, in large part, from the patients' retrospective reports in adolescence and/or adulthood. The data show that only two patients (Biographies 2 and 3), both boys with a micropenis, did not recall having ever been involved in sexual rehearsal

TABLE 10.3

Juvenile Sexual Rehearsal Play

Biography	Participation In Sexual Rehearsal Play	Outcome
1. B.O.	Periodic, sporadic	Traumatic guilt
2. H.E.	None	Deprivation
3. M.O.	None	Deprivation
4. R.H.	One episode recalled	Deprivation
5. K.A.	Periodic, sporadic	Traumatic discipline
6. M.E.	Periodic, sporadic	Traumatic discipline
7. K.O.	Periodic, sporadic	Dismay

play. Each was loath to have his very small penis seen by others. So also was the boy (Biography 4) with extensive postsurgical scarring and a poorly reconstructed hypospadiac penis. He recalled only one episode of attempted sex play with a girl playmate, and then no more. Among the seven patients, these three boys had the most obviously defective genital appearance.

The four patients (Biographies 1, 5, 6, and 7) who in childhood repeatedly engaged in sexual play recalled the negative outcome. In Biography 1, the patient blamed himself for the accidental death of the girl who had recently been his playmate in sex rehearsal. Punishment and humiliation followed the sexual play episodes in Biographies 5 and 6. In Biography 7, the play resulted in dismay when the girl discovered that she had no vaginal opening. In none of the seven cases was the outcome of juvenile sexual rehearsal play undilutedly positive.

Stigmatization

Inspection of Table 10.4 shows that each of the seven patients experienced some degree of stigmatization in childhood. As opposed to the other previously discussed precursors of paraphilia, a history of childhood stigmatization is the characteristic shared in all seven cases. In each case, it was the special status of being born with a congenital defect that rendered the child particularly vulnerable to stigmatization. The categories of stigmatization (Columns I to VI in Table 10.4) are as follows.

Syndrome Concealment/Denial

One of the most insidious ways for a child to become stigmatized is to make the topic of his/her condition totally unspeakable. In the present

TABLE 10.4

Childhood Stigmatization

Biography	I Syndrome Conceal- ment/ Denial	II Nosocomial	III Excessive Safeguarding	IV Pejorative Teasing and Labeling	V Inadvertent Ascertainment
1. B.O.	No	No	Yes	Yes	No
2. H.E.	No	No	Yes	Yes	Yes
3. M.O.	Yes	No	No	Yes	Yes
4. R.H.	No	No	No	Yes	Yes
5. K.A.	Yes	Yes	Yes	Yes	No
6. M.E.	Yes	Yes	Yes	Yes	Yes
7. K.O.	No	No	No	No	Yes

sample, parental concealment and/or denial of the syndrome proved to have a stigmatizing effect on three patients (Biographies 3, 5, and 6), as shown in Column I, Table 10.4.

In Biography 3, the patient was about seven years old when he had enough courage to share with his mother the disturbing self-diagnosis of micropenis. His mother put him off with a vague promise of a doctor's visit. The promise did not materialize. Instead, the mother eventually took the boy to a neurologist for an attention-deficit disorder and academic underachievement. Thus, the boy construed that his sex problem was not to be talked about. Until the neurologist referred him to Johns Hopkins for evaluation of his micropenis condition, he had a lonely struggle with the unspeakable monster of his genital handicap.

In Biographies 5 and 6, the parents' evasiveness indicated that these girls had something wrong with them. In Biography 5, the mother made it clear that talking about anything pertaining to the first four years of life, prior to sex reassignment, was forbidden.

In Biography 6, the authentic diagnosis of the child's genital condition was removed from the family vocabulary. The only explanation the parents offered to their daughter was that she had undergone surgery for a hernia. They failed to explain the rationale for genital examinations, which proved to have an adverse effect on the child. As in Biography 3, the child's correct diagnosis was denied; as a substitute for the unspeakable diagnosis of her-maphroditism, the mother confabulated a false diagnosis of brain damage. Thenceforth, the child was subject to unnecessary evaluations for special placement in a program for brain-damaged children.

Nosocomial Stigmatization

Nosocomial stigma compounded childhood stigmatization in four cases (Column II, Table 10.4). In Biographies 5 and 6, the girls felt stigmatized by being exposed to many doctors during genital examinations and procedures the rationale for which they did not understand. In Biography 5, the girl's own words were, as she looked back on genital examinations and exposures in childhood, that they "made me feel like a prostitute." In Biography 6, nosocomial stigma became focused in the suspicion evoked by her surgeon's enigmatic remark, when she was seven years old, that she had "definitely feminine hands." This remark reinforced a hazy premonition that there was something wrong with her feminine gender status. In Biography 2, the boy became silently angry with the stigmatizing implication of routine questioning, during physical examinations, as to whether he was satisfied with the size of his micropenis. In Biography 4, the long-term stigma, written into his record, was that he was mentally retarded, instead of electively mute while hospitalized and undergoing surgery on his deformed penis.

Excessive Safeguarding

The strategies by which parents deal with a defective or chronically ill child are polarized. At one pole, aversion toward the defect or illness is generalized to the child and is manifested as some form of child abuse. On the opposite pole, there is excessive safeguarding and protective oversupervising of the child. There were four patients who became stigmatized in consequence of their parents' policy of excessive and unreasonable safeguards, prohibitions, and restrictions (Column III, Table 10.4).

In Biography 1, the patient became an obsessive focus of his mother's attention. She closely monitored her son's activities to make sure that she did not overlook any sign of developmental abnormality, not only those attributable to hypothyroidism. In her unremitting quest for perfection as a mother of a hypothyroid child, she enrolled in professional training courses and became a special education teacher.

In Biography 2, the parental safeguarding strategy was based on a false assumption that close supervision of the child's activities outside of the family would prevent him from public exposure of his genital defect. From an early age, the child was made aware of strict limitations concerning participation in group play, using a toilet in the presence of other children, or being seen in the bathtub. The boy's compliance with parental instructions proved beneficial insofar as he successfully avoided being ridiculed and teased at school. It was the overemphasizing of his special status within the family that conveyed stigmatization.

In Biography 5, the mother's secret misgiving about the femininity of her daughter, whose diagnosis was male hermaphroditism with androgen insensitivity, was manifested as unreasonable insistence on exclusively stereotypic feminine behavior. The mother's hidden agenda was, in fact, to protect herself from being confronted with any evidence in the daughter of so-called masculine traits.

In Biography 6, the patient was cast in the role of an eternal child by reason of parental restrictions and limitations on developing autonomy. The mother justified such restrictive supervision by citing not her daughter's history of sexual ambiguity and sex reassignment, but her miniature size and fragile constitution.

Pejorative Teasing and Labeling

Children who are in some way different from their age mates are sometimes stigmatized by the very term used by others to define the difference, especially if the term is used in a jeering or taunting way by age mates.

Column IV of Table 10.4 shows that only in Biography 7 was there no evidence of this type of stigmatization, its absence being contingent on the late age at which atresia of the vagina was finally recognized and diagnosed. In Biography 1, the boy was classified at school as a slow learner, and he attributed his exclusion from the play of other children to his failure to "catch on" to the rules of their games. Biography 2 was that of the boy who bitterly resented the label of being satisfied with his small penis because of what he considered the stupidity of young doctors who questioned him. In Biography 3, the boy misconstrued taunts of "fatso" and "slow poke" as being contingent on the size of his penis. Biography 4 is that of the boy who was falsely labeled as mentally retarded by housestaff physicians who misconstrued elective mutism as deficient intelligence. Analogously, in Biography 5, the girl was also falsely labeled, in this instance by the mother, who confabulated a diagnosis of minimal brain damage. In Biography 6, stigmatization was displaced from the genital ambiguity to the short stature, and the girl was teased as a "midget."

Inadvertent Ascertainment

It is a common practice for professionals and even more common for parents to believe that they are sparing a child by withholding information about his/her clinical history, treatment, and prognosis. Walls have ears, however. There are many ways in which a child may discover information more or less inadvertently, and then, putting two and two together, come up with a worrisome and stigmatizing proposition.

As Column V in Table 10.4 shows, there was only one case (Biography 1) in which it seemed reasonably clear that the patient had not undergone the experience of having information secretly withheld from him. In one other case (Biography 5), whereas information was withheld between ages four and eleven, in the psychohormonal counseling program the child was given an explanation conceptually suited to her age about her condition and prognosis at age 11 yrs 5 mos. In the remaining five cases, the children did make discoveries that for a period of time remained their own private stigmatizing secrets.

In Biography 2, self-ascertainment as a potential transexual derived from reading newspaper reports on the Christine Jorgensen case, widely publicized at that time. The idea of sex reassignment was too stigmatizing for him to be able to make overt inquiry about its applicability to himself. In Biography 3, the parents' silence necessitated that the boy discover for himself, by comparison, that his penis was indeed very small. His mother ignored his discovery, even after he told her about it. In Biography 4, inadvertent self-discovery of a perineal scar triggered the nagging suspicion that the scar was, in fact, a miniature vagina. In Biography 6, the patient was seven years old when a nightmarish dream revealed the truth, concealed by the parents, about her having formerly been a boy. In Biography 7, the patient was about eight years old when her newly acquired knowledge about penovaginal intercourse prompted her attempt at vaginal self-examination, and the secret discovery that she had no vaginal canal.

CHAPTER 11

Prevention and Treatment

During the period of history when the seven subjects of this study were born and grew as young children, it was not possible to take specific measures to prevent the development of paraphilia. The explanation is simple, namely, that it was not then known that a paraphilia has precursors in early life. A widespread professional opinion was that paraphilias appear, de novo, in adolescence or adulthood. In fact, the precursors may, in some instances, be traced as far back as to the delivery, or even earlier, to prenatal life. In Biographies 2, 3, 4, and 6 of the present series, the stigma of genital defect, which contributed subsequently to the development of a paraphilia was, indeed, obvious at birth.

In these four cases, professional ineptitude when confronted with the newborn baby's genital defect was transmitted to the parents. Their own ineptitude was, in turn, transmitted to the child who, being inept, had no strategy other than improvisation for dealing with the contingencies of having been born defective. The erotosexual outcome in these four cases was, at adolescence and maturity, a paraphilic lovemap. The outcome was the same in Biography 5, even though the transmission of ineptitude from professionals to parents to child did not begin until the diagnosis of male hermaphroditism was first made at age 5 yrs 4 mos.

Biographies 1 and 7 differed from the other five insofar as the manifestation of professional ineptitude began not as something done wrongly, but as something left undone. The omission was a failure to recognize that the child's lovemap was developing with a paraphilic error, the prodromal origin of which the child did not dare to disclose.

In all seven cases, the ultimate culprit responsible for the failure of early prevention of paraphilia in the lovemap is the powerful sex negation of the sexual taboo to which our society is heir. At all stages of medical education, it is the sexual taboo which can be held responsible for a deficiency in professional training concerning the principles of case management in syndromes of birth defective genitalia, first in the delivery room, and subsequently during the years of juvenile and adolescent lovemap development.

Throughout the world, it also is the sexual taboo which can be held responsible for the failure of medical institutions to establish specialty clinics in pediatric and ephebiatric sexology. In consequence, there is no agreed-upon body of scientific and medical knowledge by which to gauge whether a child's lovemap is developing normophilically or paraphilically. Correspondingly, there is no agreed-upon method of effective corrective intervention in the developmental years of childhood even when, as in six of the seven present cases, the need for it was evident. The prevention and/ or correction of erroneous lovemap formation during childhood both are still at the trial-and-error stage.

One of the factors responsible for this state of affairs is the pervasiveness of the sex-negating power of the sexual taboo beyond the confines of the clinic and the family into the juvenile peer group, into the community at large, and into the media where it is transmitted in print or, very potently, electronically. From an early age, all children are at risk to become entrapped by the negative sanctions of the sexual taboo in the no-win situation of a Catch-22, namely, of being damned if they do admit to having broken the taboo and damned if they don't. The offense may have been to have thought forbidden thoughts, to have had forbidden conversations, or to have engaged in forbidden activities, like sexual rehearsal play.

All seven of the children in the present series were, in the juvenile years, as well as later, entrapped in a Catch-22. The entrapment was acute for all of them, but particularly so for those six who had to guard the secrecy of their defective sex organs. Like the proverbial drowning man who drags down his would-be rescuer, not one of them was able to take advantage of the possibility of rescue when it was offered in the course of psychohormonal counseling. Only with time and the sophistication of age were they finally able to break out of the trap, and talk openly with someone older than themselves.

Being able to talk brought relief, sufficient in magnitude to have prevented suicide in at least one youth (Biography 2), and in others to have perhaps averted serious psychopathology. Talking treatment did not, however, bring about a complete cure or remediation of the paraphilic lovemap. In Biography 7, after effective surgical remediation of the defective vagina, the paraphilic content of the lovemap went into major remission, except for occasional return in narrative imagery. In Biography 6, the paraphilic content of the lovemap became enacted less frequently as sexual intercourse became less frequent with advancing age. In the other five cases, according to the evidence available, there was, over time, no recognizable increase or decrease in the intensity or frequency of the paraphilic imagery and/or enactment.

In only one instance (Biography 4) was the paraphilia homicidally life threatening. In another case (Biography 1), it could have been law-breaking had the fantasy been put into practice. These were the two cases in which talking treatment might have been augmented with antiandrogenic hormonal treatment with Depo-Provera (medroxyprogesterone acetate). The details of this treatment are in Money (1987). It is an elective treatment, and neither patient has elected to try it as of the present time.

An alternative antiandrogenic hormone is cyproterone acetate, used in Europe and Canada, but not yet cleared by the FDA (Federal Drug Administration) for use in the United States. In some patients, the effect of Depo-Provera is augmented if the hormone is used in conjunction with lithium carbonate which, in other patients, has proved beneficial when used alone (see also Chapter 1, "Neuropathological Determinism").

CHAPTER 12

Genesis of Paraphilia:
Hypothetical Concepts and Principles

Temporal and Causal Contingencies

Prospective biographical outcome of the development of paraphilias, as in the present series, demonstrates phenomenological sequences and contingencies that are related temporally, but not necessarily causally. Having a sample of a magnitude many times greater than seven would offer no guarantee of being able to discover causal explanations of paraphilia. Even a small sample of seven, however, is sufficient to generate hypotheses relevant to future investigations of the cause or etiology of paraphilia. There are, for example, hypotheses of predisposition or vulnerability.

Genomic Vulnerability

The chromosomal data from even so few as seven cases demonstrated that, if there is a genetic vulnerability, it is not restricted to a particular sex-chromosome karyotype, for three karyotypes were represented, namely, 46,XX; 46,XY; and 45,X/46,XY.

On the basis of clinic and court statistics, it is widely held that paraphilias occur more often in men (46,XY) than women (46,XX). There are three studies which indicate that the 47,XYY karyotype (the supernumerary-Y syndrome), known for its association with pathologically impulsive behavior, constitutes also a vulnerability factor for the development of paraphilia

(Money, et al., 1970b, 1975; Schiavi, et al., 1988). There is, as yet, no evidence that specifically implicates all or a part of the Y chromosome itself, either directly or indirectly in the genesis of paraphilia. If a genomic error ever is implicated, its locus may be discovered by molecular geneticists engaged in mapping and sequencing the entire human genome.

Intrauterine Teratogenic Vulnerability

If a genomic error should be implicated in the development of paraphilia, there would be multiple intervening variables between the DNA of the genome, on the one hand, and the brain as the mediator of the imagery, ideation, and behavior of the paraphilia, on the other. In the case of differentiation and dimorphism of masculinity/femininity in the fetal brain, the functional influence of the genome is initially through its control of gonadal differentiation, and then through the sex steroidal hormones released by the gonad. The hormones, in turn, carry the major responsibility for sexually differentiating the brain. However, the fetal brain responds to the masculinizing/feminizing effect of hormones no matter what their origin, which may be either intrinsic to the fetus, or extrinsic, reaching the fetus from the mother, through the placenta, or by being introduced directly into the intrauterine environment.

If there is a relationship between prenatal brain androgenization and the greater vulnerability of the male brain as compared with the female brain to the eventual development of paraphilia, the current evidence does not reveal it. The high prevalence of paraphilia in 47,XYY males is not related to their testosterone levels which, in adulthood, are widely variable. Paraphilias occur in males with a prenatal history of either a high or low level of androgen. For example, a paraphilia may occur in conjunction with the 46,XY syndrome of congenital virilizing adrenal hyperplasia (CVAH), in which the level of adrenocortical androgen is greatly elevated. However, paraphilias appear not to occur in the 46,XX female counterpart of the CVAH syndrome, which is associated with hermaphroditically masculinized external genitalia. At the other extreme, paraphilias occur sporadically in the 47,XXY (Klinefelter's) syndrome, in which the typical hormonal history is one of a low androgen level. In the present sample of seven, there was no consistent relationship between paraphilia and the prenatal history of androgenization or its absence.

Socially Induced Vulnerability

Morphologically, the genotype produces its phenotype not in a vacuum, but in collaboration with its environment, some of which is actually incorporated into the organism—nutritionally, for example. Behaviorally, the same thing happens, as in the case of native language. Without a human genotype, it is not possible to have a language that is phenotypically human. Nonetheless, the phenotypic language is taken in from the social environment, typically through the ears, and becomes incorporated into the brain where it lodges permanently, ineradicable except by brain damage, a neurosurgeon's knife, a stroke, or dementia.

As in the case of language, the formation of the lovemap is contingent on incorporating into the brain various social inputs transmitted through the skin senses, the eyes, and the ears. The first phase is predominantly tactile. It originates in the infant-mother pairbond, a prerequisite of survival, and is a precursor of what will progressively unfold as more explicitly a manifestation of primate juvenile sexual rehearsal play. Studies of subhuman primates, notably rhesus monkeys (summarized in Money, 1988; see also Chapter 2, "Lovemap Biography") have demonstrated that infants reared in isolation respond to the deprivation of sexual rehearsal play with age mates by being incapable of copulating when mature, so that they do not reproduce their species. If allowed as little as a daily half-hour of social play, they have a one in three chance of ultimately achieving the adult foot-clasp postures of mounting and presenting, male and female, respectively, but they do not do so until as late as two years of age instead of around nine months of age. Even so, they have a low birth rate as adults. The nonachievers fail to breed.

There are some tribal cultures that do not incorporate sanctions and penalties against juvenile sexual rehearsal play. The Aboriginal Australian culture of Arnhem Land is one example (Money, et al., 1970a; see also Marshall and Suggs, 1971). In the Aboriginal Arnhem Land culture, it was not possible to find any examples of paraphilia.

In the cultures of Christendom, as of other great religions, sanctions and penalties against juvenile sexual rehearsal play add up all too often to be a de facto repudiation of normophilic, boy-girl, heterosexually developing lovemaps in childhood—if not repudiation, then indifference toward the health or pathology of juvenile lovemaps, and neglect of their development.

There are four ways in which juvenile lovemaps are developmentally vulnerable to socially induced pathology, namely, when the child-rearing policy is one of:

—explicitly neglecting to monitor and reinforce healthy sexual rehearsal play;

—abusively punishing and humiliating children for engaging in sexual rehearsal play;

—prematurely inducting children into sexual rehearsal play out of synchrony with their developmental age;

—coercing children into age-discrepant sexual rehearsal play, and/or inflicting bodily injury.

These policies are effective in inducing lovemap pathology insofar as they constitute juvenile sexual rehearsal play as a form of entrapment, the consequences of which are that you're damned if you do try to quit, and damned if you don't. Thus, to admit to age-discrepant sibling incest brings reprisals, whereas not to admit it, brings no relief. This no-win dilemma is yet another example of what is known popularly as a Catch-22.

In the human species, the critical developmental period for juvenile sexual rehearsal play, during which the developing lovemap is most vulnerable and most susceptible to socially induced pathology, though it has not been absolutely defined, would appear to be between the ages of approximately four or five and eight or nine. These are the ages ascertained when data are retrievable in retrospective studies of adult paraphiles in the clinic. They are consistent with the anteroceptive data in the seven cases of the present study.

Opponent-Process Principle

When a lovemap develops paraphilically, the imagery, ideation, and behavior that become incorporated into the lovemap and change it from a normophilic into a paraphilic one is not, at the outset, sexuoerotically charged. In paraphilic masochism, for example, the pain and humiliation of abuse, discipline, and bondage that become incorporated into the lovemap begin by being a tragedy of suffering. Subsequently, they metamorphose into a triumph of euphoria. While being whipped or tortured, the paraphilic masochist experiences not pain and suffering, but the cumulative ecstasy of sexuoerotic arousal and orgasm. That which was once aversive and avoided changes, and becomes attractive and addictive.

The psychological principle by which this change from aversion to addiction takes place was first enunciated by Richard Solomon as the principle of opponent-process learning (Solomon, 1980) (see also, Chapter 2, Opponent-Process). The practice of free-fall parachute jumping provides an example. The novice is scared to death at first. Then, after a few practice jumps, his fear vanishes and is replaced by euphoria. From then on, he is "hooked" on free-fall parachute jumping, as a sport, if not a career, in the manner of an addict "hooked" on heroin. The parallel is close, for the euphoric equivalent of the addict's heroin would be the parachutist's own endorphins, opiate-like neurochemical substances, released within the brain itself in response to danger and the threat of injury. In paraphilia, opponent-process cancels the danger or threatened consequences of some particular experience, and makes it sexuoerotically exciting instead. The specificity of the association between the initially threatening experience and the genitalia differs in each individual case. So also does the individual's vulnerability to the threat. A threat that terrifies one child may be trivial to another.

In the present series of seven cases, the initial threatening experience that became incorporated into the paraphilia according to the principle of opponent-process was in six cases directly related to the genitalia, by reason of their birth-defective status. In the seventh case, the threat of reprisal for engaging in boy-girl genital play, instead of fading into insignificance, appeared to materialize insofar as the boy interpreted his girlfriend's death in an auto accident as divine retribution.

Paraphilic Fugue State

The pattern of behavior that becomes paraphilic is, as a sequel of opponent-process, disconnected from being experienced as aversive and forbidden, and reconnected with being experienced, conversely, as attractive and addicting. The changeover may not be limited to only the change from aversion to addiction, but may be accompanied by a more extensive change, to such a degree that it qualifies as an altered state of consciousness. The altered state may itself be so extensive as to qualify as the second of two personalities, each dissociated from the other, as in the syndrome of multiple (dual) personality. In the majority of cases, however, it is phenomenologically more accurate to refer to the altered state as a paraphilic fugue (see also Chapter 1, Neuropathological Determinism).

There are some paraphilic patients who are clinically and electroencephalographically diagnosed as epileptics, and a rare few whose paraphilia has been controlled concurrently with the control of epileptic seizures by neurosurgery. There are some paraphiles in whom the onset of a paraphilic fugue may itself resemble a temporal-lobe epileptic seizure of the type known also as a psychomotor seizure or psychomotor equivalent. It is noteworthy for not being detectable on a standard EEG. Possibly, brain-wave abnormalities are present only in the course of an actual paraphilic attack, and they may be too deep for detection except by implanted electrodes or one of the newly developing, noninvasive methods of brain imaging.

Among the seven patients of the present study, there were two for whom there was a record of observational evidence of the appearance of a paraphilic fugue state (Biographies 1 and 4). In the other five cases, such evidence as existed was in the patient's verbal reporting only.

Ruminative Schizoid Obsessionalism

There are some patients in whom recurrent paraphilic fugue states are separated by intervals of return to a mental state that other people judge not to be normal, but strange. It is a state of being painfully socially inept, and perseveratively ruminative and obsessional, with ideas that become paranoidal, and imagery that is vivid and possibly dangerously threatening to self and others. This is the type of paraphilia that shares an autistic boundary with schizophrenia. In both syndromes, the phylogenetic neurobiology for falling in love and pairbonding is intact, whereas that for social troopbonding is severely impaired (Money, 1986b, Chapter 10). A high degree of social ineptitude greatly reduces the chances of meeting a potential lover in an ordinary sociable way, and perhaps constitutes a vulnerability predisposing to the development of paraphilia. In Biography 5, and to a lesser degree Biographies 3 and 6, in the present series, the patient qualified as both socially inept and paraphilic.

Periodicity

Reiteration of the sequence of fugue state followed by nonfugue state followed by fugue state, and so on, indefinitely, constitutes a manifestation of cyclicity in which the cycles are not necessarily of regular onset and duration. Rhythmicity, periodicity, cyclicity, and pulsatility are widespread as biological regulatory mechanisms in both health and pathology. In psychopathology, the classic example is the cyclicity of manic-depressive or bipolar disorder.

There are some cases of paraphilia in which paraphilic periodicity and manic-depressive periodicity overlap. More frequent reiteration of the paraphilic ideation and imagery in dreams and fantasies heralds the transition from being more depressed to less erotically depressed, and from being less to more able to achieve orgasm. Concurrently, there is an increased likelihood that the paraphilic fugue state will overlap with manic excitement and issue in the enactment of paraphilic behavior.

The association of paraphilic with bipolar disorder was not diagnostically obvious in any of the seven cases in the present series.

Bipotentiality and Bisexuality

The sexual differentiation of the human embryo is in three stages: unisexual or undifferentiated; ambisexual or hermaphroditic; and duosexual or differentiated as either male or female. This three-stage paradigm applies also to lovemap development which begins as undifferentiated or unisexual, then becomes ambisexual or bipotential, and then, in the duosexual stage, differentiates to become monosexually either homosexual or heterosexual, or remains bisexually androgynous (or gynoandrous).

In the development of vandalized lovemaps, there may be predisposing precursors at stages one and two, but vandalizing itself belongs to stage three. A vandalized disfigurement may be superimposed on a lovemap that has progressed from the bipotentiality of stage two to differentiate, at stage three, as monosexually homosexual or heterosexual. Alternatively, at stage three, the lovemap may be bisexual.

Hypothetically, it is possible that the homosexual resolution of the bipotentiality of stage two will be affected by the same succession of precursors and determinants responsible for shaping a lovemap into a paraphilic one.

The evidence from the present series of seven biographies is more confirmatory than disconfirmatory of this hypothesis. In three of the seven cases (Biographies 1, 3, and 7), there was evidence of a transitional bisexual phase of which the monosexual outcome was heterosexual. In Biography 3, bisexual ideation was vaguely recalled, and had involved the idea of being a girl instead of a boy with a micropenis, whereas in Biographies 1 and 7 it was more definite, but probably within the limits of what might be found in random sampling of nonparaphilic individuals. Among these three cases, it was only the one woman (Biography 7) who established a regular and lasting heterosexual partnership. She was married. In a fourth case (Biography 2), the outcome of the transitional bisexual phase was homosexual. After several failures, which he attributed to having a micropenis, the patient settled into a compassionate, housemate relationship devoid of genital involvement.

In the three remaining cases, the resolution of the bipotentiality and the outcome of the transitional phase was a continuation of bisexuality. There were two women (Biographies 5 and 6) and one man (Biography 4) in this group. Only in Biography 6 was there a regular partnership. This woman also married. The remaining man and woman of this group of three had lovemaps so grossly anomalous that a reciprocally matching one in a partner was not encountered. In other words, these two lovemaps effectively precluded reciprocal pairbonding.

Long-term pairbonding is contingent on the reciprocal matching of the lovemaps of any two partners. When one of the partners has a paraphilic lovemap, reciprocal matching is not an easy possibility. In some instances, as in Biographies 3, 4, and 5, the specifications of the lovemap are so quirky, that there is no reciprocally matching one to be found. In others, short-term, transient, or multiple partnering is a built-in feature of the lovemap, which also was somewhat so in Biography 1. By contrast, the long-term pairbonding in Biographies 2, 6, and 7 demonstrates that reciprocal matching of a paraphilic lovemap is not an utter impossibility. The proverbial adage that there is someone for everyone is not entirely sugar-coated!

Bibliography

American Psychiatric Association. *Diagnostic and Statistical Manual of Mental Disorders,* Third Edition. Washington, D.C.: American Psychiatric Association, 1980.

Bandura, A. and Walters, R. H. *Social Learning and Personality Development.* New York: Holt, Rinehart and Winston, 1963.

Benjamin, H. *The Transsexual Phenomenon.* New York: Julian Press, 1966.

Bloch, I. *The Sexual Life of Our Time: A Complete Encyclopaedia of the Sexual Sciences in Their Relation to Modern Civilization.* New York: Falstaff Press, 1937.

Bullough, V. L. *Sexual Variance in Society and History.* New York: Wiley, 1976.

Carnes, P. *Counseling the Sexual Addict.* Minneapolis, Minn.: Comp Care, 1986.

———. *Sexual Addiction.* Minneapolis, Minn.: Comp Care, 1985.

Comfort, A. (ed.). *The Joy of Sex: A Cordon Bleu Guide to Lovemaking.* New York: Crown Publishers, 1973.

Danish, R. K., Lee, P. A., Mazur, T., Amrhein, J. and Migeon, C. J. Micropenis: II. Hypogonadotropic hypogonadism. *Johns Hopkins Medical Journal,* 146:177–184, 1980.

Darwin, C. *On the Origin of Species by Means of Natural Selection.* Cambridge, Mass.: Harvard University Press, 1964 (1959 ed. in facsimile).

Eibl-Eibesfeldt, I. *Love and Hate: The Natural History of Behavior Patterns.* New York: Holt, Rinehart and Winston, 1971.

Ellis, H. *Studies in the Psychology of Sex.* 2 Vols. New York: Random House, 1942.

Flor-Henry, P. Cerebral aspects of sexual deviation. In *Variant Sexuality: Research and Theory* (G. D. Wilson, ed.). Baltimore, Md.: Johns

Hopkins University Press, 1987.

Freud, S. Three Essays on the Theory of Sexuality. In *The Standard Edition of the Complete Psychological Works of Sigmund Freud.* London: Hogarth Press, 1953–1976.

Gagnon, J. H. and Simon, W. *Sexual Conduct: The Social Sources of Human Sexuality.* Chicago: Aldine, 1973.

Gebhard, P. H., Gagnon, J. H., Pomeroy, W. B. and Christensen, C. V. *Sex Offenders: An Analysis of Types.* New York: Harper and Row, 1965.

Graham, S. *A Lecture to Young Men.* Providence: Weeden and Cory, 1834. Facsimile reprint edition. New York: Arno Press, 1974.

Groos, K. *The Play of Animals: A Study of Animal Life and Instinct.* New York: Appleton, 1898.

Haeberle, E. J. *The Birth of Sexology: A Brief History in Documents.* Privately published. Copyright, 1983, by Erwin J. Haeberle.

Hamill, P. V. V., Drizd, T. A., Johnson, C. L., Reed, R. B., Roche, A. F. and Moore, W. M. Physical growth: National Center for Health Statistics percentiles. *American Journal of Clincal Nutrition,* 32:607–629, 1979.

Hoenig, J. The development of sexology during the second half of the 19th century. In *Handbook of Sexology* (J. Money and H. Musaph, eds.). Amsterdam/London/New York: Excerpta Medica, 1977.

Hoffman, M. *The Gay World: Male Homosexuality and the Social Creation of Evil.* New York: Basic Books, 1968.

Jorgensen, C. *Christine Jorgensen: A Personal Autobiography.* New York: Paul S. Eriksson, 1967.

Karpman, B. *The Sexual Offender and His Offenses.* New York: Julian Press, 1954.

Kellogg, J. H. *Plain Facts for Old and Young, Embracing the Natural History and Hygiene of Organic Life.* Burlington, Iowa: I. F. Segner, 1888. Facsimile reprint edition, New York: Arno Press, 1974.

Kinsey, A. C., Pomeroy, W. B., and Martin, C. E. *Sexual Behavior in the Human Male.* Philadelphia, Penn.: Saunders, 1948.

Kinsey, A. C., Pomeroy, W. B., Martin, C. E. and Gebhard, P. H. *Sexual Behavior in the Human Female.* Philadelphia, Penn.: Saunders, 1953.

Kline, P. Sexual deviation: Psychoanalytic research and theory. In *Variant Sexuality: Research and Theory* (G. D. Wilson, ed.). Baltimore, Md.: Johns Hopkins University Press, 1987.

Krafft-Ebing, R. von. *Psychopathia Sexualis with Especial Reference to the Antipathic Sexual Instinct: A Medico-Forensic Study.* Chicago: Login Brothers, 1931.

Lombroso, C. *Criminal Man.* Montclair, N.J.: Patterson Smith, 1972.

————. *Crime: Its Causes and Remedies*. Boston: Little, Brown, 1913.

Lorenz, K. Z. *King Solomon's Ring: New Light on Animal Ways*. New York: Crowell, 1952.

Ludmerer, K. M. *Genetics and American Society: A Historical Appraisal*. Baltimore, Md.: Johns Hopkins University Press, 1972.

Mantegazza, P. *The Sexual Relations of Mankind*. New York: Eugenics Publishing Company, 1937.

Marks, I. Phylogenesis and learning in the acquisition of fetishism. *Danish Medical Bulletin*, 9:307–310, 1972.

Marshall, D. S. and Suggs, R. (eds.). *Human Sexual Behavior: Variations in the Ethnographic Spectrum*. New York: Basic Books, 1971.

Masson, J. M. *The Assault on Truth. Freud's Suppression of the Seduction Theory*. New York: Farrar, Strauss, Giroux, 1984.

Maudsley, H. *The Physiology and Pathology of the Mind*. New York: Appleton, 1967.

Migeon, C. J., Brown, T. R. and Fichman, K. R. Androgen insensitivity syndrome. In *Pediatric and Adolescent Endocrinology* (Z. Laron and P. Tikva, eds.). Basel: Karger, 1981.

Miller, N. and Dollard, J. *Personality and Psychotherapy*. New York: McGraw-Hill, 1950.

Moll, A. *The Sexual Life of the Child*. New York: Macmillan, 1912.

————. *Libido Sexualis: Studies in the Psychosexual Laws of Love Verified by Clinical Case Histories*. New York: American Ethnological Press, 1933.

Money, J. *The Psychologic Study of Man*. Springfield, Ill.: Charles C. Thomas, 1957.

————. Sexual dictatorship, dissidence and democracy. *International Journal of Medicine and Law*, 1:11–20, 1979.

————. *The Destroying Angel: Sex, Fitness and Food in the Legacy of Degeneracy Theory, Graham Crackers, Kellogg's Corn Flakes, and American Health History*. Buffalo, N.Y.: Prometheus Books, 1985.

————. *Lovemaps: Clincal Concepts of Sexual/Erotic Health and Pathology, Paraphilia, and Gender Transposition in Childhood, Adolescence and Maturity*. New York: Irvington, 1986a.

————. *Venuses Penuses: Sexology, Sexosophy, and Exigency Theory*. Buffalo, N.Y.: Prometheus Books, 1986b.

————. Treatment guidelines: Antiandrogen and counseling of paraphilic sex offenders. *Journal of Sex and Marital Therapy*, 3:219–223, 1987.

————. *Gay, Straight and In-Between: The Sexology of Erotic Orientation*. New York: Oxford University Press, 1988.

————. Paleodigms and paleodigmatics: A new theoretical construct applicable to Munchausen's syndrome by proxy, child-abuse dwarfism, paraphilias, anorexia nervosa and other syndromes. *American Journal of Psychotherapy,* 43: 15-24, 1989a.

———. *Sex Sagas: Lovemaps of Twelve Matched-Pair Biographies in Clinical Sexology and Hermaphroditism.* Unpublished manuscript, 1989b.

Money, J., Cawte, J. E., Bianchi, G. N., and Nurcombe, B. Sex training and traditions in Arnhem Land. *British Journal of Medical Psychology,* 43:383-399, 1970a.

Money, J., Clarke, F. C., and Beck, J. Congenital hypothyroidism and IQ increase: A quarter century followup. *Journal of Pediatrics,* 93:432-434, 1978.

Money, J., Gaskin, R., and Hull, H. Impulse, aggression and sexuality in the XYY syndrome. *St. John's Law Review,* 44:220-235, 1970b.

Money, J., Lehne, G. K., and Pierre-Jerome, F. Micropenis: Adult followup and comparison of size against new norms. *Journal of Sex and Marital Therapy,* 10:105-116, 1984.

———. Micropenis: Gender, erotosexual coping strategy, and behavioral health in nine pediatric cases followed to adulthood. *Comprehensive Psychiatry,* 26:29-42, 1985.

Money, J. and Lewis, V. Longitudinal study of IQ in treated congenital hypothyroidism. In *Brain-Thyroid Relationships.* Ciba Foundation Study Group No. 18 (M. P. Cameron and M. O'Connor, eds.). London: J. & A. Churchill. Boston: Little, Brown, 1964.

Money, J. and Pruce, G. Psychomotor epilepsy and sexual function. In *Handbook of Sexology* (J. Money and H. Musaph, eds.). Amsterdam/London/New York: Excerpta Medica, 1977.

Money, J., Wiedeking, C., Walker, P., Migeon, C., Meyer, W., and Borgaonkar, D. 47,XYY and 46,XY males with antisocial and/or sex-offending behavior: Antiandrogen therapy plus counseling. *Psychoneuroendocrinology,* 1:165-178, 1975.

Nelson, M. M. and Forfar, J. O. Associations between drugs administered during pregnancy and congenital abnormalities of the fetus. *British Medical Journal,* 1:523-527, 1971.

Pfaefflin, F. The connection between eugenics, sterilization, and mass murder in Germany, 1933-1945. *Medicine and Law,* 5:1-10, 1986.

Pinkava, V. Logical models of variant sexuality. In *Variant Sexuality: Research and Theory* (G. D. Wilson, ed.). Baltimore, Md.: Johns Hopkins University Press, 1987.

Rees, H., Bonsall, R., and Michael, R. Preoptic and hypothalamic neurons accumulate (^{3}H) medroxyprogesterone acetate in male cynomolgus monkeys. *Life Sciences,* 39:1353-1359, 1986.

Reinisch, J. M. and Sanders, S. A. Early barbiturate exposure: The brain, sexually dimorphic behavior, and learning. *Neuroscience and Biobe-*

havioral Reviews, 6:311–319, 1982.

Schiavi, R. C., Theilgaard, A., Owen, D. R., and White, D. Sex chromosome anomalies, hormones and sexuality. *Archives of General Psychiatry,* 45:19–24, 1988.

Sheldon, W. H., Hartl, E. M., and McDermott, E. *Varieties of Delinquent Youth.* 2 Vol. Darien, Conn.: Hafner, 1970.

Sheldon, W. H. and Stevens, S. S. *The Varieties of Temperament: A Psychology of Constitutional Differences.* New York: Hafner, 1970.

Solomon, R. The opponent process theory of acquired motivation. *American Psychologist,* 35:691–712, 1980.

Soloway, M. S. Treatment of prostatic cancer: Newer forms of androgen deprivation. *Postgraduate Medicine,* Vol. 80, July 1986.

Steinach, E. *Sex and Life: Forty Years of Biological and Medical Experiments.* New York: Viking Press, 1940.

Steckel, W. *Disorders of the Instincts and the Emotions, the Parapathiac Disorders: Peculiarities of Behavior,* Vol. I. *Wandering Mania, Dipsomania, Cleptomania, Pyromania and Allied Compulsive Acts.* New York: Boni and Liveright, 1924.

———. *The Autobiography of Wilhelm Stekel: The Life Story of a Pioneer Psychoanalyst* (E. A. Gutheil, ed.). New York: Liveright, 1950.

Stoller, R. *Perversion: The Erotic Form of Hatred.* New York: Pantheon, 1975.

Sulloway, J. *Freud, Biologist of the Mind.* New York: Basic Books, 1979.

Tjio, J. H. and Levan, A. *The Chromosome Number of Man. Heriditas,* 42:1–6, 1956.

Tissot, S. A. *A Treatise on the Diseases Produced by Onanism.* Translated from a New Edition of the French, with Notes and Appendix by an American Physician. New York, 1832. Facsimile reprint edition in *The Secret Vice Exposed! Some Arguments Against Masturbation* (C. Rosenburg and C. Smith-Rosenburg, advisory eds.). New York: Arno Press, 1974.

Weinrich, J. D. *Sexual Landscapes: Why We Are What We Are, Why We Love Whom We Love.* New York: Charles Scribner's Sons, 1987.

Wilson, E. O. *Sociobiology: The New Synthesis.* Cambridge: Harvard University Press, 1975.

Wilson, J. D. and Foster, D. W. (eds.). *Williams Textbook of Endocrinology* (7th Ed.). Philadelphia, Penn.: Saunders, 1985.

Name Index

Bandura, A., 34
Barr, M., 75
Benjamin, H., 85
Bekhterev, V., 34
Benkert, K. M., 25
Binet, A., 20, 33, 34, 36
Bloch, I., 25, 35
Boelsche, W., 36
Bonsall, R., 32
Bowlby, J., 15
Bullough, V., 18, 25

Carnes, P., 36
Comfort, A., 177

Danish, R. K., 96
Darwin, C., 21, 26, 27
Dollard, J., 34

Eibl-Eibesfeld, I., 28
Ellis, H., 41

Fenichel, O., 39
Fliess, W., 38
Flor-Henry, P., 31
Forfar, J. O., 96
Foster, D. W., 58

Freud, S., 17, 27, 36–38

Gagnon, J., 34
Gebhard, P., 41
Graham, S., 40
Groos, K., 40

Hackett, W., 18
Haeberle, E. J., 20
Haeckel, E., 26, 27, 36
Hamill, P. V. V., 58
Hartl, E. M., 23
Hirschfeld, M., 31
Hitler, A., 24, 146
Hoenig, J., 33
Hoffman, M., 88
Hull, C. L., 34

Jackson, J. Hughlings, 27
Jorgensen, C., 84, 158, 193

Kaan, H., 20
Kallmann, F., 96
Karpman, B., 17, 39
Kellogg, J. H., 40
Kinsey, A., 24, 41
Kline, P., 39

Subject Index